Surviving Child Sexual Abuse

Dedication

For all the incest survivors we have known, without whom we could not have written this book, and for our children, Nicholas, Alison and Diarmuid.

Surviving Child Sexual Abuse

A Handbook for Helping Women Challenge their Past

Liz Hall
Siobhan Lloyd

The Falmer Press

(A member of the Taylor & Francis Group)
New York • Philadelphia • London

UK   The Falmer Press, Rankine Road, Basingstoke, Hampshire
RG24 0PR

USA   The Falmer Press, Taylor & Francis Inc., 1900 Frost Road,
Suite 101, Bristol, PA 19007

First published in 1989, reprinted 1990

British Library Cataloguing in Publication Data
Hall, Liz
Surviving child sexual abuse: a handbook for helping women
challenge their past.
1. Sexual abuse victims. Psychotherapy
I. Title II. Lloyd, Siobhan
616.89′14

ISBN 1–85000–478–1
ISBN 1–85000–479–X pbk.

Typeset in 11/13 Bembo by Chapterhouse, The Cloisters, Formby
Printed in Great Britain by
Redwood Press Limited, Melksham, Wiltshire

Contents

List of Tables

List of Figures

Acknowledgments

The idea for this book came to us, with some help, one sunny afternoon in mid-1987. We were bemoaning the fact that there were lots of books on the theoretical aspects of sexual abuse but none, to our knowledge, which described the process of giving help to incest survivors. We decided to try to fill that gap.

It has taken eighteen months to put our thoughts together and during that time we have been helped and encouraged by a network of supportive friends, colleagues and family. Writing has had to compete with many other demands on our time, and we have often had to fit it in late at night and at weekends.

All the incest survivors we have known over the past six years have made a major contribution to this book. Without them we would never have begun to understand the reality of childhood sexual abuse and its consequences for women. To these women we would like to express our thanks, our admiration for their courage in challenging their past and for allowing us to be part of that process.

For both of us our learning and the roots of our work lies in the rape crisis movement. We were part of a women's collective which established a Rape Crisis Centre in Aberdeen in the early 1980s. Incest survivors were in contact with the Centre from the first day the telephone lines were opened. We all started our learning at that point, and we have continued to learn with every woman who has made contact with the Centre. Our thanks go to all the members of the collective, and in particular to women who were involved in the early days.

We should also like to acknowledge the following colleagues who encouraged us to put pen to paper, shared ideas or read and commented on drafts of our material: Brenda Flaherty, Sue Hunt, Sandra Malley, Alison Peaker, Elizabeth Shiach and Patricia Smith. Colleagues in the Social Work Department, University of Aberdeen and the Community Psychology Department and Area Psychology Service of Grampian Health Board have also given support and advice at different stages. Christine Cox, our editor at Falmer Press deserves thanks too, for her support of our original ideas and her willingness to extend deadlines.

We acknowledge Charlotte F. Hoffman and Sheila L. Sisk, and Pandora Press, for giving us permission to reprint some poems from their book *Inside Scars: Incest recovery as told by a survivor and her therapist*.

We should also like to thank friends and family who kept us going when our energy was flagging and our spirits low. We owe special thanks to Graham and Greg and to our children, one of whom may have been too young to notice his mother's preoccupation, and two who will certainly be delighted to know that their mother has finally completed the book!

Finally, but by no means least, our thanks to Margaret Donald for her professional competence in deciphering our messy and never-ending manuscript, her positive and sensible suggestions and her eternal goodwill and patience on the word-processor.

Preface

In recent years, child sexual abuse has attracted increasing attention from the legal profession, politicians, policy makers and the media and from workers who are involved in helping children and their families. Attention has focused largely on the plight of children who are in abusive situations or who have been abused in the recent past, and on the issues raised in working with these children and their families. As a consequence of changes in attitudes and professional practice, there is now some hope that future generations of children may be able to ask for and receive help if they are being sexually abused.

For many adults such help was not available to them as children and, as a result, they have carried the long-term effects of sexual abuse into their adult lives. Some of them have been referred to mental health and social work agencies with a variety of problems, the roots of which lie in their experience of having been sexually abused. In the past they may have found it difficult to talk about their childhood experiences, fearing that they would not be believed or that they would encounter negative attitudes from the professionals whom they approached for help. There are also adults who have been unable to seek help. They may continue to remain silent unless they can feel confident that they will be heard and sympathetically understood. There are, sadly, some adults for whom the consequences of childhood sexual abuse are so severe that long-term hospitalization or even suicide results. It is to be hoped, however, that a growing awareness and understanding about sexual abuse and its effects among professional helpers will enable appropriate support to be offered to all adults who have suffered this form of abuse and who choose to seek help.

One of the most significant recent developments has been the growing voice of incest survivors themselves, speaking out about their childhood experiences. This has had a number of effects. Firstly, it has encouraged other incest survivors to disclose details of their experiences, and in doing so, to acknowledge problems which are common to all incest survivors. This has also contributed to our knowledge of the effects of childhood sexual abuse. Secondly, it has led to an increase in the number of adults who seek help once they discover that it is possible to come to terms with their childhood ordeal. It has also forced the helpers with whom incest survivors are in contact to evaluate the assumptions on which their work is based and the therapeutic methods which they use. For us, this has been a difficult but rewarding process, which has enabled us to feel more confident in our work with incest survivors.

In 1983 we started working with a small number of women who had experienced sexual abuse as children. Since then the number of women coming forward to seek help has increased dramatically, and we now work with them in individual and group settings. From the outset we were acutely aware of the lack of published material relating to the long-term effects of childhood sexual abuse and appropriate therapeutic methods for use in working with adult survivors. Material about how to ask critical questions in therapy or how to respond to disclosure was not widely available and we have had to learn largely through our personal experience of working with incest survivors. This book is a reflection of that learning and a means of sharing it with others who are involved in helping survivors of childhood sexual abuse. We hope that it will be of interest to mental health and social workers in statutory and voluntary agencies, primary care workers, rape crisis groups, voluntary counselling schemes, incest survivor groups and other resources which offer support to women. We also hope that the book will be read by incest survivors themselves. It is inevitable therefore that its contents will cross professional, training and agency boundaries.

For a number of reasons the book concentrates on women who have been sexually abused. In the first place, we are writing from our own experience, which has been that of working entirely with female survivors. We do acknowledge, however, that many of the issues addressed will be relevant to male incest survivors. These men may face other difficulties which are as yet unclear and little understood, since relatively few of them have come forward to talk about their experiences. Secondly, we are concentrating on female survivors of sexual abuse because of our current understanding of childhood sexual abuse which indicates the predominance of male family members abusing female children.

The book will focus on sexual abuse within the immediate or extended family. We do acknowledge that many of the issues addressed will apply equally to situations where the abuser is a trusted adult outside the family and, to a lesser extent, to incidents of abuse by a stranger. As more women decide to seek help, it is likely that helpers will meet women who have been subjected to ritualistic and sadistic abuse by family members and others. The particular issues facing these women is beyond the scope of this book, but it is important to acknowledge that they do exist.

We have tried to write the book as free as possible from jargon in the hope that it will be accessible to a wide audience. We acknowledge that readers will be selective in their use of its contents and we hope that it can be used as a source book, to be referred to on specific issues or to gain a wide understanding on a range of topics.

The book starts with a definition of terms used in the text and an examination of the ways in which helpers have previously responded to disclosures of sexual abuse.

Some of the personal and professional issues which arise for helpers who offer support to incest survivors are then addressed, paying particular attention to the importance of examining personal attitudes and values, and acknowledging any life experiences which may inhibit or add to the effectiveness of the work. A summary of the long-term effects of sexual abuse follows, together with an analysis of the factors which may lead a woman to seek help. The theme of disclosure is analyzed in depth, together with a woman's right to remain silent. This is followed by a description of the main themes in therapeutic work with incest survivors, paying attention to methods which can be used in the work. A summary of issues which arise in working with individuals, with groups, and in family settings is given, along with details of a range of methods which can be used in therapeutic work. The book concludes with an examination of some of the training issues which arise, together with prospects for inter-professional work. It is hoped, therefore, that the book will offer material which is of value to helpers and incest survivors alike, that it will act as a sourcebook for useful therapeutic methods and that it will encourage other helpers to develop confidence in offering help to women who have been sexually abused.

Finally, we recognise the crucial role which incest survivors themselves play in helping others, including helpers who may have suffered sexual abuse, to acknowledge experiences in their past. For some helpers, therefore, the book may provoke memories or bring the pain of parts of their own childhood to the surface. Nonetheless, we hope that incest survivors will not be deterred from seeking support for themselves or from giving help to others. We also hope that helpers who have not been abused will use the book to increase their understanding and gain confidence for their work with adults who were sexually abused as children. Our experience has taught us to evaluate and appraise our own work. It has also taught us that there is no substitute for listening to and learning from incest survivors themselves.

Liz Hall
Siobhan Lloyd

Aberdeen
November 1988

Behind the Human Wall

I can hear a noise behind the wall
Like a child crying.
The wall is very high and thick
And still I hear the sound of crying.
Who's in there?

It's me, help me!
I'm trapped, I feel I'm in prison.

Who built this wall and trapped you behind it?

My parents, with their hate and aggression, they didn't love me. They pushed me behind this wall and built the wall brick by brick, day by day, month by month, year by year and they have left me here as a child and I can't break through. The wall is thick, yet I'm afraid of what's on your side. The world frightens me, yet it's lonely behind the wall. I don't know who cares any more for me, yet I'm cold behind the wall. I want this wall to fall down, yet I'm frightened of what will get in with me if I let the wall down. I will get invaded by insects, horrible black creatures crawling all over me. Just that feeling makes me want to stay here.

Then you are a prisoner behind the wall
and the only way out is to break through.

Please, help me, I'm confused, I've been here for so long!
The wall can only be broken the way your parents built it,
Brick by brick, day by day, month by month, year by year.

Why do you scream?

I'm in pain; and there's nothing to stop me from feeling this hurt that makes me scream

By an incest survivor

1   Introduction

One consequence of the increase in public interest in the issue of sexual abuse has been a dramatic rise in the number of women seeking help because of their childhood experiences. Both statutory services and voluntary organizations have had to respond to this increased demand on their resources. People working with incest survivors have also been forced to examine their own attitudes and working practices, so that women can be offered the help most appropriate to their needs. Wider issues have also been debated: the legal framework for crimes of sexual violence has been examined and prevailing theories about the nature and extent of child sexual abuse have been challenged. Most importantly our understanding of child sexual abuse has been heightened by the testimony of incest survivors themselves. This chapter covers three main areas:

- a definition of some of the key terms used in the book;
- a summary of the main theoretical perspectives that have been used to understand and explain child sexual abuse;
- a description of sexual abuse.

Definition of Terms

Child sexual abuse

Attempts at defining child sexual abuse abound in the literature available. Definitions vary according to the abuse activities included, the relationship of the child to the abuser and the age difference between the child and the abuser. Some of the difficulties in the search for an acceptable definition can be best illustrated by examining different but overlapping approaches.

One of the most widely used definitions is as follows:

> The involvement of developmentally immature children and adolescents in sexual actions which they cannot fully comprehend, to which they cannot

give informed consent, and which violate the taboos of social roles. (Kempe and Kempe, 1984).

This definition has been criticized on two counts by MacLeod and Saraga (1988):

– it takes no account of the possibility of force, or the threat of force being used by the abuser;
– it suggests that some acts are abusive only because they are not socially acceptable.

The definition does not acknowledge that young adults can also be sexually abused, even though they may be over the age of informed consent. It also ignores the fact that most children are abused by adults known to them.

Incest survivors themselves have agreed a definition which has been adopted also by campaigning groups. Their definition is:

The sexual molestation of a child by an older person perceived as a figure of trust or authority — parents, relatives (whether natural or adoptive), family friends, youth leaders and teachers, etc. (Incest Survivors Campaign, quoted in Nelson, 1987).

It is vital that incest survivors have the right to define sexual abuse as they choose. However, by including abuse by babysitters, or family friends it becomes easy for critics who still doubt the prevalence of sexual abuse to discount new statistics. The allegation can be made that the figures are misleading because they include these wider extra-familial relationships (Nelson, 1987). Nelson also argues that 'nothing should be allowed to obscure the fact that the majority of (incest) survivors suffered at the hands of a father-figure or brother.'

A third, more restricted definition is used by Forward and Buck (1981):

Any overtly sexual contact between people who are closely related or per-ceive themselves to be . . . if that special trust which exists between a child and parent figure or sibling is violated by a sexual act, that act becomes incestuous.

This definition is restricted to family relationships even though it is recognized that the abuse of trust within the family has particularly devastating effects lasting into adult-hood. Nelson (1987) concludes that:

Traditionally, professionals have ignored or played down such abuse because it takes place within the family . . . there is no good place for sexual abuse But the family is the most destructive place of all.

Sgroi (1982) uses a definition which has fewer of the problems mentioned above:

Child sexual abuse is a sexual act imposed on a child who lacks emotional, maturational and cognitive development. The ability to lure a child into a sexual relationship is based on the all-powerful and dominant position of the adult or older perpetrator which is in sharp contrast to the child's age, dependence or subordinate position. Authority and power enable the perpetrator, implicitly or directly, to coerce the child into sexual compliance.

However, its emphasis on the 'sexual act' does not cover the range of sexual activities which children find threatening or unpleasant e.g. being watched in a 'sexual' way whilst undressing or bathing. It also fails to mention the range of other types of abuse which all too frequently accompany sexual abuse.

The search for the 'perfect' definiton of child sexual abuse will doubtless continue. Whatever the outcome it should include the following elements:

– the betrayal of trust and responsibility;
– the abuse of power;
– the inability of children to consent;
– an indication of the wide range of sexual activity involved in the abuse;
– the use of force and/or threats by the abuser;
– the child's perception of a threat even if the abuse is non-coercive, threatening or non-violent.

In this way, it will acknowledge that child sexual abuse not only crosses the physical boundaries between adult and child, but it also constitutes a fundamental abuse and betrayal of the power that an adult has in relation to a child.

In this book we examine issues relating to child sexual abuse which is perpetrated by an adult who is known to and trusted by a child. We emphasize abuse which is perpetrated by family members, in particular fathers or father-figures.

Characteristics of sexual abuse

Child sexual abuse has a number of features which make it particularly difficult for the child and which cause problems for the adult survivor:

Duration of the abuse: a child may be abused by a trusted adult on one occasion only, but more frequently the sexual abuse goes on for months or years (Lukianowitz, 1972; Maisch, 1973).

Frequency of the abuse: the abuse may occur once only or several times a week over a number of years. Often, however, a child experiences sexual abuse on a daily or more frequent basis.

The identity of the abuser: most sexual abuse is perpetrated by fathers or father-figures.

Forward and Buck (1981) suggest that 75 per cent of reported abuse cases involve fathers and daughters, and that 10 per cent involve grandfathers. Brothers, uncles and cousins, or adult men who are in a position of trust with the child, e.g., youth leaders, baby-sitters, teachers, doctors have also been identified as perpetrators. It is estimated that approximately 5 per cent of the abusers of girls are female (Russell, 1986; Finkelhor, 1986).

The age of the child: for most abused children the abuse starts well before puberty. Kempe and Kempe (1984) found the median age was between nine and ten years old. Herman and Hirschman's (1977) study found that between six and nine was a common age for the abuse to start. There have been many individual cases reported where the child was under the age of six and even as young as a few months old.

Age of the abuser: evidence on the age of abusers comes from figures on convicted offenders and the accounts of incest survivors themselves. In most cases, the abuser is at least ten years older than the child. In relation to abuse by brothers and cousins, the age difference may be less, but the abuser is usually past puberty when the abuse starts.

Multiple abusers: some children are abused by several adults, including a number of family members and other adults known to the family.

Sexual abuse and incest

Incest is defined by the *New Collins Concise English Dictionary* as 'sexual intercourse between two people who are too closely related to marry'. This definition reflects the legal parameters of the crime of incest and it confirms that children who have suffered long-term sexual abuse without full sexual intercourse have no recourse in law.

We have deliberately avoided the use of the word 'incest' in the book to describe sexual abuse. The only exception is when it is used in the context of 'incest survivor'. We consider 'incest' to be a difficult, emotive and confusing word for the following reasons:

- it does not take into account the range of sexual activity which constitutes sexual abuse;
- it omits the fact that one of the 'persons' is a child and is in no position legally, emotionally or socially to consent;
- it is a word which incest survivors themselves believe implies consent;
- it is too narrow and legalistic a definition.

For all these reasons, we prefer to use the term 'sexual abuse'.

Incest survivor

Throughout the book we have used the term 'incest survivor' to describe a woman who has experienced childhood sexual abuse. The term was identified by women themselves in the 1980s as an alternative to the word 'victim' which had been in common use until that time. To describe a woman as an incest survivor suggests that:

– she is no longer powerless in relation to the abuse;
– she has identified the cause of her problems and is, hopefully, going to seek help;
– she can identify with other incest survivors, sharing elements of a common past, a common language and a common wish for change;
– it emphasizes the inner personal resources which she has used to survive the abuse.

The helper

Throughout the book we use the term 'helper' to describe the person who works with an incest survivor to help her to deal with the effects of her childhood experiences. The term is not wholly satisfactory, as the helping role may take a variety of forms and can occur in different settings. For example, the helper might be:

– a volunteer with little training, working in a voluntary organization such as Women's Aid or Rape Crisis;
– a trained counsellor working in a voluntary or professional capacity;
– a member of a profession dealing with mental health problems in adults and/or children, e.g., clinical psychologist, psychiatrist, social worker, psychiatric nurse;
– an education or community worker with a women's group;
– a trained psychotherapist or family therapist;
– a marriage guidance counsellor;
– a sex therapist;
– a minister;
– a G.P. or other medical specialist;
– workers in women's hostels;
– a worker in a community project with families;
– an incest survivor herself in any of the above situations.

Other words which might be used to describe the helper include 'counsellor', 'therapist' or simply 'worker'. In a group setting, the word 'facilitator' is often used.

We acknowledge that not all helpers will have had formal training in counselling or a type of therapy. We are aware, however, that many incest survivors are supported by women with a keen insight into the nature of sexual abuse and its effects, until they are ready to embark on a formal therapeutic process or whilst they are in the process of doing so.

Theoretical Perspectives

Two theoretical perspectives have had a major influence on the way incest survivors have been helped. These are the psychoanalytic and feminist views of child sexual abuse. This section examines the features of each perspective and considers their impact on the ways in which incest survivors receive help.

The psychoanalytic perspective

Psychoanalytic theory has had a dominant influence on our understanding of male and female sexuality. Its theoretical importance lies in the way in which a set of ideas, originating in the late nineteenth century in one section of Viennese society has dominated society's beliefs and professional practice.

Freud formulated his seduction theory about the origins of 'hysteria' and the 'neuroses' on the basis of his analyses of female patients. He was shocked to discover that large numbers of his female patients revealed that they had suffered sexual abuse. He linked the symptoms of these women with sexual trauma in their childhood.

Following the publication of his ideas, Freud was heavily criticized and he modified his original ideas. He suggested that a woman who described sexual abuse was really having incestuous fantasies and wishes towards her father. It is now generally accepted that the reasons for Freud's change of mind originated in his wish to protect his standing as a respectable member of a scientific community which had rejected his ideas. After delivering a paper on his findings to a hostile and rejecting audience he wrote, 'I felt as though I was despised and universally shunned' (Masson, 1985). In addition, the nature of family life in nineteenth century Europe meant that parents had to be respected, at any cost, and this provided a further pressure for not believing his patients. Within a few years, Freud had begun to assert that for 'girls who produce such an event (sexual abuse) in the story of their childhood . . . there can be no doubt of the imaginary nature of the accusation or of the motive that has led to it' (Masson, 1985). Giving little evidence, Freud went on to claim 'these separated scenes of seduction had never taken place, and they were only fantasies which my patients made up.'

When Freud abandoned his original theory, he did a disservice not only to his profession but to many generations of women whose childhood experiences have since been denied. Freud's followers continued to work on the assumption of childhood sexual fantasies, making this their basis for inquiry when a woman disclosed sexual abuse in analysis as an adult. One serious consequence was that an abuser's desire and capacity for initiating the abuse was ignored. Furthermore, responsibility for allowing or imagining the abuse to have taken place was seen to rest with the child. Nelson concludes:

> We can only guess how momentous might have been the consequences for several generations of incest survivors if Freud had stuck to his original theory and his followers had searched actively for an incest history in disturbed patients, from the belief that it was a major cause of mental disorder. (Nelson, 1987).

Although psychoanalytic ideas have assisted in perpetuating a denial that sexual abuse has occurred, they cannot be accused of minimizing the trauma of sexual abuse itself. The theory stresses the importance of traumatic childhood events in the emotional, social and sexual development of the individual. In particular, it has made an important contribution to our understanding of the idea of ambivalence, where a woman who has been sexually abused feels both love and hate for an abuser. He has sexually abused her, but he may be the only person in her life who has ever paid her any attention or given her affection. An incest survivor might feel that,

> Because anger towards the loved person cannot be expressed for fear of losing that person, and cannot therefore be lived out, ambivalence and linking of love and hate remains an important characteristic of later . . . relationships. Many people cannot even imagine that love is possible at all without suffering and sacrifice, without fear of being abused, without being hurt and humiliated. (Miller, 1984).

Freud's emphasis on the unconscious has implications for work with incest survivors. He believed that the way in which behaviour and personality development is influenced by forces, motivation and childhood patterns of which the individual is totally unaware. It is estimated that up to 50 per cent of survivors of child sexual abuse are not aware of these experiences and yet there are many signs and symptoms that may lead to a suspicion that a woman has been abused.

Freud's discussion of mechanisms that the individual uses to defend him or herself against emotional and physical pain are also important. Freud stressed the importance of recovering the repressed or suppressed memories in order to help the individual make sense of his/her problems. This is a cornerstone of work with incest survivors.

In the final analysis, however, psychoanalytic theory operates within a patriarchal ideology. It fails to make any links between powerlessness, violence and sexuality. By denying the reality of sexual abuse it has sentenced thousands of women to 'confused guilty silence, whilst exonerating the abusers' (Scott, 1988).

The feminist perspective

In the mid 1970s, women began to question seriously the assumptions made by Freud in relation to child sexual abuse. At the same time, the issue was being brought to public attention not by professional workers or politicians, but by women in Women's Aid, Rape Crisis and Incest Survivors' Groups and by incest survivors themselves. Feminist practice in relation to sexual abuse has come from the initiatives of the women's movement in relation to rape and domestic violence. It has raised awareness both nationally and internationally about the numbers of children being abused, about the emotional and social effects of the experience and questioned why men sexually abuse children.

Theoretical work from feminist writers began to be published in the early 1980s (Rush, 1980; Herman, 1981; Nelson, 1982). Moving personal accounts from incest survivors have also begun to appear (Allen, 1982; Ward, 1984; Spring, 1986; Sisk and Hoffman, 1987) and biographies and novels have also been important (Morris, 1982; Walker, 1982; Angelou, 1984).

A feminist analysis examines the kind of society we live in and sees child sexual abuse as part of the spectrum of male dominance over women and girls. The learning of social roles, and of gender identity take place initially in the family and are transmitted through male and female sex-roles. As Ash (1984) indicates:

> The feminine role confers passivity, dependence and subordination and casts the female as the emotional caretaker of other family members. The masculine role confers mastery, control and dominance, and casts the man as protector and material provider for the family unit. Father–daughter sexual abuse, like rape and violence against women, occurs in a society which has historically viewed women and children as the property of their male protectors, and which has supported the use of male aggression to maintain dominance.

The contradictions of our society are therefore acknowledged. Men are assumed, through their role as partners and fathers, to protect their women and children, particularly from other men, and yet are sanctioned in their use of aggression to maintain their dominant status, both within the family and in society generally. Our society encourages the exploitation of women and girls through advertising, pornography and the beliefs about rape, a fear with which all women live, serving to keep them watchful and in need of protection from men.

Feminism argues that deep-rooted social attitudes about male dominance and power encourage crimes such as wife-beating and rape and until these attitudes have changed, no amount of work with convicted offenders will seriously reduce the number of these crimes. It calls for the re-evaluation of a system which causes male violence. The belief is that a society without male violence will only happen when society itself changes.

A feminist analysis also sees 'the problem of masculinity' at the centre of any explanation of child sexual abuse. It asserts that we live in a patriarchal society which is reinforced by the social structure of the family, with father as the power holder, mother as nurturer and children as dependent. Male power is also held responsible for the silence surrounding sexual abuse as mothers and children have no power to break that silence. A need to maintain the family identity prevents a revelation of the truth, since to tell would risk isolation. The analysis also goes some way towards explaining the incidence of sexual abuse of girls. Current estimates suggest that between one in five and one in eight girls are sexually abused by a male adult before the age of 16. Clearly, this level of incidence can only be explained by broad factors, and not the psychopathology of an individual man.

Feminist theory has also challenged Freudian ideas and developed new ways of thinking about mothers, abusers and children in families where child sexual abuse has occurred.

Mothers: the image produced by society is of a carer and nurturer whose role is to reproduce and develop a happy family. Her function is to provide emotional and physical care and to be sexually available to her partner. A mother is, therefore, held to blame when one of *her* children is sexually abused by *her* partner, because she works, leaves home, fails to protect *her* children, does not see the abuse, does not hear her children, fails to sexually satisfy her partner, because she is not a well-adjusted woman or chooses a man who abuses their child.

A feminist analysis of mothers in families where child abuse has occurred sees her as isolated, conforming to a feminine role-model where she is the arbiter and carer of everyone else in the family and the keeper of secrets, thus rendering her powerless.

Children: feminist theory has strongly voiced the view that, if children really did share the sexual desires and feelings of adults, they would respond to the 'courtship gestures' which adults use on one another (Nelson, 1987). Instead it points to the means of coercion and holding out of favours which abusers use to maintain a child's silence. Feminism is unequivocal in asserting that responsibility for sexual abuse of children and adults lies with the perpetrator of the abuse.

Abusers: feminism challenged the way in which characteristics that are cited in child abusers have allowed responsibility for the abuse to be deflected from them. By labelling the abuser as a psychopath, alcohol-dependent or paedophile, his behaviour is to some extent excused as needing treatment. Instead, feminism asserts that abusers should accept responsibility for their actions, thus allowing children to rid themselves of the burden of guilt which they universally feel.

The aims of feminist practice with incest survivors has four main tenets:

- to reverse the victim-blaming and mother-blaming practices of the past;

- to emphasize the importance of talking, support, self-help and education for incest survivors;
- to influence policy-making in relation to sexual abuse. This might include campaigning for more women-centred resources such as women's therapy centres and refuges for incest survivors;
- to influence practice within statutory and voluntary settings through discussion and training.

The main shortcoming of a feminist analysis is that it is ideological, and places the responsibility for everything on the structure of society. This does not allow for individual differences between families. It has little to say about male children who are sexually abused, or about the small number of female abusers. The argument about male children may be unfounded, however, if one accepts that male children, like women and girls, share the same status of powerlessness and dependency within families.

It also fails to address adequately the issue of a child feeling betrayed by her mother because her mother may know about the abuse and do nothing. We recognize the major difficulties faced by both mothers and daughters in breaking the secret of sexual abuse, but we are also aware that some mothers participate in, condone or encourage the abuse. This leaves the child in an impossible position, with no close adult in whom she can trust and ignores a situation where the mother is the only or main abuser of her child. This is particularly difficult for an incest survivor, as the silence and taboos surrounding sexual abuse by mothers are much greater than when a child is abused by male relatives. She may be faced with more disbelief and a greater lack of understanding than is normally the case. Finally, the emphasis on male power, whilst consistent with the testimony of incest survivors, does not acknowledge that sexual abuse is especially problematic because it is sexual. Many of the long-term effects (e.g., sexual problems, fear of being touched, body image difficulties) result from the sexual nature of the abuse.

It is our view, however, that a feminist analysis offers a dynamic approach to the issue of child sexual abuse. It is the approach which has informed our thinking and practice and it underpins the content of this book. Identifying power rather than sexuality as the basis for an abuser's motivation, and emphasizing the importance of talking, support, self-help and education for incest survivors and those who work with them, are all crucial. It also offers hope for change. The growth in women's self-help groups and in the number of professional workers who practice from a feminist perspective confirm this hope. Finally, feminism itself is always open to new ideas. The details of its theoretical perspective are continually under review as new research evidence is presented and new ideas are discussed and applied.

Practice Implications of the Theoretical Perspectives

The implications for incest survivors

Now that incest survivors are coming forward in increasing numbers to ask for help, their collective strength has grown and they are no longer prepared to remain silent. In the past, countless women have been referred to psychiatric hospitals, social work departments, sex, marital and family therapists for treatment of the symptoms of sexual abuse. Many have received appropriate help, but many others have remained silent about their childhood. Help for these and many other women has been restricted to treating the symptoms of their problems rather than their root cause. In addition, a woman may have been helped as part of another system or group — a marriage or family, for example, rather than as a person in her own right. In the last decade, however, an incest survivor has been more likely to receive help for herself in her own right, to work on the root cause of her problems.

Implications for helpers

In the past there has been a general reluctance on the part of professionals to identify and acknowledge the effects of child sexual abuse. This partly reflects a lack of knowledge, but it is also symptomatic of a general unwillingness to believe that sexual abuse occurs. Recently, however, as the issue is debated more publicly, professionals have had to re-examine their practice and the assumptions on which it is based. This, together with the growing confidence of incest survivors themselves, has helped to ensure that women who have been abused will no longer feel so isolated and silenced.

The Meaning of Sexual Abuse

In this section we outline the range of sexually abusive behaviour and activities that are perpetrated on children. It does not make easy reading, but we feel that it is important to understand what might be involved when a woman says she has been sexually abused. A knowledge of what abuse entails also enables helpers to anticipate disclosures and to become more accepting of information which is extremely difficult to describe and equally difficult to share.

There is clearly a continuum of abuse (Sgroi *et al.*, 1982), which ranges from an adult exposing his genitals to a child at one end of the spectrum, to rape, accompanied by violent and sadistic abuse at the other. The examples of sexual abuse given in subsequent pages are not isolated incidents; many of them have been disclosed by numerous women.

Context of the abuse

Sexual abuse can take place:

- in every day situations such as bath-time or bed-time;
- always in the same location, e.g., a child's bed, abuser's bed, on a chair in the living room;
- at the same time of the day or week (e.g., Thursday evenings when the child is left alone with the abuser);
- with or without being clothed;
- as part of a wider range of physical or sadistic abuse;
- in a 'special' place away from the child's home e.g., in a car, shed, or building used for community activities;
- in a fleeting way as the child and adult come physically close to each other e.g., the abuser fondles the child's genital area as he passes her on the stairs or in a swimming pool;
- possibly to maximize the child's sense of guilt it can take place in her parents' bed, or in the presence of other children;
- in a context where the child is rewarded by money or presents for the sexual contact.

Most incest survivors have been exposed to a variety of sexual activities. It may be difficult for them to pinpoint the start of the abuse but it often quickly escalates in both frequency and range. What follows represents a picture of the continuum of the sexual abuse of children.

Sexual abuse: a continuum of abuse

The abuser watches the child in an intrusive or sexual way as she has a bath, goes to the toilet or gets dressed and undressed.

The abuser exposes his penis to the child.

The abuser persuades or demands the child to undress and expose her genitals to him.

The abuser has the child sitting/lying on his lap in such a way that her body movements, pressure and position cause him to have an erection.

The abuser masturbates himself in front of the child, perhaps to ejaculation.

The child is told to masturbate herself.

The child is told to masturbate her abuser, perhaps until he ejaculates.

The abuser fondles the child, touching her in a gently stroking manner. This may begin by him touching her entire body, or focus on certain parts of her body — breasts, nipples, bottom, vaginal opening, clitoris, lower abdomen, inner thighs.

The abuser fondles the child in a painful and rough way, e.g., pulling or biting her nipples.

The child is told to fondle the abuser — his body, or parts of it, e.g., penis, buttocks, legs.

The child is forced to kiss her abuser on the mouth, often in an overtly sexual way, e.g., French kissing.

The abuser rubs his penis against the child's body
against the child's thighs
against the child's buttocks
in her genital area
against other parts of her body.

The abuser places his penis in the child's mouth.

The abuser ejaculates in her mouth.

The abuser uses his mouth and tongue to stimulate the child in the genital area, or internally in her vagina.

The abuser ejaculates over her body or face.

The abuser ejaculates on the child or himself and forces her to lick up his semen.

The abuser penetrates the child's body by inserting his fingers into:
her vagina
her anal opening
her urethra

The abuser penetrates the child's body with his penis in:
her vagina
her anal opening
her urethra

The abuser uses everyday objects e.g., pen, banana, cucumber, sticks, other long thin objects to penetrate the child in:
her vagina
her anal opening
her urethra

The abuser uses sexual or gynaecological objects, e.g., vibrator or vaginal dilator to penetrate the child in:
her vagina

her anal opening
her urethra

The abuser uses weapons, e.g., gun, sword or dangerous objects, e.g., glass bottle, broken glass or knife to penetrate the child in:
- her vagina
her anal opening
her urethra

The abuser involves the child in sexual games, e.g., strip poker.

The abuser deliberately/accidentally induces sexual arousal and orgasm in the child.

The child is made pregnant by the abuser.

Involvement of others in the abuse

The child is forced to watch the abuser having sexual contact with another adult.

The child is forced to watch the abuser sexually abusing another child.

The child is forced to be involved in sexual activities with another child, e.g., sibling.

The child is offered for sexual purposes by the abuser to friends and relatives.

As above, but the friends and relatives then sexually abuse the child.

As above, but for money, gifts or other inducements.

The child is forced to become a child prostitute.

The child is forced to be part of a sex ring.

The child is forced to be involved in pornographic activities, e.g., photographed in overtly sexual poses, forced to dress in adult clothes, tied and bound as part of the sexual abuse.

The child is forced to watch the abuser being involved in sexual activity with an animal.

The child is forced to be involved in sexual activity with animals.

Related abusive activities

The child is forced to agree to the sexual activity.

The child is forced to ask her abuser to involve her in a particular sexual activity.

The child is told to repeat after her abuser the sexual activities he intends to involve her in.

The child is told to write a letter to her abuser asking him to involve her in certain types of sexual activity.

The child is forced/expected to say that she enjoyed the sexual activity.

The child is expected to wear certain clothes during the sexual activity.

The child is expected to interpret an abuser's verbal and non-verbal signals that he wishes sexual activity with her to occur, e.g., a look at the clock, certain gestures or verbal instructions which always precede the abuse.

The child is verbally abused, e.g., 'your body is like . . .'

The child is verbally humiliated in front of others.

Physical abuse

A child who is being subjected to sexual abuse may also experience physical abuse. The sexual abuse may form part of a range of physical abuse which is perpetrated on all the children in the family. Alternatively, the physical abuse may be limited to its use as a means of keeping one child silent about the sexual abuse. The following are common forms of physical abuse:

The abuser hits the child with his hands or fists
   on her body
   on her head
   in the genital area

The abuser hits the child with an object
   on her body
   on her head
   in the genital area.

The abuser shakes the child.

The abuser throws objects, e.g., iron, sticks, bottles at the child.

The abuser throws the child against a wall or furniture.

The abuser bangs the child's head on a wall or funiture.

The abuser dislocates or fractures the child's limbs.

The abuser burns the child with:
   cigarettes/matches

an iron or fire
boiling water/fat.

The abuser pulls the child's hair.

The abuser pulls the child around by her hair.

The abuser kicks the child.

The abuser cuts the child with a sharp object, e.g., razor blade, broken glass, knife, sharp implement:
on her face and neck
in her genital area
on other parts of the body.

The abuser traps the child's fingers in a door or drawers.

The abuser puts his hands round the child's throat.

The abuser keeps the child's face under water.

The child is whipped with a belt, rope, etc.

The abuser cuts/shaves her hair (including pubic hair).

Other forms of abuse

There are other forms of abuse that often accompany sexual abuse. They are sadistic or cruel in nature or they may be a result of neglect. They may include some or all of the following:

The child is deprived of food and drink.

The child is kept away from other family members.

The child is locked up, kept dirty and not fed.

The child is deprived of items necessary for her physical health, e.g., inhaler for asthma, hearing aid, spectacles.

The child's food and drink are contaminated:
with unpleasant tasting substances
with mould
with semen
with urine or faeces
with paraffin/petrol.

The child is prevented from sleeping by:
    being constantly woken up (e.g., shining a torch in her eyes, making loud bangs, by
        blowing whistles)
    being made to stand up all night.

The child is left by herself for long periods with no food or drink.

The child is forced to stand for hours.

The child is tied up.

The child is locked up in small confined area, e.g., cupboard, small attic or cellar room,
    coal bunker.

The child is thrown out of the house.

The child is forced to smoke large numbers of cigarettes.

The child is forced to drink a quantity of alcohol.

The child is forced to drink methylated spirits/paraffin.

The child is forced to take tablets or other medication to excess.

The abuser urinates/defecates over the child.

The abuser urinates in front of the child
    on the floor
    into the fire
    into a bucket.

The abuser uses a range of objects to frighten the child, e.g., weapons, sharp imple-
    ments, masks etc.

The abuser uses insects to:
    hurt the child (e.g., wasps, bees)
    frighten her
    threaten her during sexual and physical abuse.

Unnecessary medical procedures are carried out on the child by the abuser, e.g.,
    enema, injections.

Wounds are deliberately re-opened.

The child's or family's pets are injured or killed in front of the child.

The child is forced to make 'impossible' choices, e.g.:
    the child is banned from a room/house and permitted to return only if she agrees to
        sexual activity;

the child is locked in a cupboard/cellar/attic/other room and released only if she agrees to sexual activity;

the child is forced to choose between herself or another child being sexually abused;

the child is forced to choose between various forms of abuse that will be carried out e.g., sexual abuse versus a violent beating; being burnt versus being locked in a dark room;

the child is forced to choose between herself being physically and/or sexually abused or a pet being hurt or killed;

the child is forced to choose between being put out of the house or being subjected to sexual abuse.

Cold water is thrown over the child and warmth is then denied.

The abuser damages possessions valued by the child, e.g., toys, musical instruments, books, records.

The abuser uses treasured possessions of the child in the abuse.

The abuser criticizes or misuses activities valued by the child, e.g., religious activities, musical activities, sport.

Presents are given which are then withdrawn or destroyed.

Presents are given which contain frightening or disgusting objects.

The child is forced to be involved in ritual abuse, e.g., Black Magic, witchcraft, or systematic torture.

Faced with this list for the first time, helpers may feel a range of emotions including disgust, anger, guilt and helplessness. These are all normal reactions and are developed when we consider the full implications of child sexual abuse for helpers in Chapter 2.

2 Issues for the Helper

Working with incest survivors raises a number of important issues for the helper. These should be considered before starting the work and reviewed while it is in progress. Helpers need to consider their personal history, attitudes, beliefs and prejudices about sexual abuse. They also need to have an understanding of their own sexuality, since the ability to discuss matters relating to sex and sexuality in an open and specific way is also important. Sex and sexual abuse are still enveloped in embarrassment, shame, fear, ignorance and secrecy. This serves to confuse and cloud the reality experienced by an incest survivor and compounds the hidden nature of the subject.

This chapter explores issues which should be addressed by anyone working with incest survivors. The issues include:

– challenging the myths about sexual abuse and examining the helper's own attitudes;
– the gender of the helper;
– self-disclosure;
– effects on the helper's family relationships;
– emotional reactions to working with incest survivors;
– training and supervision.

Challenging the Myths about Sexual Abuse

Many commonly held beliefs about the incidence and meaning of sexual abuse have been challenged in recent years. These beliefs have enabled professionals and society at large to fail to acknowledge the prevalence of sexual abuse, its resulting pain and the damage it carries for children and adult survivors. The myths and their consequences for incest survivors have been well documented elsewhere (Nelson, 1987; MacLeod and Saraga, 1988). Table 2.1 provides a summary of these myths, together with established facts about child sexual abuse. It is worth noting here that, in addition to large-scale research studies, the testimony of incest survivors themselves through personal accounts and incest survivors' groups, has done a great deal to challenge the myths.

Table 2.1:   Sexual Abuse: Myths, Consequences and Facts

Myth	Consequence	Fact
Incest/sexual abuse never happens	Survivors' and children's accounts dismissed as fantasy	Sexual abuse is widespread
		At least one in eight girls experiences abuse before the age of 16
	Disbelief by helpers	
	Consequences of abuse ignored	The abuse often lasts for years
Children are sexually provocative	Children and survivors are blamed for the abuse	Adults are responsible for interpreting a child's behaviour as provocative
	The child or adult survivor feels guilty and confused	Children do not behave in an overtly sexual way unless they have previously been abused
	Ignores the threats and bribes used by abusers to make child participate in the abuse	
Incest only occurs in certain communities/cultures/classes	Helpers do nothing	Sexual abuse happens in all sorts of families, communities and social classes
	Prevents adults accepting responsibility for their actions	
	Perpetuates silence about child sexual abuse	Men who abuse come from all walks of life
Mothers are to blame (they collude with the abuser)	Removes responsibility for the abuse from the abuser	Mothers find it hard to believe that their partner/relative is an abuser
	Compounds guilt for a mother	Mothers may also be abused by their partner/relative
		Some mothers know about the abuse and do nothing
		Mothers may be threatened with violence if they disclose
		Disclosure forces a mother to choose between her partner and her child
		Some mothers do participate in the abuse

Table 2.1: (Continued)

Myth	Consequence	Fact
Men who abuse are deviant	Removes responsibility for the abuse from the abuser Allows excuses to be made for the abuser	Biased research sampling has created the myth by only studying convicted offenders It is not normal to sexually abuse a child but many abusers appear to be normal in all other respects Some abusers do have alcohol/psychiatric or other problems
Abusers have been abused in their own childhood	Justifies cycle of abuse theory Assumes that people cannot change because of their past Survivors may be seen as potential abusers by helpers and themselves Assumes that only people who have been abused are capable of child abuse	Most female incest survivors do not abuse their children Many male incest survivors do not abuse their children The experience of being abused can affect parenting skills
Sexual abuse is the product of a dysfunctional family	Pays less attention to power structures within families and society Ignores the causes of sexual abuse and its effects on a family	Power within most families is unequal Families do not sexually assault children but many men do Dysfunction is a consequence of abuse, not necessarily the cause of it
Sexual abuse does not do the child any/much harm	Accounts of sexual abuse are dismissed by helper Survivors told they were too young for it to matter Survivors told to forget about events in their past Survivors told not to worry about something that happened only a few times	Short and long-term consequences of child sexual abuse are now recognised to be considerable

Table 2.1: (Continued)

Myth	Consequence	Fact
Children and adult survivors lie about sexual abuse	Professionals take no notice of the child and adult survivors	Children do not have the awareness or sexual knowledge to lie about sexual abuse
		A child or adult survivor has little to gain by lying about sexual abuse

In work with incest survivors there are two central issues which relate to the myths about sexual abuse which have professional and personal consequences for the helper. These are the questions of believing and responsibility.

Believing

The myths which relate to the issue of believing are:

- sexual abuse never happens;
- sexual abuse is acceptable in some cultures;
- children, and by implication adult survivors, tell lies about sexual abuse;

Myth: Sexual abuse never happens. The first step is for a helper to acknowledge that sexual abuse can and does occur. This may appear to be stating the obvious, but continued disbelief and an inability, or unwillingness, to accept the extent to which such abuse occurs are still widespread.

We do not know how common sexual abuse by a trusted adult is. There are difficulties in interpreting the available data because:

- there is no consistency between studies in their definition of sexual abuse;
- there is no agreement on the age limits of childhood;
- early studies, carried out before 1975, were based on small clinical samples, which made it difficult to draw firm conclusions.

Finkelhor (1986) has examined the prevalence rates of sexual abuse in the United States in thirteen studies carried out between 1975 and 1985. They ranged from 6 per cent to 62 per cent for females, and 3 per cent to 31 per cent for males. He concludes that the incidence of child sexual abuse is not trivial, even if one accepts the lowest prevalence rate of 6 per cent of females and 3 per cent for males. The figure of 6 per cent would give a prevalence in 1984 of 62.7 million children under the age of seventeen experiencing sexual abuse (Fields, 1988).

In Britain there have been two recent studies of the problem (Baker and Duncan, 1985; West, 1985). The MORI survey conducted by Channel 4 and analyzed by Baker had a sample of 2019 people. 10 per cent said they had been sexually abused by the age of sixteen. 13 per cent refused to answer and 77 per cent said they had suffered no such abuse. The survey reported that one in eight girls and one in twelve boys in the total sample had suffered sexual abuse. When the figures for abuse by a family member were abstracted, there were five girls for every boy.

Overall, there is some indication that the figures may be an under-estimation. The MORI survey, for example, had a 13 per cent refusal rate. The researchers noted that some respondents refused to answer questions because they did not want to recall painful memories. This was confirmed by a large random survey (Russell, 1986) where definitions of sexual abuse were carefully chosen and interviewers were selected and trained before matching with possible respondents in terms of age, race and class. The study concluded that almost one in five women of all ages had been sexually abused by a family member before the age of sixteen.

Myth: Sexual abuse only occurs in certain communities/cultures/classes. Early studies (Flugel, 1926; Guttmacher, 1951) concluded that sexual abuse was more likely to occur in isolated communities, in families where there was a strong influence of alcohol, in working class families, in poor families, in cultures where men and women did not conform to traditional sex roles, in families where men themselves were abused or where women who were abused in childhood married abusers and became colluding mothers. The sampling methods of these studies and their conclusions have been challenged by Cavallin (1966), MacLeod and Saraga (1988) and Nelson (1987). Susan Forward examined data relating to the abusers of almost three hundred women treated in her practice. She concluded that:

> They come from every cultural, economic, racial, educational, religious and geographical background. They are doctors, policemen, prostitutes, secretaries, artists and merchants. They are heterosexual, bisexual and homosexual. They are happily married and four times divorced . . . they are emotionally stable and they have multiple personalities. (Forward and Buck, 1981).

Myth: Children, and by implication adult survivors, tell lies about sexual abuse. Children do not have the explicit knowledge to enable them to talk about this sort of sexual activity unless they have experienced it. Dismissal and disbelief of adult survivors' accounts can be destructive, driving them away from sources of help or causing them more distress with the professional denial of what they know to be a reality.

Personal and professional implications

Once a helper has acknowledged the prevalence of sexual abuse, the personal and professional implications need to be considered.

Personal implications include:

– wondering when the helper will meet someone socially who tells her/him of experiences of being sexually abused;
– fear of discussing any aspects of the work with friends or family members in case a close friend/relative discloses sexual abuse in their past;
– wondering if any male friends or acquaintances abuse their children in this way;
– fear for the safety of her/his own children with male friends, relatives and babysitters;
– wondering if behaviour with her/his own children could be construed as abusive;
– beginning to feel that every conversation leads to the subject of sexual abuse;
– wondering if she/he is one of the many adults who have forgotten or repressed the experience of childhood sexual abuse.

It is understandable and normal for heightened awareness to lead to these feelings. If they cause the helper to lose a sense of perspective, however, they should be raised in supervision.

Professional implications include:

– wondering how many incest survivors have been 'missed' in past work;
– fear of being 'overloaded' with incest survivors;
– concern about asking routine questions about childhood sexual abuse for fear of being unable to cope with the number of women who might disclose;
– fear of being over-zealous in looking for signs of sexual abuse.

Again, these feelings are understandable. They should be discussed in supervision if they become problematic.

Believing individual women

Whilst we are now beginning to accept the frequency and reality of sexual abuse in general, helpers may still have a tendency towards scepticism about the disclosures of individual women. They should remind themselves that:

– a woman has little to gain by lying about sexual abuse;
– if a helper can believe everything else that a woman has told about herself, there is no reason to doubt the sexual abuse;
– incest survivors have learnt to minimize the effects of sexual abuse and this can

make it easier for a helper to minimize or deny the harm which the abuse
caused;
- an incest survivor may minimize the frequency or nature of the abuse;
- an incest survivor may not feel justified in having any help because the abuse is in
the past.

A helper has a responsibility not to diminish or deny the effects of a woman's childhood experiences. It is also important for the helper to give the woman's history of
childhood sexual abuse an important place in the way she/he helps a woman.

Responsibility

The myths which relate to the issue of responsibility for the sexual abuse are:

- children are sexually provocative;
- children do nothing to stop the abuse so they must enjoy and encourage it;
- mothers are to blame because they collude with the abusers;
- sexual abuse is the produce of a dysfunctional family;
- the abuser is sexually deviant, mentally ill, abuses alcohol etc.

Myth: Children are sexually provocative. Young children have strong needs for physical
and emotional affection and reassurance from their parents. They are also capable of
sensual feeling and enjoyment. This does not mean, however, that they understand
their behaviour in the way that adults do, nor that they see any sexual meaning in the
verbal and non-verbal messages they give to adults. An acknowledgement that
children are sexual beings does not imply that they are physically or emotionally ready
to engage in a sexual relationship. It is sometimes easy for a helper to forget that a
child's sexuality is open to interpretation and exploitation by adults. The point is well
made by Jackson (1978) who suggests that to interpret a wide range of child behaviour
as sexual has mistakenly imposed the language of adult sexual experience on the
behaviour of children. It should never be forgotten that it is adults who are responsible
for interpreting a child's behaviour as sexual.

Myth: Children do nothing to stop the abuse so they must enjoy and encourage it. A helper
may feel that a child could have told another adult or done something to stop the abuse
as she got older. These suggestions take little account of the threats and bribes which
have been used to maintain a child's silence. For some children, the relationship with
their abuser is the only semblance of affection they have ever received. This can make
them reluctant to condemn their abuser, and only adds to their sense of blame and
complicity. Finally, many children do not recognize that the abuse is wrong until they
are older, and because it is done by someone they trust and care about, assume that it is
'normal' behaviour.

Myth: Mothers are to blame because they collude with the abuser. Mothers are often referred to as 'the silent partner' in families where incest has occurred. They are held to be responsible for the abuse on three counts:

- inadequate or flawed personalities;
- abandonment of wifely and motherly duties and therefore forcing daughters into a maternal or adult role;
- failure to take action on the abuse even when they know that it is going on.

Nelson (1987) carefully dismantles all three assertions by looking at the difficult choices facing mothers in families where sexual abuse occurs and at the feelings of powerlessness experienced by them. She suggests that it is easy to absorb an ideology of motherhood which asserts that mothers should be with their children twenty-four hours a day, and that they should accept responsibility if things go wrong. If children are being abused, the argument goes, then their mothers should somehow know about it. Often the anger expressed by survivors at their mothers is taken as evidence that they knew what was going on. If an abused child or adult survivor manages to tell her mother that she has been sexually abused by a family member or other trusted adult, the mother's reaction is often one of loss. She has lost her view of herself as a partner and as a protective mother, and her relationship with her family will never be the same again.

Myth: Sexual abuse is a sign of a disorganized, dysfunctional family. This myth ensures that the focus of concern is the family, rather than individuals within a family who perpetrate or have been subjected to sexual abuse. Sexual abuse is interpreted as a symptom of what is wrong in a family rather than the cause of it. The problem is perceived to be the underlying dysfunction of the family. This theory offers no explanation as to why the overwhelming majority of abusers are men, nor does it place responsibility for sexual abuse firmly with the abuser. An alternative perspective is to identify sexual abuse as the problem, and the disorganized family as a consequence of the abuse. Either way, the issues are never clear-cut.

Myth: Men who sexually abuse are deviant. Abusers have been variously described as deviants, as the product of their own abused childhood, obsessive in their compulsion to abuse, mentally ill, alcohol-dependent or sexually deviant. Whilst some abusers *are* sadistic, violent, mentally ill or disturbed in other ways, they have also been described by incest survivors as normal men and responsible fathers in other respects. If an abuser is seen as normal by his family, friends, neighbours and colleagues, it becomes harder to believe that he is totally responsible for sexually abusing a child. The only logical explanation is that some of the blame must lie with the child, her mother or anyone else who can be implicated.

Personal implications

– helpers need to acknowledge the reality of male power in relation to women and children within families;
– helpers may feel the need to reassess their relationships with their own partners and children.

Professional implications

If responsibility for the sexual abuse is placed with the abuser, the helper should accept that an incest survivor is not guilty of getting herself abused, failing to stop the abuse or failing to protect her siblings. These are all adult responsibilities. Once a helper has accepted this, she/he will be able to help the incest survivor to handle the issues of guilt and responsibility more objectively.

There are, nonetheless, some outstanding issues for helpers:

– helpers should make the distinction between responsibility for the abuse and responsibility for failing to protect the child;
– they should acknowledge that a mother has failed her child if she knew about the abuse and did nothing. She is, however, left with a considerable dilemma if her partner is the abuser;
– financial and social considerations may weigh heavily with a mother who knows about the abuse and does nothing;
– professional pursuit for evidence of mother-collusion can threaten the entire therapeutic process, erecting a permanent barrier between mother and daughter;
– helpers should not automatically label a mother 'collusive' if she did not know the abuse was happening, or if she did nothing. They should recognise the complexities of mothers' situations and feelings and explore these with incest survivors. It can be helpful to note that:

> For many survivors, part of their anger with their father is that he denied them the possibility of a good relationship with their mother: therapy ought not to collude with this. (MacLeod and Saraga, 1988).

– helpers also need to acknowledge that some mothers do participate in or set their children up for being sexually abused, e.g., in child prostitution or pornography;
– helpers need to acknowledge that a few abusers are so mentally ill that they do not know what they are doing;
– incest survivors often forget that they were children at the time of the abuse. It is easy for helpers to do the same.

The Gender of the Helper

In this section we will examine the gender issues which are critical in working with incest survivors. In itself the start of any therapeutic contact is likely to make an incest survivor feel very anxious. She is alone in a room, often with only one other person. There may be no-one else nearby and she may feel threatened as she did as a child. To be faced with a male helper in this situation can be so difficult for some survivors that they cannot stay.

The female helper

The female helper starts off with a number of advantages. The majority of incest survivors have not been abused by women, and therefore tend to feel much safer in the presence of women. They are more likely to be able to discuss the sexual details of the abuse with a woman because they do not fear that she will become sexually aroused by them.

The female helper may have more empathic understanding of an incest survivor's position because she is likely to have had to confront her own vulnerability, victimization or position of inequality in other contexts, including her own family. She may have experienced sexual situations in which she has felt threatened or not in control. She can convey to the incest survivor that women can be competent and in control of their lives. This enables her to identify positively with an incest survivor. There is an inherent danger here, however, that the female helper may be seen by an incest survivor as a 'superwoman' who manages her life well and never has any problems!

Physical comfort, which can be very useful in facilitating the healing process, is likely to be more acceptable and less threatening from a female helper.

The major source of conflict for an incest survivor with a female helper involves her relationship with her mother and other significant female relatives who did not protect her from being abused. She is likely to transfer many expectations and feelings about significant women in her life on to the helper. This can raise concerns about caring and competence, a desire to protect the helper, and mixed feelings of anger, neediness and disappointment.

There are a number of negative reactions that female helpers can show in working with incest survivors (see Table 2.2). These should be examined in detail when they occur during the helping process. They can be unhelpful and can even result in the incest survivor terminating her contact.

Table 2.2: Issues for the Female Helper

Potential difficulties	Consequences	Action by helper
Disbelief/denial about sexual abuse	It is worse for an incest survivor if another woman disbelieves her	Review beliefs and evidence about sexual abuse
Overidentifies with incest survivor, becomes overwhelmed with fears of helplessness and despair	Distances herself from incest survivor Gets angry Difficulties in listening to the incest survivor	Get supervision and support to maintain objectivity
Remembers sexual abuse from her own past	Angry with incest survivor for triggering memories Too distressed to continue work	Seek help for herself and stop working with incest survivors in the meantime
Takes on role of rescuer	Unable to set a limit on referrals May engage women in help who are not yet ready Burn-out	Get supervision and support Set limits on the work
Over-involvement with a woman's problems	Risks reducing incest survivor's control over her life Helper angry or distances herself from incest survivor Unable to set boundaries or limits on the work Burn-out	Seek supervision and support Set limits
Anger towards abuser	Ignores any positive feelings, comments, incest survivor makes about abuser	Support to offload anger Supervision to understand feelings
Frustration or anger at slow pace of recovery Feels that incest survivors should not continue to behave as victims	Lack of understanding of incest survivor's situation and continuing feelings of helplessness Personal beliefs impede work	Get supervision Discuss justification for anger

Table 2.2: (Continued)

Potential difficulties	Consequences	Action by helper
Becomes sexually aroused at details of survivor's abuse	Incest survivor may be unaware of this as it may not be obvious Helper feels guilty/embarrassed/angry	Try to discuss in supervision
Excessive need to be a 'good mother' to compensate for incest survivor's early experiences	Leads to over-involvement	Get supervision Explore if this is a general feature of work or relates to one incest survivor
Difficulty with terminating contact	Incest survivor feels she is not really coping after all Intrusion of helper's needs – can't let go	Discuss helper's needs in supervision
Unable to accept that mothers could not know/do not protect their children from the abuser	Misunderstanding of the abuser and his behaviour	Discuss in supervision
Does not fully understand incest survivor's reactions to the abuse, especially if it was limited to fondling or masturbation	Minimizes her reactions Incest survivor feels misunderstood and withdraws	Review understanding of long-term effects of child sexual abuse
Difficulties in validating woman's experience because of own view of women's role in society	Believes some of the myths about sexual abuse Indicates that problems are less to do with the abuse and more to do with a woman's personality	Read survivor's accounts of their past and some feminist literature on sexual abuse

The male helper

The legacy of bad feelings about men in general that the incest survivor has carried from her childhood can inhibit or prevent the start of any therapeutic work with a male helper. If she can tolerate these feelings, and come through the initial stages, there are a number of important benefits for her. First, she can discover that not every man will abuse her, be only interested in her sexually or exploit her. Secondly, she can learn that it is possible to trust a man, perhaps for the first time in her life. Finally, her attitude towards men can improve significantly by experiencing the helper's concern and understanding for her without fearing that he will abuse her trust.

Unfortunately, issues that repeat her childhood experiences are likely to be a constant source of difficulty with a male helper. She is likely to expect betrayal, intrusion and that he will overwhelm her with his apparent power over her. She may even expect him to sexually exploit or abuse her.

Physical comfort from a male helper during a period of distress is another issue which creates echoes of her childhood. Incest survivors have problems with touch in any case, but comfort from a male helper whom she perceives to have power over her, is likely to bring many of her childhood feelings to the surface. If these can be resolved, comfort from a male helper can be very reassuring and beneficial. Unfortunately, her distress is likely to be at its highest initially and during periods of disclosure, neither of which are easy times to learn to trust a man in this way.

Beyond these specific issues, there are other problems which women can have in relation to male helpers. They may be particularly noticeable in a group setting. Firstly, women often have difficulty discussing sexual matters with a man. Secondly, women are likely to be more passive and less assertive with a man and to defer to him. In work with an incest survivor, where encouraging her to take control of her life and of her past is one of the key aims, she may be more likely to acquiesce to a male helper's ideas and decisions and find it difficult to challenge him sufficiently to become a woman in her own right. Finally, women find it harder to express their anger to a man, and may try to protect him from it, fearing his reaction.

So far, we have examined an incest survivor's potential problems with a male helper. There are, however, a number of unhelpful reactions from the male helper himself. These are summarized in Table 2.3.

In a one-to-one therapeutic setting, we believe that most incest survivors find it easier to work with a female helper, particularly in the early stages. Some women will always find it impossible to entertain the possibility of working with a man. It is vital, therefore, that incest survivors should, where possible, be given the choice of a female helper from the outset.

In group settings, there is often a debate about whether the group leaders should both be female or whether one should be male and one female. It is thought that having a male and a female group leader facilitates the working through of the conflicts from the incest survivor's family situation. It may be, however, that the male-female combination could be too close to the original family situation for the survivor to find it helpful. Incest survivors who join a group in the latter stages of their therapeutic work, may be able to tolerate these difficult feelings. Women nearer the beginning may need careful preparation for the group with particular reference to the gender of the helpers. Having two female workers as group leaders overcomes many of these difficulties, and avoids feelings of passivity, powerlessness and unassertiveness that women can feel in the presence of a man.

Table 2.3: Issues for the Male Helper

Potential difficulties	Consequences	Action by worker
Possible over-identification with abuser	Incest survivor feels betrayed	Discuss in supervision
	Helper excited by sexual aspects of the abuse	Review the work
Over-emphasizes sexual aspects of the abuse rather than issue of power	Incest survivor feels that he is only interested in the sexual content	Review understanding of sexual abuse and its effects
	Incest survivor disgusted and withdraws	
Sexually aroused by details of the abuse	Incest survivor may be very aware of male sexual arousal	Discuss in supervision to examine effects of the woman's history on him
	Incest survivor feels betrayed and angry	If unresolved, stop working with incest survivors
	Withdraws from helping situation	
	Helper feels guilty, becomes over-compensating or distant	
	In rare cases could lead to therapeutic relationship becoming sexual and thus repeating the abuse	
Feels guilty about being male/about thoughts and actions in relation to his and others' children	Overcompensates to show that he is a 'safe' man	Examine own experiences with supervisor
	Overprotects incest survivor and own family	
Feels anger towards abuser	Ignores any positive feelings/comments that the incest survivor makes about the abuser	Support to offload anger Supervision to understand feelings
Does not fully understand incest survivor's reactions to the abuse, especially if it was limited to fondling or masturbation	Minimizes her reactions Incest survivor feels misunderstood and withdraws	Review understanding of long-term effects of child sexual abuse

Table 2.3:   (Continued)

Potential difficulties	Consequences	Action by worker
Difficulties in validating woman's experience because of own view of woman's role in society	Believes some of the myths about sexual abuse Indicates that problems are less to do with the abuse and more to do with a woman's personality	Read survivor's accounts of their past and some feminist literature on sexual abuse

Self-Disclosure

Work with incest survivors frequently demands a relatively high level of self-disclosure on the part of the helper. The helper can find that she/he is open about personal experiences as they relate to issues raised by the survivor. Self-disclosure should never be used to discuss any personal difficulties which the helper might be experiencing. Problems can be caused, for example, if a helper inappropriately discloses a history of sexual abuse. This can result in an incest survivor's problems being overshadowed or minimized. It can also severely test the therapeutic relationship.

Effects on Helper's Family Relationships

Working with incest survivors can raise issues in relation to a helper's partner and children. It is important to be aware of these at the outset. They vary according to the gender of the helper.

The female helper

Anger: when a female helper works with an incest survivor for the first time, she is likely to feel anger towards all men for the consequences of the actions of one of them. These feelings are common but can become harmful, however, if they begin to affect her relationship with a male partner, colleagues or friends. They can be compounded if the helper is unable to explain the reasons for her anger. Although it is not appropriate to discuss details of her work, the helper should at least try to say to her partner:

- that she is working with women who have been sexually abused;
- how the work makes her feel;
- what she would find helpful from her partner if she comes home angry or upset about a disclosure from an incest survivor (e.g., a quiet space for a short while, a hug, something to take her mind off her work or several cups of tea).

Discussing issues relating to sexual abuse with a male partner: the issue of male power is usually present when men and women discuss sexual abuse together. It is now generally acknowledged that child sexual abuse is a reflection of wider power relationships between men and women in society. This in itself can make the issue difficult to discuss, even with a supportive male partner or colleague. Female helpers should try to voice their fears and feelings to their male partners, before deciding whether it will be helpful to discuss it further.

Trusting male partners: when a helper learns from incest survivors about the context in which sexual abuse occurs, what it entails and the threats and bribes which are used to maintain silence, she can seriously question whether she can trust a male partner with her own children. She might find herself saying:

> 'I know that he wouldn't ever abuse any of our children but I've found myself watching how he plays with them . . . '

She might find herself becoming over-vigilant at home, watching the way her partner relates to their children, how and when he cuddles, bathes or dresses them. She might find herself making excuses for being present when she would normally be doing something else, or curtailing her own activities so that she is at home as often as possible. Again, this is a normal reaction, if experienced in moderation, and it will pass. It is hard to share with a partner, however, since it implies a lack of trust. It could also seriously damage the trust which exists between partners if it persists. A sensitive partner will notice the signs and raise it himself. Otherwise, the helper should share her feelings in supervision or with other helpers in order to get them into perspective before she raises it with her partner.

Effects on her sexual relationship with a male partner: a helper's own sexual relationship can be affected by work with an incest survivor, especially during periods of disclosure and she may find herself rejecting her partner. More disturbing, however, is the experience of a flashback if a sexual experience with a partner reminds her of something which an incest survivor has disclosed. This can be very upsetting both for the helper and her partner. It should be discussed with her partner to resolve the specific problem as well as having a general discussion with a supervisor to examine ways of coping with the situation.

The male helper

Guilt: there are two issues for a male helper in relation to feelings of guilt. Firstly, he will be acutely aware that an incest survivor was abused by a man, and this leads to him feeling guilty on behalf of all men. Secondly, if he is a parent, he can become more aware of his own children, particularly his daughters, in a physical way. Both issues should be discussed in supervision.

Fear: a male helper can sometimes have fears about how he treats his own children. After hearing about the way an abuser started to abuse his child, he may no longer have any certainty about what is acceptable behaviour between father and child, e.g., in relation to nudity, bathing, privacy, cuddling. Discussing these fears with his partner and in supervision will help him to gain some perspective on his own behaviour.

Effects on his sexual relationship with a female partner: having listened to an incest survivor describing distressing sexual experiences a male helper may begin to question his own sexual relationship. He may need to reassess what is acceptable or pleasurable to his partner by discussing aspects of their sexual relationship together. For male helpers too, difficulties can arise if he has a flashback to a distressing experience for an incest survivor when he is engaged in similar sexual activity with his partner. Again, he should discuss this in supervision before deciding whether to raise it with his partner.

For all helpers

Fears for safety of helper's children: the over-protectiveness which some incest survivors experience towards their own children can also be felt by helpers. They can find themselves becoming reluctant to engage a babysitter, allowing their children to play outside, spending the night in a friend's house or going on a school outing for fear of encountering a potential abuser. These signs of anxiety are often picked up by a partner or friends if they know that the helper is working with incest survivors. Again, by discussing them in supervision the helper can be reassured that her/his feelings are normal and that they will pass.

Sexuality of the helper: crucial to the process of giving help to incest survivors is the helper's understanding of her/his own sexuality and sexual development. Account should also be taken of personal standards in relation to adult nudity in the home, bathing with children, openness about sexual matters and ease of discussion of sexuality and so on. Helpers should also be aware of the ways in which their own personal standards and boundaries affect their perception of an incest survivor's experience. Chapter 10 outlines some of the ways in which training can address the issue of sexuality. The most important factor is that helpers are comfortable with their own sexuality and the ways in which they express it.

Common Emotional Reactions to Working with Incest Survivors

Work with incest survivors often produces emotions and reactions in the helper which can affect both the therapeutic relationship and style of work. It is essential that helpers are aware of their reactions and examine them carefully, perhaps with the help of a supervisor, colleague, or other support person.

Some reactions are the result of an empathic response to the incest survivor. For example, the helper can become very distressed after a detailed disclosure of sexual abuse, because the woman herself is very upset. However, it ceases to be empathic if the helper is unable to contain her/his feelings and reacts inappropriately.

Example: Joanne was very distressed disclosing that her father violently raped her when she was 10. The helper reacted initially by feeling upset too, but could not hold her distress and burst into tears. Joanne was then concerned about the helper's reaction, to such an extent that she minimized her own feelings and also the importance of the incident she had been discussing.

This section now examines the common reactions of helpers to disclosure and their consequences for therapeutic contact and work. It is necessary to discuss these during support and supervision so that they do not impede the work. This is especially relevant if a helper finds that she/he is reacting in a way that keeps on producing the same problems in the work. For example, the helper may find that she/he tends to react angrily to all disclosures of abuse.

Guilt

This is expressed in a number of ways. The helper might say:

- I feel bad about having had a good childhood;
- I was spared what she experienced;
- I feel guilty because I'm angry about what happened to her. She's suffered enough;
- I feel guilty for thoughts about and behaviour towards my own children;
- I made the woman feel suicidal because I asked her for details about the sexual abuse;
- I feel guilty that I felt aroused by her disclosure.

These feelings can lead to the helper being unable to say or ask about things that might hurt the incest survivor, or not wanting to hear any more about the sexual abuse. In addition, the helper may have difficulty in setting realistic limits on work with a particular woman in order to compensate for her/his feelings of guilt.

Fear

This can be expressed in the following ways:

- she might kill/hurt herself if she tells me what happened;
- she'll feel worse if she tells me, and I'm frightened for her;
- I am frightened to listen to her in case it reminds me of something bad from my own childhood;
- I'm scared of how I'll cope with my own feelings.

These feelings result in the helper not asking a woman about the abuse, thus giving an impression that a woman's history of sexual abuse is too difficult to discuss.

Anger and Rage

These are expressed in the following ways:

- how could anyone do that to a child?
- how dare he/they (abusers in general) do these things?
- why on earth didn't she do something to stop it?
- and where was her mother while all this was going on?
- she made me remember what happened to me;
- I feel angry with her because she won't forgive the abuser;
- I feel angry because she won't move on in the work.

These reactions are common but can lead a helper to disbelieve and minimize the abuser's responsibility for the abuse. A helper can easily mistake her/his anger for the incest survivor's anger, resulting in a blind spot about the woman's true feelings. As we have already noted, the helper's anger with a particular woman's abuser can spread to anger with men in general. This can result in problems with male colleagues, friends and family members.

Shock/Horror

These feelings are often experienced when a helper starts to work with incest survivors, when she/he listens to women who have experienced both physical and sexual abuse, and when the abuse has had particularly sadistic features. They are expressed in the following ways:

- surely nobody could do anything so dreadful to a child;
- I feel sick and horrified by the appalling things which this woman has had to suffer;

– I can't bear to listen. It's too horrible;
– could a child really survive all of this?

High levels of shock or horror about the nature and extent of the abuse will lead to the helper distancing him or herself from the woman as a self-protective mechanism. The helper may avoid asking the woman for details of the abuse or may find it impossible to believe her. This is likely to result in the therapeutic contact being shortened if allowed to go unchecked.

When an incest survivor is disclosing particularly violent and sadistic abuse, the helper can experience nightmares. These should be shared with a supervisor or support person.

Dread

This is related to reactions of shock and horror and occurs particularly during periods of detailed disclosure about the incidents of abuse. It is expressed by the helper saying:

– what else is she going to tell me?
– I don't want to ask in case she tells me something even worse;
– where is it all going to end?

Again this is liable to lead to the helper distancing him or herself from the woman, and not allowing her to disclose the details of the abuse.

Grief, sadness and distress

These are very common reactions and occur both during disclosure of memories when the woman herself gets upset, and during periods when the woman is grieving over the losses which are a result of the abuse.

They are expressed in the following ways:

– I get so upset by what she's telling me that I don't want to hear it;
– I wish I could make it all go away for her (and for me).

This leads once again to the helper becoming distanced from the woman for fear of getting upset. An incest survivor herself may suspect that her helper is overwhelmed by her distress and she in turn may try to protect the helper. This is not helpful for the incest survivor.

Disgust

Feelings of disgust occur most often during periods of detailed disclosure about the sexual abuse. They are also common if the helper has only just started working with incest survivors. After some time, most helpers can cope with these feelings because they can anticipate what a woman has to tell. They are expressed in the following ways:

– this makes me feel sick. I don't want to listen any more;
– how could he do anything so sick/ base/ obscene to a child?

The incest survivor is likely to pick up these feelings in her helper, and she may protect the helper by not disclosing any more details of the abuse.

Feeling overwhelmed and burnt-out

This often occurs when the helper is going through a particularly unpleasant period of disclosure with a woman or if the helper is trying to work with too many incest survivors at any one time. It is expressed in the following ways:

– I can't bear to hear anyone else say they have been sexually abused;
– I can't remember which woman I'm talking to – they've all merged into one;
– I don't want to hear any more;
– I'm too tired to hear any more disclosures.

If these feelings emerge with an individual woman, it can lead to the helper becoming distressed and exhausted, and results in a general distancing from her. As a consequence the helper may try to get the woman to minimize the effects of the abuse rather than helping her to face very distressing events from her past.

If a helper is trying to help several incest survivors at any one time, it is essential to have supervision and support. Attempts should be made to set clear limits both on the number and amount of time spent with incest survivors. It may also be time for the helper to take a break!

No emotional reaction

Whilst overwhelming emotional reactions in the helper are troublesome, being totally unaffected can also produce difficulties. Helpers sometimes express this in the following ways:

– I don't/can't feel anything;
– I shut myself off so that I won't feel anything;
– this incest survivor might affect/contaminate me with her feelings.

These feelings are likely to make an incest survivor think that the helper is not interested in her. A lack of response may also indicate that the helper has learnt that the expression of feelings is dangerous. A complete absence of emotional expression is not uncommon in people who have themselves been abused (see Chapter 3).

Idealization of the incest survivor

This is expressed in the following ways:

- it is a great privilege to work with her;
- I admire her for surviving and for her courage;
- my problems are nothing compared to hers;
- she had done so well.

It can lead the helper to minimize an incest survivor's pain, suffering and problems, and make it difficult for her to express her vulnerabilities and distress. At the beginning of therapeutic work it over-emphasizes an incest survivor's achievement in surviving her childhood experiences at the expense of acknowledging the bad feelings which she has about herself.

Delight/praise

Expression of a helper's more positive emotions is necessary but can be problematic. Statements such as:

- I am pleased that she finally got round to telling me;
- she is doing so well;

can encourage an incest survivor to continue doing the work, but can also encourage her to carry on just to gain the helper's approval, rather than because it meets with her own needs and wishes. A woman who has been abused can also find it extremely difficult to hear and believe praise. As a consequence, she may not be able to tell the helper about any of her positive achievements.

Voyeurism/sexual arousal

An extremely problematic reaction in the helper is when she/he actually gets some satisfaction, or becomes sexually aroused, by the sexual details of the abuse. The latter reaction is reported to be more common among male helpers (Herman, 1981). It may be expressed in the following ways:

– I enjoy hearing all the details of what happened to her;
– I want to know everything that happened. It's so interesting hearing what an adult can do to a child;
– it turns me on to hear the sexual details;
– I feel guilty because I have these feelings;

This can lead to the woman distancing herself or even refusing to attend the helping agency because she feels misunderstood or abused once again.

Rescueing/over-protective reaction

A common reaction is the desire to help any incest survivor who comes to the helper's attention without regard to setting reasonable limits on numbers. The helper feels a need to protect incest survivors from feelings of vulnerability, pain and distress. It can be expressed in a number of ways:

– I must protect her from getting upset. She's had enough pain already;
– she's too fragile/vulnerable for me to ask any detailed questions about the abuse;
– I'll try to make everything all right by keeping her safe.

This clearly ignores the incest survivor's inner strengths and resources and can lead to a very slow pace of recovery.

Other Issues for the Helper

Rejection

Most incest survivors are extremely sensitive to being rejected. They expect to be rejected and can easily interpret aspects of the helper's behaviour as rejecting. For example, not returning a phone-call, appearing to be tired during a session, not reading a piece of writing immediately, being late for a meeting with the incest survivor, getting her name wrong, can all be interpreted as signs of rejection or lack of interest on the part of the helper.

Testing out

Some incest survivors test out the helper to see how much they can be relied on. This testing out may take the form of lying, threatening suicide or making huge demands of the helper in terms of time and emotional commitment. It is important for the helper to have a consistent attitude, setting limits with a woman where necessary. A helper may have to endure a long period of testing before a woman can begin to accept that the helper is prepared to work on her problems with her.

Confidentiality

This is always a problem for women who have been sexually abused. Many express concern about what information will be shared with other agencies or colleagues, and how much will be kept in records. These issues must be considered carefully by the helper, especially in health or social services agencies where records can be seen by other staff members. It is recommended that helpers should discuss the agency's normal procedures and practice regarding record-keeping and confidentiality with the woman herself.

For a helper there may be additional concerns, as it is often necessary and helpful to tell a supervisor or support person the details of the sexual abuse which a woman discloses. This is essential if the helper becomes distressed or overwhelmed by the disclosures. An incest survivor should be told that, from time to time, her helper may discuss her with a colleague, but that the information will remain confidential.

Regression

During disclosure work, some incest survivors regress to being a small child. This is explored in detail in Chapter 9. In this situation, the helper can be a trigger for the regression to occur. Regression demands high levels of support and involvement from the helper, a safe place in which to allow the regression to occur and time to allow the woman to return to her normal adult state afterwards.

Working with several members of the same family

Considerable problems can be caused if the helper is seeing several members of the same family separately because of their individual needs. The helper is likely to hear conflicting perceptions of events and there will be reasonable concerns about confidentiality regarding information from other family members.

The helper will also find that therapeutic work proceeds at very different rates for different family members. Sometimes, a helper will be asked to help a woman's sibling with expectations that the brother/sister will gain as much as the woman herself from getting help. Unfortunately, this does not always happen as the sibling may feel pressured into seeking help, or may not be able to use the helper in the same way as his/her sister.

It can be particularly stressful if the helper is working in a setting where sexual abuse is not generally acknowledged or where she/he is the only person involved in working with incest survivors. It can result in a lack of immediate support which exacerbates the sense of isolation. In these circumstances the helper should seek support from others working in this field, while bearing in mind the issue of confidentiality.

Incest Survivors as Helpers

Many incest survivors want to help other abused women with their problems, in a professional or voluntary capacity. Table 2.4 summarizes the ways in which a helper's personal experience of childhood sexual abuse might enhance or hinder work with other incest survivors.

Table 2.4: Incest Survivors as Helpers: Some Advantages and Areas of Difficulty

Potential Advantages	*Potential Areas of Difficulty*
Can immediately identify with the incest survivor	Greater possibility of survivor becoming over-involved
No difficulty about believing her	Own past may intrude inappropriately (My experience was worse than/not as bad as yours)
Easier to help disclosure	May bring previously forgotten memories to the surface
Can accurately guess what survivor is trying to say	Some issues may be more difficult to deal with (e.g. sexuality, physical abuse)
Helps survivor to break the silence ('me too')	May get angry with other survivors because they are not 'trying' hard enough to come to terms with their past
Reduces isolation	

Many incest survivors have forgotten all or some of their childhood experiences, and this can create difficulties in helping other survivors. Forgotten memories, flashbacks and nightmares can be triggered by hearing another survivor's history. It is essential for any helper who finds him or herself in this situation to seek support and help before she/he continues working with women who have been sexually abused. This may necessitate transferring an incest survivor to another helper in order to allow time for the helper to deal with her/his own past.

Training Issues

Chapter 10 examines aspects of training in more depth, but here we should note that the minimum training needs for anyone offering support to incest survivors should include:

- acknowledging the helper's own life experiences and how these could help or hinder work with incest survivors;
- recognising the consequences of childhood sexual abuse;
- reading life stories of incest survivors;
- becoming open about using language specific to sexual abuse;
- ensuring that adequate supervision and support is available when undertaking work with incest survivors.

Anyone contemplating work with incest survivors should ask themselves a number of questions when she/he feels ready to start the work. The answers will give an indication of their readiness and motivation:

- do I feel prepared to do the work?
- do I feel ready to do the work?
- have I talked over the implications of doing this work with my partner?
- have I done any reading/preliminary training about sexual abuse?
- do I have adequate support for the work?
- do I have adequate supervision for the work?

3   Problems in Adulthood

Factors in Childhood Relating to the Development of Problems

In the last decade, there has been a gradual accumulation of empirical evidence indicating that a history of child sexual abuse is associated with considerable mental health and adjustment problems in adulthood, long after the abuse itself has stopped (Bagley and Ramsay, 1986; Finkelhor, 1984; Fromuth, 1986). There are a number of factors in childhood which are relevant to the development and severity of these problems (Browne and Finkelhor, 1986; Lister, 1982; Russell, 1986). These include:

Traumatic sexualization: (Browne and Finkelhor, 1986) This occurs when a child is subjected to sexual activity. Consequently she develops misconceptions about sexual behaviour and norms, learns to associate sexual activity with bad feelings and may confuse sex with love and affection;

Betrayal: The child's trust and vulnerability are betrayed by adults who are in a position of trust with the child and should therefore be protecting and caring for her;

Powerlessness: The child is powerless in that her wishes and needs are constantly undermined and disregarded. She is forced into experiences that leave her fearful and from which she is unable to protect herself;

Stigma: The child's sense of being stigmatized results from the many negative messages associated with sexual abuse. They may come directly from the abuser who blames or condemns her, or from other adults who imply blame and shame to the child about the sexual abuse. Additionally, her perception of cultural and religious taboos may convince her that she should feel guilty, bad or ashamed;

Enforced silence: The child is expected, told or forced by use of threats, to keep the secret of sexual abuse. Lister (1982) emphasizes that this enforced silence is important in the development of adult mental health problems. It encourages the woman to continue to live in fear and isolation with considerable feelings of guilt and shame. He states that 'in silence, the pain and subliminal memories of pain festered'. Once this silence has been broken, the adult survivor can be terrified that the abuser's threats will come to fruition, and yet relieved that the burden of secrecy is removed. She may feel a sense of disloyalty towards her family for breaking the secret, and this may cause difficulties during any therapeutic work (Gelinas, 1983).

Factors Relating to the Nature of the Abuse

Duration and frequency of the abuse: there is strong evidence linking the duration and frequency of the abuse with the severity of its long-term consequences (Bagley and Ramsay, 1986; Browne and Finkelhor, 1986; Tsai and Wagner, 1978). However, it is also clear that a single incident of sexual abuse can produce very significant problems for a woman in her adult life.

Type of sexual abuse: there is some suggestion that the type of sexual abuse is related to its damaging effects (Russell, 1986), but the empirical evidence is as yet inconclusive.

Relationship with the abuser: greater damaging effects are reported following sexual abuse by a father or father figure (Russell, 1986). The effects of being abused by other family members may depend on the degree of trust in the relationship. It is also possible that abuse by trusted neighbours or babysitters can be more damaging than abuse by distant relatives.

Use of physical force: an association between the abuser's use of force or violence and the degree of later long-term effects has been confirmed in a number of studies (Finkelhor, 1979; Russell, 1986).

The number of abusers: the empirical research does indicate greater traumatic effects where the child has been subjected to abuse by several individuals. In our experience, for women who were sexually abused by both parents, or were abused by one parent with the knowledge and encouragement of the other, the negative consequences are more severe.

The age of the child: there is some suggestion that the younger the child at the start of the abuse, the greater the consequences in her adult life (Gil, 1988).

These explanations for the occurrence and severity of the long-term consequences of child sexual abuse should be used only as a guide since significant problems can and do result from a single incident of sexual abuse by a more distant relative. What is clear, however, is that being sexually abused as a child by a trusted adult does have a number of long-term consequences for mental health and relationships in adult life. The evidence from research studies has enabled us to construct a picture of the common problems of adult incest survivors that is remarkably consistent regardless of the family background and severity of the abuse. These difficulties should therefore be construed as the *normal* consequences of child sexual abuse though their pattern varies from one individual to another.

The Long-term Consequences of Sexual Abuse

Table 3.1 summarizes the long-term consequences of sexual abuse. Clearly not all the problems are present in every incest survivor and their severity varies from one woman to the next. They do provide a sobering account, however, of the real and severe difficulties faced by many women as a result of their childhood experiences.

Low self-esteem

Low levels of self-esteem are fundamental to many incest survivors' difficulties. Kempe (1980) reported that sexually abused children revealed a view of themselves as defenceless, worthless, guilty, at risk and threatened from all sides, especially from their parents. This picture continues into adulthood with a woman often displaying overwhelming helplessness, hopelessness and an extremely negative view of herself. The self-esteem problems are compounded by the extreme sense of guilt and shame that most incest survivors carry about the sexual abuse and their inability to stop it. Self-blame often generalizes to other experiences in adulthood, leading to further situations where a woman is taken advantage of and exploited.

Incest survivors normally have a very negative self-image. They feel bad about many aspects of their life. They express guilt about their failings, particularly in meeting the demands of others, and they blame themselves constantly for things that go wrong. This leads to difficulties in liking and accepting themselves, in accepting that anyone else might like them, want to be with them, or care about them which can result in further isolation and alienation. This poor self-image and self-esteem is at the root of victim behaviour, and underlies much of the depression, alcohol and drug abuse and relationship difficulties experienced by incest survivors. A lack of assertiveness, feelings of powerlessness and helplessness are also consequences of low self-esteem which lead to a failure to protect themselves from further abuse and to a denial of emotional needs.

Incest survivors often fail to see the many emotional strengths and resources

Table 3.1: Summary of Long-term Consequences of Child Sexual Abuse

Low Self-esteem	Further Assault/Revictimization
Confusion	General Fear of Men

Emotional Reactions
  – guilt
  – anger and rage
  – sadness and grief
  – complete absence of emotional
    reaction
	Interpersonal Difficulties
	  – in relationships with men
	  – in relationships with women
	Sexual Problems
	  – impaired sexual arousal
	  – difficulties with orgasm

Depression	– lack of sexual motivation

Anxiety Problems
  – generalized anxiety
  – panic attacks
  – specific fears and phobias
  – pronounced startle response
	– lack of sexual satisfaction
	  – guilt during sexual contact
	  – vaginismus
	  – pain during intercourse

Isolation and Alienation	Problems with Touch

Bad Reactions to Medical Procedures
  – hospital admissions
  – gynaecological procedures
  – dental procedures
	Parenting Problems
	Abuse of Self
	  – self mutilation and injury
	  – suicidal attempts

Physical Complaints	Substance Abuse
Sleep Disturbance	– alcohol – drugs

Eating Disorders
  – compulsive eating and obesity
  – bulimia
  – anorexia nervosa
	– tranquillizers
	Compulsive and Obsessional Problems
	Under-achievement in Education and
	Occupation

Dissociative Problems
  – perceptual disturbances
  – flashbacks
  – nightmares/bad dreams
  – out-of-body experiences
	Difficulty in Sustaining Positive
	Experiences
	Smaller Negative Effects

Problems with Trust	
Victim Behaviour	

which have enabled them to survive and cope with the negative consequences of their childhood experiences. Thus, a negative helpless picture of themselves persists, although they may show great courage, fortitude and determination in dealing with problems in their lives. Part of their difficulty in seeing these positive aspects of themselves is that they have experienced little positive feedback about their good qualities, especially when they were children.

Confusion

Incest survivors often experience intense confusion about the nature of their difficulties, the causes of their problems and about the reactions of others to them. Gelinas (1983) suggests that this confusion, in the absence of severe psychiatric problems, is one of the most common indicators that a woman has been sexually abused as a child. It is likely that their confusion originated in childhood, partly as the result of a lack of understanding about the sexual nature of the abuse, and partly because the child was abused and hurt by an adult whom she could have reasonably expected to protect and care for her. Her difficulty in understanding or making sense of the childhood experiences continues into adulthood.

Emotional reactions

Guilt: guilt is the predominant emotional response of most incest survivors. It relates to their feelings of responsibility for the sexual abuse and generalizes to many situations and relationships. The high levels of guilt about childhood experiences can be attributed to several factors (Tsai and Wagner, 1978):

- silence about the abuse, suggesting that the abuse was an experience to be ashamed of and not to be revealed to others;
- feelings of responsibility for the sexual abuse, often compounded by the reactions of the abuser and other significant adults blaming the child;
- failing to stop the abuse, giving the incest survivor the idea that she 'allowed' it to continue;
- any feelings of physical arousal she felt during the abuse.

As a child, therefore, she learns to feel guilty about the abusive experiences. Without the reassurance that she was not responsible for the abuse, these feelings continue into adulthood, and lead her to feel guilty about all aspects of her life and any problems encountered by people she is close to. This in turn results in a lowering of her self-esteem, the establishment of depression and a sense of hopelessness.

Anger and rage: some incest survivors show considerable anger and hostility towards the world in general, and family and friends in particular. This manifests itself in angry outbursts, aggression and an ability to produce conflict in many situations. It is extremely disruptive for relationships and can lead to isolation from other people. As with the guilty feelings, the anger is unfocused and is displaced from the childhood experiences into adulthood.

It is a set of complex responses to the abuse and abuser, and to other potentially protective adults, especially the mother. It relates to the widespread occurrence of sexual abuse, and to the fact that so much was lost through the experience of being abused. For example, it is not uncommon to find incest survivors becoming extremely angry because they perceive other people to have normal, caring sexual relationships, and good relationships with their parents and children. Anger and hostility are also used as a protective shield preventing others from getting close (Hays, 1985). Many incest survivors have never learned appropriate ways of dealing with their anger, and frequently turn it in on themselves. This leads to self-mutilation, alcohol and drug abuse and suicidal attempts.

Sadness and grief: many incest survivors experience periods of extreme sadness which they are unable to understand. They rarely appreciate the extent of the losses in their lives which are due to being sexually abused (e.g., loss of normal relationships with parents, of normal childhood and adult opportunities, of normal emotional development). This sadness can have all the signs of an unresolved grief reaction (see Chapter 9), and may result in considerable depression. The incest survivor is usually confused by the intensity of these emotional reactions and her lack of explanation for them (Hays, 1985).

Complete absence of emotional reaction: as we will see in Chapter 6, when a child is being sexually abused she will often learn to dissociate herself from the abuse and its accompanying feelings. Such dissociation usually continues into adulthood, with the result that the incest survivor remains unaware of emotional reactions and can be devoid of any emotional expression. She may therefore describe the abusive experiences without feeling, and may misinterpret, ignore or deny the existence of any signs of emotion.

Depression

Periods of depression and low mood are common in incest survivors (Bagley and Ramsay, 1986; Browne and Finkelhor, 1986). During these times, it is usual to find intensification of feelings of guilt, very low self-esteem, withdrawal from social contact, and sometimes an inner deadness or lack of emotional reaction (Herman *et al.*, 1986). Suicide attempts, disturbed sleep and eating patterns and marked changes in weight are common occurrences.

Incest survivors often come into contact with psychiatric services when they are depressed. In-patient treatment may be necessary for those who experience severe depression, and anti-depressant medication and electro-convulsive therapy (ECT) may be used. For a woman who has not felt able to discuss her childhood experiences at all, these contacts with the statutory services can help to maintain her capacity to cope with normal life. Because her secret remains unbroken, however, the medical responses listed above do not enable her to deal with the root cause of her difficulties.

Anxiety problems

Most incest survivors experience considerable anxiety, as well as multiple fears, often of phobic intensity. Anxiety shows itself in three main ways:

- it is experienced physically, e.g., headaches, dizziness, dry mouth, palpitations, pains/tightness in the chest and other parts of the body, sweating, shaking and nausea. It is accompanied by physical exhaustion, sensitivity to noise, and sleeping problems;
- anxiety affects an individual's behaviour, in that it leads to avoidance of feared situations, difficulties in making decisions, restlessness, constant checking of tasks already done and irritability;
- anxiety affects an individual's way of thinking. Following the work of Beck and his associates (Beck, 1976) it is possible to identify the types of negative thinking that occur during periods of anxiety and depression (see Chapter 9). These negative thoughts contribute significantly to the maintenance of high levels of anxiety, and form part of a vicious circle of physical anxiety leading to avoidance and negative thinking. This, in turn, leads to further physical anxiety.

Panic attacks: a panic attack is defined as a distinct episode that is characterized by the following features:

- a high level of anxiety;
- strong physical reactions (dizziness, heart palpitations, sweating, shaking, trembling, nausea, feelings of unreality, going hot and cold, chest pains, breath-lessness/choking sensation);
- loss of the ability to plan, think or reason;
- a very strong desire to escape from the situation;
- a strong fear of doing something uncontrolled, e.g., of going 'crazy', or of dying.

A panic attack is usually experienced during periods of high anxiety, but it may come out of the blue. It is usual for panic attacks to become more frequent during recall of the details of sexual abuse.

Specific fears/phobias: incest survivors often have a number of specific fears which can be extremely disabling, and can lead to a woman avoiding certain situations. They can be categorized as follows:

- Places that have similar qualities to the place where the abuse occurred, for example visiting a house that has many of the same characteristics (room lay-out, stairs, colour of decor, etc.) as the house she lived in during the time of the sexual abuse. Similarly, claustrophobia (intense fear of being in a confined space) is quite common for women who were abused in a small room.

Example: Moira was abused by her father in a small dark attic room. As an adult she experienced intense anxiety and panic attacks in a number of confined spaces — lifts, attic rooms, sitting as a passenger in a car or being on a crowded bus. These symptoms led her to avoid all these places.

- Specific phobias e.g., of animals, insects. These may relate directly to the abusive situation where her abuser may have used her fears of animals/insects to frighten and threaten her further. Even without this direct link to the abuse, incest survivors often experience insect phobias. Insects are seen as dangerous, out of their control, able to creep in unseen and behave in incomprehensible ways. The women themselves often come to see their insect phobias as a way of describing the abuse situation.
- Phobic reactions to violence are particularly common in women who have experienced physical as well as sexual abuse, and result in avoidance of all violent or potentially violent situations in everyday life and of all violent scenes on television, video or films.
- Phobic reactions to sexual activity or nudity in the media are frequently experienced by incest survivors. This results in avoidance of television, video or film material which portrays sexual activity or nudity. A woman may also avoid situations such as sporting activities or a visit to the beach where people may not be fully clothed.
- Situations in which high levels of anxiety or panic attacks have been experienced previously. The woman is likely to anticipate further anxiety/panic symptoms and become frightened of the symptoms themselves. Over-sensitivity to any physical signs of anxiety is common, and leads to predictions that she will have further unpleasant symptoms or panic attacks and so she will try to avoid being in similar situations. This can rapidly generalize to other situations, and can lead to agoraphobia (complete avoidance of all places outside her home).
- Situations that generate fear that the woman herself describes as irrational or unfounded. These can then become the focus of all her anxiety symptoms and can lead to considerable disruption of her everyday life.

Example: Penny described being frightened of plugging in any electrical equipment for fear that the electrical socket would harm her in some way. She knew these fears were unfounded but continued to avoid electrical equipment, with obvious consequences for her everyday life.

Pronounced startle response: incest survivors often exhibit a significant startle response to any sudden noises e.g., ringing of the telephone or door bell. It is as if they are on edge all the time listening for noises. Most describe this response beginning when they were children.

Isolation and alienation

A sense of isolation and loneliness is often experienced by an incest survivor. She often prefers to lead an isolated life even within the context of her family. In this way, the secret of the sexual abuse can remain unbroken. She frequently fears that others will find out or guess about her childhood experiences, and will blame her, so it becomes safer to remain withdrawn from people. From childhood, she is likely to have felt alienated and different from her peer group because she has had experiences that cannot be discussed openly. The sense of being different results from the many negative associations and feelings, e.g., feeling bad, dirty, ashamed and guilty, that she has with the abuse. These feelings may have come directly from her abuser who may have blamed her or at least communicated a sense of shame. They may have come from other adults whom she tried to tell, or from the child's own knowledge about the fact that the sexual activity was wrong (Finkelhor and Browne, 1986). This sense of being different from others usually inhibits the formation of close relationships, and, without the reassurance that she is not to blame for the abuse, will continue into adulthood.

Negative reactions to medical procedures

Hospital admissions: routine admission to hospital can produce difficulties. For an incest survivor, being in hospital represents a lack of control, a lack of privacy, having unexplained procedures done to her, often by male doctors, and a feeling of being trapped. Hospital admission can therefore result in distress, panic or extreme hostility within the woman. Admissions to psychiatric hospitals produce a number of different reactions including:

- a sense of safety;
- fears of being trapped;
- fears of being in hospital for ever;
- fears that she is going 'mad';
- extreme anger and hostility.

Gynaecological procedures: internal vaginal examinations, cervical smear tests, and pregnancy and fertility investigations often produce acute panic and flashbacks for an incest survivor. Procedures under general anaesthetic are not usually so difficult, although a woman may express fears that a male doctor might abuse her whilst she is under the anaesthetic.

Dental procedures: visits to the dentist revive memories of being trapped in a potentially painful or frightening situation. If her dentist is male a woman may avoid attending the dentist until it is absolutely necessary, and then may only manage to undergo treatment with the help of tranquillizers.

Physical complaints

A number of physical problems are often noted in incest survivors. Most commonly headaches, stomach problems, chronic backache, psychosomatic pains and illness, cystitis, asthma and eczema are found (Faria and Belohlavek, 1984). It has also been documented that epileptiform seizures, sometimes called pseudo-epilepsy or hysterical epilepsy, are to be found in incest survivors (Gross, 1980). Goodwin *et al.* (1979) suggest that at least 10 per cent of 'hysterical seizures' are associated with childhood sexual abuse. For incest survivors who have a confirmed diagnosis of epilepsy, the frequency of epileptic fits can greatly increase during flashbacks and recall of memories of sexual abuse.

Example: Julie had been diagnosed as epileptic as an adolescent. Her epilepsy was well controlled with minimal anti-convulsant medication. Suddenly, during her twenties when she got married, the frequency of fits increased dramatically. Increased medication made little difference, and it was only when she disclosed that her marriage had revived memories of being sexually abused by her uncle during childhood, that her epilepsy reverted to its previously well-controlled level.

For women who have experienced very severe sexual abuse, gynaecological problems, pelvic infections, and the effects of damage to genital and rectal organs may continue to cause problems well into adulthood.

Sleep disturbance

Disrupted sleep patterns are very common in incest survivors, especially at times of extreme distress or when they are reliving the memories of their abusive past. Recurring nightmares and bad dreams often occur, and may lead to a fear of going to bed.

Eating disorders

There is growing evidence that between one-third and two-thirds of women with eating disorders have experienced childhood sexual abuse (Oppenheimer *et al.*, 1985).

Compulsive eating and obesity: compulsive over-eating and its associated weight gain and loss of self-esteem is often part of an incest survivor's difficulties with control. Meiselman (1978) noted that a third of her sample of abused women were significantly overweight.

Bulimia: this involves secret bingeing and self-induced vomiting and is accompanied by extreme feelings of guilt and shame. Oppenheimer *et al.* (1985) found that as many as two-thirds of women with bulimia had been sexually abused before the age of fifteen.

Anorexia Nervosa: anorexia is characterized by self-starvation, purging through laxatives, self-induced vomiting, distorted body-image, cessation of menstruation and very significant weight loss. Sloan and Leichner (1986) presented evidence linking anorexia with a history of childhood sexual abuse.

Dissociative problems

Many children who have been sexually abused learn to deal with the abuse by denying its reality, by dissociating themselves from it or by repressing it partially or completely. These methods of dissociation and their implications for diclosure will be discussed in more detail in Chapter 6. However, it is clear that these dissociative processes are rarely totally successful and evidence that a woman has been sexually abused as a child often breaks through in quite frightening ways.

Perceptual disturbances

A number of perceptual disturbances are experienced by most incest survivors (Ellenson, 1985, 1986). They can be visual, auditory, olfactory and related to taste and touch, or more usually some combination of these.

Visual disturbances: these include:

- Shadowy figures: these are nearly always described as dark, featureless shapes, usually male, and evil or dangerous. Seeing such figures at night-time at the foot of the bed is very common. During the day-time, these figures are often seen to move quickly and furtively.
- Partial figures: the face, eyes or hands of the abuser, or of an unknown male, are often seen, especially during sexual activity.
- Elaborated images: sometimes the perceptions of male figures are more ela-

borate in detail. Clear pictures of the abuser are often seen and may be super-imposed on a partner in sexual situations.

- Movement in peripheral vision: seeing a rapidly moving object or person out of the corner of the eye is common.
- Images of objects used during the abuse: where the woman's abuser has used objects (e.g., knife, rope, bottle), or insects (e.g., spiders), to frighten or abuse her, images of these often occur and add to her fear and terror.

Auditory disturbances: these include:

- Intruder sounds: these occur mostly at night and include footsteps, heavy breathing, bumps, scrapes, doorknobs turning, doors and windows being opened and closed or tampered with, and creaking floorboards.
- Vocal sounds: these usually take the form of a child crying, screaming or calling out, hearing the child's name called out by an adult known to the survivor. Sometimes, an incest survivor will hear words spoken by the abuser or by herself during the abuse.
- Booming sounds: these are less common but usually sound like a heavy door banging shut or an explosion.
- Persecutory/hostile/threatening voices: these are heard particularly by women who have been subjected to prolonged violent or sadistic abuse. The voices often condemn her and may encourage her to do something violent to herself or others. Sometimes, these voices are interpreted by the woman as the voice of the devil.
- Sounds associated with the abuse: women sometimes hear sounds that were present before and during the abuse, e.g., music, creaking floorboards, radio sounds, running water.

Tactile sensations: a sensation of being touched by a human hand or face is common among incest survivors expecially when they are in bed. Ellenson (1986) suggested that this occurs less frequently than visual and auditory disturbances. For women who have experienced physical abuse along with the sexual abuse, tactile sensations often relate to the physical abuse.

Sensations of pain: during recall of abusive incidents or during flashbacks, it is quite normal for an incest survivor to experience sensations of physical pain. These sensations frequently amount to re-experiencing the abuse. Internal and external genital pain, pain in the chest and ribs (due to the experience of a heavy body weight on top of her) or in other parts of the body are common.

Perception of smells: smells that have particular associations with the abuse or the abuser are often experienced by incest survivors. Common examples are bodily and sexual smells, and the smell of cigarettes and alcohol.

Perception of taste: this often occurs in conjunction with perception of smells and usually involves being able to taste body and sexual secretions.

Recurring illusions: these are common and occur with visual or auditory sensations. They can include:

- a sensation that there is a threatening evil male entity in the room, sometimes described as a monster or demon;
- a sense of a poorly defined evil presence.

Flashbacks

Memories of childhood incidents return in the form of flashbacks which occur frequently and are beyond the control of the woman herself. A flashback has several distinguishing features:

- it occurs when she is suddenly and unpredictably taken back to an abusive incident in her childhood;
- the flashback produces a vivid recollection or picture of this incident and included the intense emotional reactions and physical pain experienced at the time, and visual, auditory and tactile memories of the abuse itself. At times, the incest survivor may experience such intense flashbacks that she feels as if she is re-experiencing the abuse. Bleeding from the genital area can be triggered by a flashback;
- it can be triggered by an experience in the present that instantly reminds her of the sexual abuse. Common examples of such triggers are:

  - the tone of someone's voice;
  - sexual situations including sexual positions, arousal, being touched in certain places;
  - touching certain fabrics e.g., blankets, nylon shirts;
  - hearing certain sounds e.g., music, heavy breathing;
  - hearing certain words spoken;
  - seeing a man who resembles her abuser in some way (clothes, facial appearance, build);
  - certain smells e.g., alcohol, cigarette, sexual or bodily smells.

Example: Mandy experienced flashbacks every time she heard military bands playing march tunes. Her father was a member of an army band and regularly sexually abused her on the way to ceremonial occasions at which he was playing.

– it can be triggered by an experience in the present that is apparently unrelated to the abuse itself. These triggers may involve general reminders of her childhood, discussions with friends about sex, families, discipline methods or children, and conflict with family members.

Flashbacks are very alarming experiences, and often lead to fears of ensuing 'madness', increased self-mutilation and suicidal attempts, and alcohol and drug misuse. For some women who have experienced very violent abuse over a number of years, the flashbacks often occur in large numbers, and as one is dealt with, it is replaced by others. Flashbacks are also particularly common during therapeutic work and when an incest survivor is experiencing a flashback, it is usual to see changes in body position, breathing rhythm and ability to maintain eye contact. A woman will often avert her gaze or appear to be gazing into the middle-distance. Her body movements may clearly indicate that she is re-experiencing the abuse, with avoidance actions and obvious discomfort in the genital area being common.

Nightmares and bad dreams:

The sleep patterns of an incest survivor are often disturbed by nightmares. They can be very realistic and appear to be exact replications of various incidents of abuse. The content of nightmares can therefore be used as a basis for disclosure. Nightmares are accompanied by extreme emotional reactions of distress, terror or pain. The consequences for the woman range from a fear of going to sleep to suicidal attempts, and may involve increased self-mutilation, running away, and drug and alcohol misuse. The bad dreams of an incest survivor are often characterized by fear, being chased or trapped, or they include a child being hurt in some way.

Out-of-body experiences:

An incest survivor often describes feelings of being 'out of her body' and floating (Briere and Runtz, 1986). She may feel that situations and experiences are unreal, and that she is watching herself go through life as though she were another person. She can often trace this dissociative process back to the abusive situation, where she learnt to survive by believing that the abuse was not really happening to her but to someone else. It enabled her, therefore, to escape from any unpleasant or painful feelings associated with the abuse.

Problems with trust

Sexual abuse of a child by a trusted adult is not only a physical violation of the child, but also represents a betrayal of the trust that the child has for the adult. The child rapidly learns therefore that it is not safe to trust others. This is compounded by the secrecy, blame and shame attached to the abuse which results in her being unable to tell anyone, and these problems with trust continue into adulthood and create difficulties in establishing and maintaining relationships. Incest survivors often see trust as an all-or-nothing matter i.e., they believe they should trust totally or not at all. In addition, they do not pick up normal cues about the levels of trustworthiness in others.

Victim behaviour

Incest survivors often behave as victims believing they have no rights or choices. They therefore feel helpless, submissive and compliant to others. They often have no recognition of their own emotional needs or personal space, and allow others to violate both on a regular basis.

Revictimization/further assault: incest survivors are particularly vulnerable to being sexually assaulted or raped as adults (Fromuth, 1986; Russell, 1986). Russell also indicated that incest survivors are more likely than non-abused women to have physically violent husbands and to be sexually assaulted within marriage. It suggests, therefore, that the experience of childhood sexual abuse may prevent a woman from learning how to protect or assert herself as an adult.

General fear of men

Some incest survivors have a general fear of men which results in avoidance of any situations where they might have to speak to or pass too near a man (e.g., shops, medical facilities, walking down a busy street). It can be difficult for them to call in tradesmen to do essential repairs, and even the usual regular calls of the milkman or window-cleaner for payment of bills can cause alarm and fear.

Interpersonal difficulties

The problems faced by an incest survivor in her relationships with others are often coloured by mistrust and insecurity. Forming and sustaining relationships can be difficult. Baker and Duncan (1985) suggest that this results not only from the experience of being sexually abused as a child, but also from the abuser's misuse of his power and responsibility, from the betrayal of her trust, and from the distortion and disruption of family relationships. Normal emotional development of a child in this situation is likely to be disrupted especially if the sexual abuse remains hidden, ignored or condoned by other significant adults. Even more problems result if both parents are involved in abusing the child, thus giving her no respite from the abuse. Further difficulties arise because abused children are often prevented from having normal childhood friendships, leading to additional isolation.

Relationships with men: many incest survivors report difficulties in relating to men. Courtois (1979) found that over three-quarters of her sample of incest survivors had such problems and their relationships were characterized by disappointment, fear, hostility, mistrust and the likelihood of betrayal. Herman (1981) also reported that many incest survivors tend to over-value and idealize men. These problems have several consequences:

- avoidance of relationships with men: complete life-time avoidance is relatively rare, although many survivors go through long periods of avoidance of relationships with men;
- avoidance of long-term intimate relationships with men: some abused women avoid close relationships with men and end up being involved in brief unsatisfactory relationships instead;
- difficulties in long-term intimate relationships with men: many incest survivors do manage a significant close relationship with a man, but this can be fraught with problems because of its parallels with the abusive childhood relationship;
- oversexualized relationships: many incest survivors have difficulties in distinguishing between affection and sex. Sex may therefore be used to gain attention and affection (Herman, 1981), or conversely a man's affection is seen to be genuine and worthwhile only if the relationship is sexual (Jehu and Gazan, 1983). Brief unsatisfactory sexual relationships with men are thus more likely to occur, and the survivor may be seen by others as promiscuous.
- prostitution: it is now well-established that many prostitutes were sexually abused as children (James and Meyerding, 1977; Sheldon, 1987). As children, they may have been given rewards for the sexual activity or for maintaining the silence which, when combined with their poor self-esteem and self-image, made them more vulnerable to prostitution. Female adolescents who run away from home to get away from sexual abuse are more likely to be exploited and abused and may get involved in prostitution (McCormack *et al.*, 1986). It is, however, relatively unusual for adult women to seek help during a period of prostitution;
- abusive relationships: incest survivors often become involved with men who mis-treat them (Meiselman, 1978; Tsai and Wagner, 1978). This probably

results from the woman's poor self-esteem, leading her to believe that she deserves to be abused or mistreated. She is likely to have never learnt to assert or protect herself in relationships, particularly if her mother was never able to. It is not uncommon for a mother in such families to assume a passive and submissive role, to be depressed and demoralized and to behave like a victim;

– marriage: many incest survivors marry early to get away from home and the abuse. These early marriages often fail because the legacy of the sexual abuse intrudes and causes problems with trust, sexuality and intimacy. The divorce and separation rate is known to be higher in women who were abused as children (Russell, 1986). Many incest survivors do manage to continue with marital relationships, but in our experience, these are more likely to be successful for women who were abused by men who were not in the father role (e.g., uncles, grandfathers, cousins).

– jealousy: some incest survivors feel so insecure in a relationship with a man, that jealousy of him, his thoughts and actions can lead to considerable problems. This can erupt in accusations that any time her partner looks at another woman on television, films, at work or in the street, he is obviously wanting to have sex with that woman. It reflects the survivor's low self-esteem, confusion about sexuality and deep insecurities about relationships with men.

Relationships with women. Difficulties in relationships are not confined to those with men. An incest survivor often has problems with trusting other women, partly as a reflection of her feelings about her mother. Her relationship with her mother may be coloured by feeling betrayed, let down, rejected or ignored, and these feelings intrude into relationships with other women. This can prevent the development of normal supportive relationships with women. Severe mistrust of women results if the survivor has actually been abused by her mother or other female relatives.

Lesbian relationships: there is a suggestion that lesbian women are more likely to have a history of child sexual abuse than heterosexual women (Jehu and Gazan, 1983). Obviously, one cannot judge whether the experience of sexual abuse results in their sexual orientation. Meiselman (1978) noted that lesbianism tended to emerge after several years of unhappy and unsatisfactory heterosexual relationships. A common fear expressed by incest survivors after the failing of a marriage or a heterosexual relationship is that they might be lesbian. This fear can inhibit them from having any relationship with a woman.

Sexual problems

These are almost universal among incest survivors and take a number of forms. It is very often the occurrence of sexual problems which encourages a woman to seek help and to disclose the childhood sexual abuse.

One of the major difficulties for an incest survivor in a sexual relationship is that sexual activity in itself can produce flashbacks to the childhood sexual abuse. It can take the form of a brief image (e.g., seeing the face of the abuser) or a vivid memory which is very disturbing to her. They may occur when her current sexual partner touches her in ways that remind her of her abuser, makes demands or forces her into unwanted sexual activity, and when there are certain bodily and sexual smells. When these flashbacks occur, the woman is likely to experience feelings of intense anxiety, panic and distress, and immediately 'freeze' physically. This will obviously disrupt any on-going sexual activity, and is likely to restrict the range of and motivation for sexual experiences.

Once flashbacks have occurred in this way the woman is likely to anticipate further problems so that even very limited sexual contact begins to produce anxiety. As a result, sexual activity may be avoided completely, with difficulties for the woman's partner and associated guilt for the woman herself. Beyond these very general problems, incest survivors often have a number of specific sexual difficulties (Gelinas, 1983; Sheldon, 1987):

Impaired sexual arousal: for some women, sexual arousal appears to be disrupted (Becker *et al.*, 1982). This may result from the intense anxiety produced by flashbacks as described above, as it is well known that high levels of anxiety can impair arousal level. Resulting restrictions on sexual activity may then limit sexual stimulation. For some women, sexual arousal is completely lacking (Jehu *et al.*, 1985), either because she dissociates herself totally from potential sexual sensations or because she does not allow herself to be aware of any stimulation she is receiving from her partner.

Difficulties with orgasm: it is well documented that incest survivors often have orgasmic difficulties (Meiselman, 1978; Becker *et al.*, 1982). Orgasm may be possible in certain circumstances e.g., with a new partner, with a patient and undemanding partner or during certain types of sexual activity (McGuire and Wagner, 1978). Where orgasm does occur, it is often not associated with pleasure. If it is pleasurable, this can be extremely threatening and can lead to intense feelings of guilt especially for women who have experienced sexual arousal during the sexual abuse. If a woman experienced sexual arousal in association with violence, she may only become aroused as an adult if her partner is violent with her. This is deeply upsetting and confusing for her.

Lack of sexual satisfaction and motivation: lack of interest in and motivation for sex is quite common, and may be partly a result of depression, problems with the sexual partner or generalized negative feelings about physical contact. Lack of sexual satisfaction has also been found in incest survivors (Tsai and Wagner, 1979).

Guilt during sexual contact: for the incest survivor who is able to participate in a sexual relationship, she is frequently overwhelmed with feelings of guilt either for enjoying the sexual activity, becoming aroused or for initiating any part of the sexual contact. This usually relates to feelings experienced during the sexual abuse.

Vaginismus: this is a condition that occurs quite frequently in incest survivors. It involves an involuntary reflex response of the outer vaginal muscles and of the perineum to any threat of vaginal penetration.

Pain during intercourse: incest survivors often report pelvic pain especially during intercourse (Gross *et al.*, 1980). This may be due to internal injuries resulting from the sexual abuse, to chronic vaginal infections, or to anxiety leading to extreme muscle tension and pain.

Problems with touch

Fundamental to all close relationships is the issue of touch. Many incest survivors find it extremely difficult to tolerate being touched physically. This results in:

- fear and avoidance of crowded and social situations in case someone brushes against her;
- inability to shake hands when being introduced to someone;
- any physical contact on greeting or leaving friends or family members;
- refusal to allow anyone to physically comfort her when she is distressed;
- extreme problems in intimate or sexual relationships;
- fears that she will contaminate/infect someone through her touch;
- difficulties in touching her children;
- problems with medical and dental examinations;
- dislike of hairdressing.

This problem with touch can affect many aspects of an incest survivor's life, and lead to increased anxiety.

Parenting problems

For incest survivors with children, there are a number of common difficulties:

Difficulties in meeting her child's emotional needs: some incest survivors have problems with their parenting skills partly because they did not experience adequate parenting when they were children. They may be unaware of a child's emotional needs, or may over-compensate for their own difficult childhood by being unable to set appropriate boundaries and limits for the child.

Overprotection of children: fears for the safety of a child, especially if the child is left in someone else's care, are usually very pronounced. This may extend to fears that the child's father will abuse the child. If the woman's abuser is still alive and in contact with her family, she will be justifiably vigilant, and fearful when her children are in his presence. These fears can lead to general over-protection of the children and can some-times prevent the children from becoming independent. She may also underestimate the risk of abuse to her children, believing that there was something about herself as a child that singled her out for abuse.

Fears that she will abuse her child: an incest survivor often fears that she will abuse her child because she believes that sexual abuse runs in families or that an abused child becomes an abuser as an adult. These beliefs are confirmed for her if she is in any way angry or frustrated with her children. She is unable to distinguish normal methods of discipline from the abuse she experienced, with the result that her children may not get appropriate disciplining.

Difficulties in showing physical affection towards children: incest survivors are often fright-ened to comfort or show physical affection towards their children for fear they will be seen as an abuser. This shows the confusion they have about the boundaries between physical affection and sexual closeness. Therefore many incest survivors are very frightened to touch their children in any way. This means that physical care of their children becomes problematic, and normal parenting tasks such as bathing, dressing, nappy-changing, toilet-training are difficult.

Difficulty in protecting her child: if an incest survivor has not remembered her experience of being sexually abused, or has not recognized its effects, she may be unaware of signs that her children are in danger or may not be able to react appropriately to them. For example, if one of her children is being abused, she may be paralyzed by fear, deny that her child could be abused or ignore any warning signs. She may be unable to deal appropriately with other potentially difficult situations such as allowing a child to play at a friend's house without adequate supervision, asking a young child to run errands for her, or allowing children to cross roads before they are old enough to do so safely.

Actual abuse of her child: for some survivors, the obvious lack of adequate parenting in their own childhood, and the lack of an appropriate model of parenting, leaves them poorly equipped to deal with the demands of caring for their own children. A lack of warmth and an inability to be protective leaves her children vulnerable. Without help this can sometimes result in abuse and neglect (Goodwin *et al.*, 1981), thus perpetuating a cycle of abuse and deprivation. As yet, we do not know the percentage of female incest survivors who do go on to abuse or neglect their own children, although our impression is that it is extremely small.

Abuse of self

This is very common in incest survivors (de Young, 1982), particularly when they are depressed, angry or remembering the details of the sexual abuse. It includes:

Self mutilation: this usually takes the form of making small cuts with a sharp object on the arms, legs and other parts of the body. These are often superficial wounds, and should be distinguished from suicidal attempts.

A woman's explanation for this type of self-injury is usually one of the following:

- the pain of these cuts diverts me from the pain of the memories;
- I know I should feel something about these memories but I don't so I cut myself to prove to myself that I can still feel pain;
- I feel so bad about myself that it doesn't matter what I do to myself;
- I don't even notice what I am doing to myself.
- I want to hurt myself because I don't deserve any better.

Other self-injury: some incest survivors go through periods of head-banging and hitting themselves. This occurs at times of particular crisis or desperation, and serves the same kind of function as the self-mutilation.

Suicidal attempts: repeated suicidal attempts (often overdoses or wrist-cutting) are common (Briere and Runtz, 1986). They occur when the pain of the past is too much, when control over her current life experiences disappears or during periods of severe depression (Gelinas, 1983). Paradoxically, incest survivors sometimes appear suicidal because they keep the means of terminating their lives always to hand in the form of pills, glass etc. Their explanation is that they need to have the safety of an 'escape route' if they feel that things are getting 'too bad'.

Substance abuse

Alcohol abuse: the use of alcohol as a way of blocking out the memories and their associated pain has been confirmed in a number of studies summarized by Finkelhor and Browne (1986).

Drug misuse: misuse of drugs such as amphetamines, cocaine, LSD and heroin is less common than alcohol misuse in adult survivors, but sometimes begins in late adolescence and continues into adulthood (Peters, 1984).

Tranquillizer dependency: Tranquillizers (e.g. Valium, Librium, Diazepam, Ativan) may have initially been prescribed to help a woman with her anxiety symptoms or sleep difficulties, but they also help to blank out memories of childhood experiences.

Compulsive and obsessional problems

Obsessional concerns with cleanliness, and fears of harming others, especially children, are not uncommon in incest survivors. This obsessional behaviour usually develops in an attempt to gain control over her anxieties and fears, or to preoccupy her sufficiently to allow her to block out the past.

Example: Alison described difficulties in dealing with household tasks. She had to do things in a set order, and could not rest until her house was cleaned in this rigid way every day. If she was interrupted, she had to start again at the beginning. She had developed this rigid routine as a way of distracting herself from her memories, fears and guilt about being sexually abused by her father.

Compulsive behaviour such as shoplifting (Winestine, 1985), and compulsive lying and stealing have been noted in women who were abused as children. The function of lying is often to prevent others from getting close or learning the true nature of her childhood experiences.

Under-achievement in education and occupation

Educational under-achievement is widespread among incest survivors, yet their poetry and writing skills indicate that many have the potential to achieve at a much higher level than they managed during their formal education. The disruption of education caused by sexual abuse during childhood and enforced silence about the abuse is known to have a significant effect on a child's ability to concentrate on and cope with formal education (Nakashima and Zakus, 1977).

Under-achievement in employment is also widespread. It partially reflects the educational difficulties, but Russell (1986) also found that unemployment was much more likely in a sample of incest survivors, regardless of educational levels.

Difficulties in sustaining positive experiences

Incest survivors often describe problems in allowing themselves to enjoy anything or in sustaining positive experiences. If they do enjoy any aspect of their lives, guilt manifests itself and manages to spoil the experience.

These difficulties usually originate in childhood where they learnt to believe:

- I don't deserve anything nice happening to me;
- If I enjoy something, I am bound to be punished;
- I am not worthy of anyone wanting to do good things for me;
- If an experience is nice, there is bound to be something nasty about to happen;
- No-one does good things to or for me without expecting something in return.

These negative appraisals of herself prevent an incest survivor from deriving pleasure, enjoyment or any anticipation of positive experiences, and they contribute to her low self-esteem and episodes of depression. Many incest survivors also present themselves in a way which denies their femininity. They see this as one way of protecting themselves against male advances.

Smaller negative effects

So far we have considered the major consequences of child sexual abuse and its associated family disruption. However, there are many smaller consequences that can disrupt or distort an incest survivor's life. These are usually habits learnt during childhood. The following examples were given by incest survivors:

- wearing pyjamas (increases feelings of safety);
- shutting all internal doors of the house before answering the door-bell (so that no-one can see what might be happening in the house);
- sleeping with the light on;
- sleeping with the bedroom door open/closed;
- sleeping along the very edge of the bed;
- always checking and double-checking that any children in the house are safe when they are in bed;
- not able to have a bath/shower with someone in the house;
- making sure that bedclothes/sheets are tucked in very tight;
- never wearing clothes of a particular colour/fabric/style;
- playing music all the time to block out memories.

The long-term effects of childhood sexual abuse as outlined here can be devastating. Many women do not attribute their current problems to their past, but they can be helped to do so. It is often the case, however, that once a woman begins to make the connections, she can confront her problems and her past with new-found energy and determination.

4 Seeking Help

When an incest survivor decides to seek help, she is taking an important first step in coming to terms with the experience of childhood sexual abuse. She may have spent months or years getting to this point, and much will depend on her finding a setting in which she feels safe enough to disclose the painful details of her past. Finding out what resources are available locally can be difficult. There are, however, a range of organizations and professional helpers who can offer support, undertake therapeutic work or refer a woman to a more appropriate source of help.

This chapter outlines the main sources of help available to incest survivors, together with information on how to make contact with them. It also examines some of the contexts in which help can be given and the issues which arise in these contexts.

Choosing a Source of Help

Until she has access to reliable information, a woman will be unable to make an informed choice about the source of help most appropriate to her needs. There are a number of questions she might ask before deciding which route to pursue. These are listed in Table 4.1. Not all of these questions will have clear or immediate answers, and they will vary according to the context in which help is given.

Where and how to get help

Table 4.2 lists the main sources of help available for incest survivors, not all of which will be available in any one locality.

Family doctor: a woman's family doctor, or G.P., can be an important source of help initially. Her G.P. may be the first person a woman tells about her childhood experiences; her/his reaction to the woman's disclosure can determine whether fur-

Table 4.1:   Questions to Ask about Sources of Help

Can I refer myself?
If not, do I need to have a letter from my doctor?
Will notes be kept on my visits?
Who will see these notes?
Will information about me be sent back to my doctor?
Can I see what is written about me?
Will I be able to get time off work to attend for help?
Will I have to pay?
Are child-care facilities available?
How regular will the sessions be?
How long will each session last?
Who will be present?
Where will we meet? e.g., hospital, own home, helper's office.
Who else will my helper speak to about me?
Can I stop attending if it gets too difficult?
How will I know when it is time to end my contact?

Table 4.2:   Sources of Help for Incest Survivors

A woman may refer herself to	*Her G.P. can arrange referral to*
Family doctor	Community or hospital clinical psychology services
Other members of primary care team (e.g., health visitors)	Psychiatric services
Walk-in counselling services	Sex therapy clinic
Counselling services at place of work or study	Psychotherapy services within National Health Service
Voluntary agencies - Incest survivors group* - Rape crisis group* - other voluntary group relating to specific problems (e.g. Women's Aid, Marriage Guidance (Relate), Anorexic Aid, Phobia group, Alcohol Advice Centre) - Women's groups in the community	A professional worker with particular interest and expertise in working with incest survivors (regardless of agency)
Social Work Department	
Some psychotherapy services (usually private)	
Private counsellor/therapist	

*Indicates services specifically for women who acknowledge that they were sexually abused.

ther help is sought or made available. A family doctor can refer a woman to other services within the National Health Service (NHS) for specialized help. Referrals can be made to a psychologist, psychiatrist or psychotherapist. A woman can usually ask her doctor for a referral to a particular individual within the NHS if she knows about someone with particular expertise or knowledge in the area of sexual abuse.

Clinical psychologists: usually work within the NHS and work in both hospital and community settings. They study psychology before undertaking the clinical psychology training. Their aim is to help people deal with their psychological difficulties by gaining an understanding of the effects of a person's history, life experiences and conditions on his/her behaviour. They work with individuals and groups using counselling skills together with a number of techniques to deal with specific problems. Although some psychologists may have the title 'Dr.', this is a research qualification, and they are not allowed to prescribe drugs.

Psychiatrists: are doctors who have chosen to specialize in the field of mental illness. They usually work in psychiatric hospitals or special units in general hospitals. Some provide services in doctors' surgeries. They can prescribe medication and may have had training in psychotherapy and counselling.

Psychotherapists: work within a number of settings (NHS, private practice, social services departments and voluntary organizations). A registered psychotherapist should have undergone recognized training, and aims to help people resolve their personal difficulties through the use of 'talking'. A psychotherapist does not necessarily have a medical training.

Social workers: work for local government and voluntary organizations, and some are attached to hospitals or doctors' surgeries. They deal with a wide range of social and emotional problems and have statutory responsibilities, including taking children into care and arranging a compulsory admission to a psychiatric hospital under the Mental Health Act. They usually have a large and varied caseload so their opportunity for doing intensive work is limited. Some local authorities have a community-based mental health team specializing in mental health problems. Social workers can be contacted through the social services department (social work departments in Scotland, health boards in Ireland), and they are listed in telephone directories.

Rape Crisis Centres: are now established in fifty-one towns and cities in Britain and Ireland (See Appendix 3). Each centre is run as an autonomous group. They provide a support service by women for women who have experienced sexual abuse in their childhood or as adults. Rape Crisis Centres usually offer telephone counselling or one-to-one support from volunteers. They may also have an incest survivors group. Rape

Crisis members also ensure that the women who contact them have control over the contact they wish to have, and help is given in a supportive, non-judgmental atmosphere where the women are encouraged to make decisions that are right for themselves.

Incest Survivor Groups: have been set up by Rape Crisis Centres, Women's Aid, in local community centres and in psychiatric hospitals. Telephone contact lines for incest survivors have been established in at least eleven towns in Britain and Ireland. There is a wide variety in the way groups operate (see Chapter 8). Contact with an incest survivors group can usually be made through a Rape Crisis Centre or Mental Health Advice Centre. Even if the Centre does not have a group, it may be able to suggest other sources of help locally.

Advice Centres: many towns now have a range of advice agencies and support groups which deal with specific issues e.g., Alcohol Advice Centre, Women's Aid, Marriage Guidance. There are also advice centres operating under the auspices of local associations for mental health. They offer a range of counselling resources, on a one-to-one basis and in groups.

Choice of Context

In addition to knowing what resources are available locally, a woman should also consider whether she will feel more comfortable in a one-to-one setting or in a group with other incest survivors. At a later stage she might also wish to do some work with her siblings, mother or in a family context.

The main distinction between the services listed in Table 4.2 is between statutory (e.g., social work department, health services) and voluntary organizations (e.g., Rape Crisis Centre). Table 4.3 summarizes the relevant distinguishing features.

Table 4.3: Statutory and Voluntary Organizations as Sources of Help

Statutory organizations	Voluntary organizations
May have to be referred by G.P.	Greater ease of self-referral
May have to wait some time if there is a waiting list	More likely to be seen soon after making contact
Setting may be formal, e.g., office, hospital	Flexibility in meeting place and time of meeting
Trained and professionally qualified staff	May be staffed by volunteers or trained workers
Records may be centralized and passed to other professionals	Each organization has own records

It is preferable for an incest survivor, if she is able to, to make use of facilities located in the community or those provided by hospital out-patient departments. Sometimes, however, it is necessary for an incest survivor to be admitted as an in-patient to a psychiatric hospital or unit, because of symptoms of severe depression, suicidal behaviour or other problems. Admission to hospital at a time of great stress can provide a number of benefits to an incest survivor:

- it allows her a period of rest in a safe place away from the pressures of her normal life;
- she can receive medication or other treatment for her symptoms;
- it allows the woman to be in a supportive and safe environment whilst she does some difficult disclosure work.

Helpers in these settings should also be aware of the potential difficulties for an incest survivor. The most obvious problem relates to confidentiality and trust:

- a woman may be expected to talk to several members of staff about her experiences. Consequently no one member has all the information to help her to deal with it appropriately;
- she may feel upset or angry if she feels that staff members are sharing her 'secrets' without her permission;
- some staff members may feel excluded if they are not told details of her experiences.

It is important that these issues are resolved by the staff team, and the woman should be assigned to an individual therapist who is able to involve her in the necessary therapeutic work. The incest survivor should also be informed about the staff team's policy regarding confidentiality.

Group and Individual Settings

A woman needs to decide whether she will feel more comfortable in a one-to-one context with an individual helper, or in a group with other incest survivors.

Individual setting

Many women choose a one-to-one therapeutic situation, preferring the confidentiality and sense of security which it offers. Individual help can be arranged by referral to a clinical psychologist, psychotherapist, psychiatrist, social worker or counsellor in a specialist advice agency. Table 4.4 lists some of the issues which can arise for an incest survivor and her helper in one-to-one therapy.

Table 4.4: Individual Help: Issues for Helpers and Incest Survivors

For the woman	Consequences for a helper
Can establish a long-term trusting relationship with someone who believes her	Concern about over-involvement or dependency. May ask, 'Will she lean on me so hard that I'll collapse?'
Details of her abuse are confidential to one person	Feels the need to share burden of the 'secret' of the abuse with colleagues for support
Work can be done at her own pace, in her own time	Pace of work may be too slow for the helper and this can be frustrating
Feels helper is someone she can rely on	May be difficulties at holiday periods or if helper is ill/absent
Intensity of the work can be frightening. Asks herself, 'Will I go mad if this carries on?'	Helper asks 'Can I get her through this?', 'Can I cope with her pain?'
Feels that she is going mad	Needs to reassure the woman that she is not going mad. Asks, 'Can I get her through this?'
Does not want to burden her helper with details of the abuse	Should emphasize the continued importance of disclosure
May not fully resolve issues of secrecy, isolation and stigma	Suggest that woman joins incest survivors' group at appropriate time
Can become over-dependent on helper	Can feel overburdened by woman's dependency

Group work

A woman may decide to move on from individual therapy to a self-help or other group. Alternatively an incest survivors' group could be her main source of support from the outset. Chapter 8 examines issues relating to groups for incest survivors in some detail. Table 4.5 lists the main advantages and limitations of groups.

Work with Families

Therapeutic work with a whole family usually involves children in families where abuse is suspected or confirmed. In adulthood, it may be beneficial for the woman to work with siblings or her mother in either a family or group setting.

Table 4.5: Group Settings: Advantages and Limitations

Advantages	Limitations
Women share burden of the abuse with others who have been through similar experiences	Group setting may be too threatening for some women
Emotional and social isolation reduced when women realise they are not the only ones to have been abused	Confidentiality may be more difficult to maintain
Can help women to face the reality of what has happened	Individuals may feel excluded or need more individual attention
Can validate as normal a woman's feelings of guilt, anger, grief, loneliness and other long-term effects	Women may need more regular support than group can offer
More established members can acknowledge progress they have made and can give hope to newer members	Hearing about the experiences of others may be too painful
Can be a place of safety to express true feelings and emotions	Reluctance to participate in group if woman feels she has not suffered as much as others in the group
Women can work together to build trust and alleviate guilt	

Table 4.6: Issues in Working with Siblings

Issues for siblings	Implications for the helper
May be first time the abuse is openly acknowledged to each other	Needs to check out knowledge with each sibling about the abuse. May need to perform mediating role
May have been abused in different ways	Ensure that both experiences are acknowledged and validated without minimizing either
May be at different stages of recovery from the abuse	Acknowledge this and take into account in the work
Abuse may have had different consequences for each sibling	Acknowledge and encourage dialogue on the issue
One sibling feels responsible for allowing abuse of others to happen	Examine threats and bribes used to maintain silence and secrecy, and issues of responsibility for the abuse
May have different views of the same event	Check out reasons for discrepancies, emphasize common elements

Work with siblings

When a child has been sexually abused by a trusted adult, she is likely to ask herself if her brothers or sisters have had similar experiences. Sometimes sisters have attended for help at the same agency. If this is the case, it may be possible to bring them together to talk about their past. Table 4.6 gives an indication of issues which might arise in this context.

Mothers and daughters

In individual therapy and in group work, the question of a mother's knowledge about the abuse is a recurring theme. A woman may want to confront her mother with issues relating to the extent of this knowledge, her failure to protect her and her responsibility for past events. An incest survivor may wish to enlist the support of her helper in confronting her mother. Clearly, this can only take place if her mother is also willing to do the work. It might be possible for a mother to undertake individual work before coming together with her daughter. Some of the issues which arise in joint work with mothers and daughters are given in Table 4.7.

Every incest survivor has the right to choose the therapeutic setting which she feels will best meet her needs and help her to come to terms with her past. Information about the resources which are available locally, the timing of her decision to seek help and the approach of a particular helper or group are all important elements in this process.

Table 4.7: Issues for Mothers and Daughters

Mothers	Daughters
Acknowledging that the abuse has occurred	Did she know about it? How could she *not* have known?
Feelings of guilt and failure to protect her child, of not being a good-enough parent	Why did she not see that something was wrong? What did she do/could she have done to stop it?
Vulnerability when confronted with the facts about the abuse	May want to protect mother from details of the abuse
Finds it difficult to cope with daughter's feelings	May want to protect mother so disguises her true feelings
Is she able to let daughter know what it was like for her, especially in her relationship with the abuser	May not want to hear. Finds it difficult to acknowledge mother's own difficulties
Mother may have been abused by the same man	Why didn't she protect me from him? She knew what he was like

5 Stages of Recovery

This chapter examines the stages of work that an incest survivor is likely to have to pass through before finally coming to terms with being sexually abused as a child. The details and emphasis of the work will vary from individual to individual, and may also reflect the setting in which the work is carried out. For example, some women may only attend a group that is time-limited and has a restricted set of aims. Others may attend for individual counselling with no time limits, or be involved in both group and individual work simultaneously. Progress through the stages is not an orderly process, since it is affected by a number of factors both within the woman and in her circumstances.

The six stages are:

- acknowledging that help is needed;
- initial disclosure of childhood sexual abuse;
- finding an appropriate source of help;
- beginning of therapeutic contact;
- the middle phase of therapeutic work;
- ending the therapeutic contact.

Stage 1: Acknowledging That Help is Needed

An acknowledgment that the woman needs some help for her present or past difficulties may come from herself, through the concern of her family, friends or work colleagues, or through agencies dealing with other members of her family (e.g. education and child health agencies). At this stage, she may not be aware that she was sexually abused or that being abused as a child could have links with her present difficulties.

Stage 2: Initial Disclosure of Child Sexual Abuse

The first disclosure from an incest survivor that she was sexually abused as a child may take place with family members or friends, or may not occur until she is established in a therapeutic relationship and has already begun to work on some of her difficulties. The reactions of those whom she first tells will determine whether she feels encouraged to seek further help. If this disclosure is made in a context where help is not available (e.g., in a community-based women's group) it is essential that potential sources of help are discussed with the woman immediately, so that she can seek them out for herself. Contact with the health service can be made through her family doctor, or she may prefer to avail herself of help from voluntary groups, social services or community agencies.

Once she has decided to seek help, there should be as little delay as possible between a woman's request for help and her first contact with her chosen helping agency. Significant delay could result in:

- a woman feeling that her history of sexual abuse is too shocking/disgusting for her to have help;
- a woman feeling rejected after she has plucked up courage to ask for help;
- a woman retracting/minimizing/denying that she has been abused;
- a woman feeling that her story of abuse is not serious enough to warrant attention;
- a woman requiring emergency or urgent psychiatric help because once she has broken the secret about her past she cannot contain the feelings associated with it any longer;
- an increase in her suicidal, or self-injurious behaviour, perhaps requiring emergency treatment.

Detailed discussion of the management of and issues arising from initial disclosure is given in Chapter 6.

Stage 3: Finding an Appropriate Source of Help

Sources of help can be found both in the statutory (medical, mental health and social services) agencies and within voluntary agencies. A woman may come to them by a number of different routes. Her selection of an appropriate source of help depends on whether she can remember or disclose that she was sexually abused. Chapter 4 discussed the various helping agencies available; where possible she should be encouraged to choose an agency that best meets her needs and circumstances.

Stage 4: Beginning of the Therapeutic Contact

Therapeutic work to overcome the effects of being sexually abused as a child begin
with a woman's initial acknowledgment that she was abused. For some incest sur
vivors, however, this acknowledgment is not possible for several reasons:

- she does not remember that she was abused;
- she does not feel ready to disclose this information;
- she does not feel safe enough to do so with the particular helper;
- she does not believe that her early experiences are having any effect on her life

In these cases, the woman may need to be involved in a therapeutic situation which
allows her to prepare herself for a confirmation that she was sexually abused as a child

Establishment of a therapeutic relationship

An incest survivor will come for help with many problems relating to her childhoc
experiences. Some of these problems may make it difficult for her to be involved in
therapeutic relationship. Her feelings of guilt, shame and helplessness, combined wit
her fears of being betrayed and exploited in close relationships, may lead her to want
run from the helper; she may fear disbelief, blame and rejection.

From the very beginning of contact, therefore, the helper should aim to establis
a relationship with the woman that will allow her to feel that she is believed and take
seriously. This will involve:

- actively listening and attempting to understand her problems from her point
  view (i.e. with empathy);
- suspending judgments and preconceived ideas about the woman and gener
  issues about child sexual abuse;
- responding warmly, with support and interest;
- allowing her to discuss her problems, her past and other issues at her own pac
- respecting her right to remain silent about any issue.

The experience of sexual abuse as a child is surrounded by secrecy. It involves a misu
of power, betrayal of the child's trust, and compounds the child's helplessness and la
of control over her situation. These issues are likely to be very much in evidence at th
stage of therapy. An assurance of confidentiality, not forcing her to talk in detail abo
the abuse and giving her choices in the therapeutic situation are vitally necessary
avoid betraying her trust and leaving her feeling helpless a second time.

Establishing a relationship with an incest survivor that is safe enough to allow h
to reveal her childhood memories and their associated pain can take a long time -
perhaps many months. She may be very tentative, ambivalent or suspicious with th
helper and she must be given time to feel secure before the work progresses.

Engagement difficulties

It may take a long time for an incest survivor to trust her helper and to engage with her. Non-attendance at initial appointments is normally seen as a sign of poor motivation in professional helping services. Attempts will need to be made to follow up non-attendance and other means of encouraging a woman to engage with her helper should be considered. These could include:

- visiting the woman in her own home initially;
- seeing the woman initially with someone she already trusts and with whom she has already shared some of her experiences;
- meeting on neutral territory. An office or hospital, for example, may have unpleasant memories or be seen as too authoritarian. Alternatively, some women feel safer out of doors;
- the layout of the room in which the woman is seen is important. Some women need to feel that they can escape quickly if necessary, so sitting near and in view of the door is important. A woman may be unable to relax if the helper is seated between her and the door;
- building up the relationship over the telephone may be necessary before a woman can risk a face-to-face meeting. This is more likely to enable the woman to feel in control and she is also able to terminate the call herself if necessary.

Framework and specific aims

Therapeutic work with an incest survivor can be a lengthy and intensive process and it is not likely to begin unless the therapeutic environment allows the woman to feel in control and offers her some assurance of confidentiality. There are five important principles which should be explained to a woman at this stage:

1   She will be gradually helped to gain control of her past so that it stops intruding into and affecting the present;
2   She will be encouraged to take more control of and exercise choice in the therapeutic situation and in her current life circumstances;
3   During her therapeutic work, she will be given control and choice of when and how much she discloses about painful and distressing memories and experiences of her past;
4   The work will proceed at a pace that she can tolerate;
5   Extra support will be given or sought from other agencies where necessary with prior discussion with the woman.

The specific aims of the work will vary from woman to woman, and will also depend on the setting in which she receives help. There are a number of aims which apply to any setting. These are outlined in Table 5.1.

Table 5.1: Aims of Work with an Incest Survivor

---

1. Helping her to gradually talk in detail about her childhood so that she gains some understanding of the effects of being abused as a child;
2. Gaining an understanding of the long-term effects of being abused;
3. Facilitating an understanding and safe release of emotional reactions;
4. Gaining an understanding of her family and its interactions;
5. Exploring the losses resulting from her childhood experiences, and helping her to reverse some of them;
6. Breaking the secret of her past with others;
7. Working specifically on the long-term effects of the abuse (e.g., assertiveness work, sex therapy, anxiety problems, depression);
8. Gaining an acceptance of the past so that it allows her to look forward to the future.

Establishing the arrangements for the therapeutic work

It is essential at the beginning of any work with an incest survivor for the helper to clarify what the offer of help entails. The issues which should be discussed with her are:

- when, where and how often the therapeutic sessions are to take place;
- the length of these sessions;
- whether the sessions will be discussed with anyone else (e.g. in support or supervision for the helper(s));
- whether the helper will be communicating with a referring agency (this is usually only necessary in the statutory services) or with anyone else (e.g., G.P.);
- whether there are any details of her experiences which the woman does not wish to be communicated to the referring agency;
- what level of or alternative arrangements for support the helper might organize for both an incest survivor and the helper during difficult periods of the therapeutic work, holidays etc.

Explanation of the therapeutic process

It is helpful at this stage to acknowledge that coming to terms with childhood sexual abuse is a painful process that can take considerable time. A useful analogy is to explain the healing process by likening it to the healing of a wound. The helper might say:

I want you to think of this process like the healing of a deep wound. First, imagine you have a deep wound on your arm. Think what would happen if you kept it covered up with plaster or a bandage for a long time. It would not heal properly and might even go septic. If you then take the plasters off, the wound will hurt a great deal, but once it has been cleaned, it will begin to heal properly. Now if we imagine that what your ... (father, uncle, brother, cousin, grandfather etc.) did to you caused a deep wound inside you, but for a number of reasons it has been bandaged up ever since. What we will be doing is gradually peeling back those bandages until the wound is exposed. This is going to hurt but then it can be cleaned and will begin to heal properly leaving just a scar. Eventually, it will stop hurting, except when the scar is knocked sharply.

This analogy is both hopeful and realistic, and offers some explanation for any setbacks.

The following information about what may happen during the process of receiving help should also be discussed:

- the process may take a long time, extending to several months or years;
- the woman is likely to feel worse before she begins to feel better;
- there will be times when she wishes she had not embarked on this process;
- it may have some effects on her relationships with her partner, her children and her own family;
- she may need time off work during or after particularly upsetting periods of the work.

At this stage the woman's courage in seeking help should be acknowledged. She should also be assured of ongoing support during the work she is about to undertake.

Difficulties at this stage

The helper must examine any factors at this stage which may inhibit the start of the therapeutic process. These are summarized in Table 5.2.

Finally, some incest survivors are extremely unsure about the benefits of receiving help or may be ambivalent about embarking on the process. If this is the case it is useful to consider the following options:

- initially she might be offered a limited number of therapeutic sessions to allow her to examine the importance and relevance of her history of being abused as a child;
- she may need more time to make her decision, and another meeting with the helper might be arranged for several weeks later in order to give her that time;
- she may need to have time to see how she will react to making her initial disclosure before committing herself to working on the problems.

Ultimately, it is the woman's choice whether she accepts the offer of help.

Table 5.2: Relevant Factors for the Start of Therapeutic Work

Issue	*Implications*	*Questions to be considered*
Motivation to work on the past	If low, she may not be able to involve herself with the work and may fail to attend meetings or appointments	Who referred her? Was she willing to be referred? Did she seek the help herself? Did she seek help for the problems of another family member (child, spouse, sibling)?
Life circumstances	If complicated, disrupted, busy or unsupported, it may be difficult to embark on the work	Is this the right time for her? Does she have very young children and little support? Is she going through another major life crisis? Does she have any support for herself?
Her willingness to get involved with a particular helper	Issues of trust, gender of the helper are critical here	Can she trust the helper? Can she talk more easily to a male or female helper? Has she any expectations or prior knowledge that the helper has worked with other incest survivors?
Previous attempts at getting help	Issues concerned with being believed, and reactions of helpers	Has she received help before and when? What were the reactions of the helper(s)? What gender were they? Was she believed and taken seriously?
Concerns about confidentiality	Concerned about trust and a manifestation of the power of the secret	Who else will find out that she has been abused? Who will be told details of the abuse? What will be written down about her in notes, letters?

Confidentiality

The issue of confidentiality should be discussed at the start of the work. The issues to be explored with the incest survivor are:

  – any statutory requirements that the helper has to communicate with the referring agency (e.g., within the NHS, helpers are expected to communicate some information to the woman's family doctor);

– any information that she does not wish the referring agency to know (e.g., if she lives in a closely-knit community, she may find it difficult to cope with the possibility of anyone in the community knowing that she was sexually abused);
– whether the helper discusses her/his work with a supervisor or support person;
– what other staff in the helping agency need to know. This is particularly relevant in situations where there is a team of helpers (e.g., in psychiatric hospital settings, Women's Aid or a hostel where the woman is living).

Stage 5: The Middle Phase of Therapeutic Work

Once a woman has accepted the offer of help, the most intensive part of the work can begin. Some women find their decision to accept help too frightening and withdraw from the helping situation fairly quickly. In our experience, most incest survivors who manage to cope with the initial stages do continue long enough to gain some benefit from the contact.

The content and process of the middle phase of therapeutic work depends largely on the needs and problems of an individual woman. Table 5.3 outlines the major issues that arise, and their likely timing in the overall process. Some issues or problems occur throughout whereas others are more likely to be present at the beginning or end of the therapeutic contact.

Levels of support

During a period of disclosure, when there is often an increased need for support, incest survivors frequently worry about becoming over-dependent on their helpers. This can also become an issue for helpers. If this is the case, it can be useful to conceptualize the process in terms of recovery from a physical injury. The helper might say:

> I want you to imagine this process is like recovering from a broken leg. When you break a leg, first you have to have bed rest, then you get on to two crutches with lots of help from the nurses. After that you learn to walk on two crutches, then one until you can manage just with a stick. For a while you will hobble about. That's what is happening here. Just now you are needing crutches but eventually you'll be able to throw them away, though you may need them back again occasionally if there are any setbacks.

This will enable a woman to see that it is quite reasonable to need and use the support that is available to her, and that there may be times when a high level of support is needed. Kenward (1987) noted that in individual work at least, the need for high levels of support occurs mainly during the early stages but may increase again about a year later before reducing to more manageable levels prior to ending contact with a helper.

Table 5.3: Issues in the Therapeutic Process Issue

Issue	Stages
Long-term effects obvious	Early stages Middle stage
Trust	Early stages and at times of disclosure
Confusion about why she needs help now	Early stages
The first detailed disclosure	Early Stages
Questions about her family	Throughout
Child-like behaviour/fears especially on disclosure	Throughout
Guilt	Throughout
Loss	Throughout
Victim behaviour	Throughout
Growing awareness of links between past and present	Throughout
Small changes in usual mode of behaviour, attitudes, perception of the past	Throughout
Emergence of clearly defined emotional reactions	Throughout
Emergence of anger and rage	Middle to later stages
Becoming a survivor	Middle and later stages
Breaking the secret with other incest survivors, family and friends	Middle and later stages
Dealing with specific problems (sexual, marital, parenting, anxiety etc.)	Middle and later stages
Confrontation of abuser and/or family members	Later stages
Forgiveness	Later stages
Growing confidence, self-esteem	Later stages
Concerns about the future	Ending
Getting ready to leave sources of help	Ending

The level of support required by an incest survivor varies from woman to woman and on the stage which she has reached in the recovery process. Weekly sessions at the outset, moving to fortnightly or monthly contact later is a common pattern.

Sometimes a woman needs much more intensive support; this can amount to daily contact, perhaps by phone. If she needs more contact than this, it is likely that a short admission to a psychiatric unit or an alternative place of safety (e.g., women's hostel or Women's Aid refuge) may have to be arranged. Use of community and voluntary organizations, church facilities (if appropriate) and community psychiatric nurse teams should be considered as additional sources of support for any woman who can continue to manage in the community.

Stage 6: Ending of Therapeutic Contact

The process of ending therapeutic contact with an incest survivor will begin once it becomes clear that her past is no longer intruding into the present, and that she has moved from being an incest victim to becoming a survivor. The management and timing of the termination of contact is important and should be done in consultation with the woman herself as the ending of contact can be painful for the incest survivor and her helper, especially when the contact has lasted a long period of time. Some women prefer not to consider this issue openly, and may terminate the contact suddenly by not keeping their last appointment. Where possible, however, the ending should be planned. It may be useful to consider some of the following strategies:

– reduction in the frequency and/or length of sessions;
– determining how many more sessions are required, setting a fixed date for the last one and spacing out the remainder to fit in before that date;
– not setting the date for a further session, but allowing the woman herself to request a further meeting. If no contact is made within say, three months, agree that the helper will make contact to discuss future sessions.

In some situations, e.g., a time-limited group, the number of sessions and the date of the last session may be fixed at the beginning. In this case follow-up meetings or sessions with an individual helper may be arranged by agreement.

At the end of any work with an incest survivor, the helper should discuss the following issues:

– the usefulness of the contact to her;
– any arrangements for follow-up and the helper's availability to see her again in the future;
– any writing that she has done for the helper. Is this to be kept, destroyed or returned?
– any contact that the helper intends to have with the agency that referred her.

These issues may be problematic if the woman terminates her contact early.

Finally, helpers should remember that incest survivors, having worked through many issues and terminated their contact with a helper, are quite likely to find that future life events can trigger off further memories. It is important therefore for a helper to operate an 'open door' policy if possible; the ability to do this will obviously reflect the demands on the helper. If an 'open door' policy is not possible, then women should be made aware of other sources of support. The original helper may also be required to accept a subsequent referral if requested by the woman herself.

Special Considerations for Women who have Experienced Physical and Sexual Abuse

For a woman who has experienced severe levels of physical and sexual abuse, usually within her family, there are a number of features that relate to the stages of therapy (Rocklin and Lavett, 1987):

- She may have great difficulty in asking for help, assuming rejection, disbelief and hostility;
- Similar fears are likely to emerge at the start of any therapeutic contact. As a result, the helper may have to be more active in engaging the woman in the work, perhaps requiring more frequent contact than would be usual. There may be a 'trial period' with the helper, the main goal being to indicate to the woman that her helper is trustworthy, concerned and not rejecting;
- Issues of trust and being believed are predominant especially at the beginning, and reassurance about these concerns is essential;
- Periods of disclosure are more likely to provoke a regression to childhood with its associated terror, despair and child-like behaviour (see Chapter 9). Higher levels of support may be needed at this time. Fears about any threats made by the abuser may also be activated at this time;
- The helper may be actively involved in 're-parenting' the woman, assuring her of safety, protection and care. This again represents the need for a greater level of involvement from the helper;
- The ending of the therapeutic contact should be planned, and involve a gradual reduction in contact over a period of time;
- Concerns about confidentiality are likely to be more pronounced particularly if the woman is still in contact with the abuser. She is likely to re-experience fear of the threats which he used to maintain her silence as a child.

Outlining the stages of recovery can be a useful exercise. It can help a woman to acknowledge the progress she has made, and it allows her to look ahead with some degree of optimism, even when she may be feeling that her pain is increasing rather than diminishing in intensity.

6 Disclosure

The long-term consequences of child sexual abuse are considerable, but many women are unable to disclose their experiences until many years after the abuse has stopped. In this chapter, we will examine the management, difficulties and consequences for a woman of her initial disclosure of a history of being sexually abused as a child, and of subsequent disclosures.

Many incest survivors attend helping agencies unaware of the links between their current difficulties and their early experiences of sexual abuse. For others, their history of sexual abuse remains hidden, sometimes even to the survivors themselves, until an event in their adult life brings the past to the surface. Gelinas (1983) has likened this process to having a 'time-bomb' inside that ticks away until a trigger in the present detonates the bomb and brings a sudden and intolerable increase in psychological difficulties and distress. Common triggers are described in Table 6.1.

The factors which influence or facilitate disclosure of a history of sexual abuse, especially when it has remained hidden for many years, are very important. Some of these lie within the incest survivor herself (Courtois and Watts, 1982; Josephson and Fong-Beyette, 1987) and are as follows:

- whether she learnt to dissociate herself from the abuse as a child;
- the reactions of others to previous attempts to disclose as a child and as an adult;
- whether she has told anyone before;
- the extent of her recall of the abuse;
- the severity of the abuse;
- her emotional reactions to the memories of the abuse;
- whether she has had close relationships with non-abusive adults during childhood.

A key factor here is the extent to which a woman has learnt to dissociate herself from the abuse and its accompanying emotional reactions when she was a child. The trauma of sexual abuse is likely to make a child feel overwhelmed, extremely frightened and anxious. The fact that the abuser is a trusted adult adds to her confusion, so much so

Table 6.1: Triggers linking Current Difficulties with Childhood Abuse

Context	Trigger
Adult Relationships	– After a long-term relationship with a man has been established – Having a sexual relationship with a man – Being in an abusive relationship with a man
The Abuser	– His terminal illness or death – Makes further demands on survivor – Denial of abuse when confronted – Fear of abuser in presence of her own children
Her Mother	– Terminal illness or death of mother – Confrontation and denial of abuse – Separation/divorce from father (where father was abuser) – Revealing that she was abused by same abuser (e.g., her father, and survivor's grandfather)
Siblings	– Disclosing their sexual abuse – Siblings' children (especially daughters) reaching age woman was when abuse started – Siblings' children in presence of abuser
Her Children	– Birth of a daughter – Daughter reaching age that woman was when the abuse started – Children in presence of abuser – Discovery that child is being sexually abused by woman's abuser or by another family member
Abusive Situation	– Rape – Physical assault – Marital abuse – Abuse in adult relationships
Experience of Loss	– Death of other important family member – Loss of job – Miscarriage/stillbirth/abortion – End of relationship
Gynaecological Examination/ Procedure	– Cervical smear test – Fertility problems requiring treatment – Pregnancy investigations
Media	– Television or radio programmes about child sexual abuse – Films depicting sexual abuse – Magazine and newspaper articles
Employment in a helping profession or membership of a woman's group	– Client/other women disclosing that they were sexually abused as children – Training/workshops/discussion on child abuse, sexuality or violence in the home

that she may even doubt the reality of the abuse. By denying this reality, she learns to dissociate herself from the accompanying psychological and physical pain, trauma and confusion.

There are a number of ways that an abused child uses to cope with and dissociate herself from the abuse. Ultimately, these methods help her survive the experience. Common examples are:

- pretending the abuse was not happening to her;
- forgetting each incident so that each time seemed to be 'the first time';
- thinking of other things e.g., a dream world, chores/homework/etc. that she had to do, whilst the abuse was taking place;
- over-breathing/breath-holding, until the abuse was over;
- pretending to be asleep;
- coming out of her body, so that she has the experience of looking down on herself during the abuse but not feeling the pain, fear or hurt until later.

As an adult, an incest survivor may, however, experience feelings without understanding their origins, because she has no conscious knowledge that she was sexually abused as a child. The process of linking her feelings and current difficulties with her early life experiences can be terrifying and very distressing. The dissociative process continues into adulthood with the following consequences:

- the abuse is not recalled at all: such total amnesia frequently occurs though there are often clues that something unpleasant has happened in a woman's childhood.

Example: Elizabeth had completely repressed memories of being raped by her grandfather at the age of six. She knew, however, that from the age of six, she had become a difficult child with eating problems, sleeping difficulties and a great fear of people. Her parents had told her that she had had scarlet fever at the age of six and had never been the same since. During therapy, some thirty years later, she started to question this explanation and suddenly recalled the sexual abuse with all its terror, pain and great distress.

The woman remembers the sexual abuse but transfers the memories to a safer place (e.g., outside the home) and to a less threatening abuser (e.g., stranger rather than father). An excellent example of complete repression of a traumatic and painful childhood is to be found in 'No Longer a Victim' by Cathy-Ann Matthews (1986), who believed she had had a happy childhood until she was in her late forties. The memories of herself as a physically and sexually abused child emerged during her training as a marriage guidance counsellor.

- The abuse is recalled but without any emotional reactions: denial or minimization of feelings is common, and may reflect the methods the woman used to cope with the abuse when she was a child;

- the abuse is recalled amidst feelings of guilt and shame: here the overwhelming nature of stronger emotions such as terror, panic, pain, aloneness, despair and rage is denied;
- Only certain incidents of sexual and physical abuse are recalled, whereas more traumatic incidents are forgotten:

Susannah initially disclosed that her stepfather had touched her from the age of seven. During therapy, she recalled that the sexual abuse had started when she was three or four and, far from involving genital touching alone, had involved sexual intercourse and oral sex.

- The memories of abuse are vague and without much detail: this often occurs with incidents that have particularly unpleasant implications, e.g., if the incident demonstrates that other important adults knew about the abuse.

Example: Jan remembered an incident of abuse when her father demanded to have intercourse with her, at the age of twelve, had then become very violent and had beaten her up. During therapy, this incident became very important, because Jan remembered that her mother had walked in and discovered her father having intercourse with her, and that physical abuse was perpetrated by both parents as a punishment for being a 'dirty' girl. In this way Jan learned of her mother's knowledge of and attitude towards the sexual abuse, and the fact that she was blamed by both parents.

Disclosure of a history of sexual abuse or of specific details about the abuse should never be sought just for the sake of disclosure. A woman should be encouraged to discuss the possibility of sexual abuse if:

- there are clues in her background or the nature of her difficulties;
- a sibling/one of her children reports being sexually abused.

She should be encouraged to disclose detailed memories if:

- she is having frequent nightmares, perceptual disturbances or flashbacks to the abuse;
- she is making links between her past and her current difficulties.

There are also factors relating to the helper which we have already considered in detail in Chapter 2. Gender, perceived empathy, understanding, trustworthiness, and the attitudes and assumptions of the helper about sexual abuse, are all important in enabling a woman to disclose sexual abuse from her childhood. The reactions of any helper in the past to a woman's attempts at disclosure are also relevant, in that many incest survivors have learnt that some therapists or helpers cannot 'hear' information about sexual abuse and treat it as an irrelevancy from the past (O'Hare and Taylor, 1983). This can lead to increased wariness on the part of an incest survivor about making further attempts at disclosure.

A woman's first contact with a helping agency is likely to involve discussions about her difficulties and the context in which they have occurred. Questions about her family, marital and work background may be routinely asked. Helpers should consider whether to ask similar routine questions about any experiences of being sexually abused. The advantages and disadvantages of routine questions are outlined in Table 6.2.

Table 6.2:   Routine Questions about Sexual Abuse

Advantages	Disadvantages
They help to remove the stigma of being an incest survivor	The helper who asks the questions may not be in a position to offer the woman help. She then feels exposed and unsupported.
	Unless help is available to her immediately on disclosure of the abuse, the woman is likely to find it increasingly difficult to cope with the burden of the secret
They enable the helper to become comfortable asking difficult questions about sexual abuse	The helper may not want to hear confirmation that a woman has been sexually abused
They raise the subject of sexual abuse in a non-threatening way	The woman may not be ready to disclose
Provides relief that sexual abuse can be discussed openly	The woman may feel that the helper is intruding
	Routine questioning may suggest to the woman that the helper views sexual abuse as no worse than other stressful life experiences
	A woman may feel trapped into acknowledging that she was sexually abused.

Initial Disclosure

The initial disclosure of a history of child sexual abuse can come in a number of ways:

- from the woman herself who has requested help to enable her to come to terms with the abuse. Here, she is taking the initiative for disclosure and can be assumed to be ready to tell the secrets of her childhood;
- from the woman herself once she has established herself in a therapeutic

situation, and feels she can trust the helper. She is taking the initiative to disclose once she has established that it is safe to do so;

- as a response to routine questions from the helper about the woman's family and sexual history;

- as a response to *specific* questions from the helper who has been alerted to the possibility that the woman had been sexually abused because of the nature of her difficulties and aspects of her history. Table 6.3 examines the potential clues that might lead to such questions.

Table 6.3: Clues to Child Sexual Abuse

Combination of some of the following factors:-

Combination of long-term effects (especially sexual problems, perceptual disturbances, fear of men or avoidance of relationships with men, self-mutilation);

Previous psychiatric history and several different diagnoses and still not much better;

No memories of childhood/over-positive descriptions of childhood;

Reasons for seeking help now (see Table 5.1);

Certain features during childhood including:
  Significant behaviour disturbance
  Running away from home
  Persistent urinary tract infections
  Sexually transmitted disease
  Frequent unexplained school absences (especially if
    evidence of physical violence in family)
  Withdrawal or isolation from peer group;

Certain features during adolescence including:
  Running away from home
  Pregnancy, especially during early adolescence
  Sexually transmitted diseases
  Pronounced fear of men
  Self-mutilation, especially cutting
  Prostitution or significant promiscuity;

Family history:
  Another child (especially sibling) sexually abused
  Evidence of violence and/or alcoholism in parents;

History of prostitution.

In this situation, the helper should take the responsibility for asking about sexual abuse as the woman may be unaware of the links between her current difficulties and her past. In this way, the helper is indicating to her that the subject of child sexual abuse can be raised, and is assisting her with the very difficult task of breaking the secret. As with routine questions, however, she may not be ready to disclose, but may feel trapped into doing so. As a result, she may fail to keep further appointments, retract her disclosure, deny its importance or refuse to discuss it further.

Therapeutic work to overcome the effects of sexual abuse begins at the moment of the initial disclosure. Unfortunately, it can also end there if the disclosure is managed in an insensitive or intrusive way. Both the style and nature of the questioning about sexual abuse and the helper's subsequent reactions are critical. Therefore, enquiry about a history of sexual abuse must be handled in a sensitive and non-judgmental way. Questions should be tentative, allowing the woman the choice to remain silent about or deny her history of sexual abuse. She should not be forced or persuaded in any way to admit that she was abused. Examples of useful questions are set out in Table 6.4.

Table 6.4: Examples of Questions to Elicit a Disclosure of Child Sexual Abuse

---

'This may be a difficult question to hear, but I am wondering whether you were ever sexually abused as a child?'

'You have been describing a number of difficulties that are often found in women who report that they were sexually abused as children. I wonder if this has ever happened to you?'

Where there is evidence that she was physically abused as a child:

'Did he ever do more than physically abuse you? For example, did he ever also sexually abuse you?'

'The problems you are describing suggest to me that something very unpleasant may have happened to you as a child. Were you ever abused, physically?' (wait for answer) 'Sexually?'

'I'm wondering if anyone touched you when you were a child in a way that made you feel uncomfortable and/or frightened.'

Helper's Reactions to Disclosure

It has been shown that if the woman perceives a negative reaction in the helper when she makes her initial disclosure, she may refuse to discuss the sexual abuse or to return for further sessions (Josephson and Fong-Beyette, 1987). Examples of such reactions are:

- if the helper ignores or minimizes the effects of being sexually abused;
- if the helper shows an excessive interest in the sexual details;
- if the helper appears very angry, shocked or disgusted by the disclosure.

Therefore, if a woman confirms that she was abused, the helper should respond positively. Examples of helpful ways of responding are as follows:

- congratulate the woman on taking the step of disclosing, and acknowledge the difficulty of doing so;
- identify child sexual abuse as a primary cause of some of her difficulties;
- do not minimize the sexual abuse even if it occurred infrequently or on one occasion;
- offer her immediate support in the days following disclosure;
- encourage her to explore her feelings about her disclosure;
- offer her therapeutic help, or assist her in finding appropriate help as soon as possible;
- ask her if she wishes to talk about the abuse. Her answer will determine the helper's course of action;
    - if the answer is Yes, encourage her to do so, but in her own time and at her own pace;
    - if the answer is No, respect her right to remain silent, but leave her with an invitation to talk about it should she change her mind;
- if she is to be referred on to another helper, she should not be encouraged to talk too much about the details of the abuse as she may not be able to cope with the accompanying emotional reactions. This is best done within the safety of an established therapeutic relationship;
- remain calm, and do not show any feelings of shock, disgust or distress. These reactions will prompt the woman to retract her disclosure, stop the contact with the helper, or remain silent;
- indicate to the woman that she is believed.

These responses acknowledge a woman's difficulty in disclosing, indicate that she is believed and is being taken seriously, and begin to help her understand that child sexual abuse has significant consequences into adulthood. It is essential that the helper avoids certain unhelpful responses (see Table 6.5) as these are likely to make the woman leave the therapeutic situation.

Once a woman has confirmed that she was sexually abused as a child, she may react in a number of ways:

- she may feel relieved that she can begin to make sense of her difficulties;
- she may be very shocked, leading to feelings of numbness and distress;
- she may feel bewildered, frightened, and/or confused;
- she may have very mixed feelings about remembering and disclosing her childhood experiences;
- she may be angry or resentful towards the helper for encouraging or enabling her to remember;
- she may be totally calm, misleading the helper into thinking that her childhood experiences held no negative feelings for her;

– in the days following disclosure, she may attempt suicide, abuse alcohol or drugs heavily or injure/mutilate herself in some way.

Table 6.5: Unhelpful Responses to Disclosure

'It's in the past. Do try to forget about it.'

'Did you enjoy it?'

'It only happened a few times, so maybe there isn't really anything to worry about.'

'You were much too little for it to have any effect.'

'That is not as bad as some sexual abuse that I have heard about.'

'Do you really expect me to believe that your father/cousin/brother/uncle etc. who is obviously such a successful man would do such a thing.'

'What a disgusting thing to have happened to you. It makes me very angry when I hear women describe these sorts of experiences.'

'Please don't go on just now. I find this sort of thing very distressing to hear.'

'But why did you let him carry on when you got older?'

'Why didn't you tell someone?'

(By male helpers) 'I'm a safe man. You can tell me.'

These are obviously strong emotional reactions. If the woman has been helped to recall the sexual abuse for the first time for many years, the helper must be alert to her needs for support, safety and reassurance, and once the confirmation of a history of sexual abuse has been made, it is useful to gather certain *general* information about the abuse:

– the age she was when the abuse started and stopped;
– the identity of the abuser(s);
– who else now knows that she was abused;
– who she told/tried to tell as a child;
– what were the reactions of those she told;
– whether she knows if any brothers, sisters or other family members were also abused.

Beyond these general facts, a woman should not be pressed at this stage for any specific details unless she indicates that she wants to talk further.

Some women may have experienced sexual abuse but still deny the fact. This may be for one or more of the following reasons:

– that she has no recollection of being abused;
– that she was abused but does not wish or is not ready to talk about it;
– that she was abused but does not wish to talk to the particular helper about it;

– that she was abused but she is too frightened to break the secret because of threats from the abuser, or fears about confidentiality;
– that she fears she will not be believed if she discloses;
– that she feels she will go 'mad', 'crack up', 'go to pieces' if she breaks the secret;
– that she thinks the helper will feel disgust or repulsion towards her.

In this situation, the helper has no choice but to respect her silence. However, she may be able to disclose at a later date when she feels ready. In our experience women who have been abused, but who cannot yet acknowledge it, often feel relieved that the possibility of child sexual abuse has been recognised and put to them by a helper.

Subsequent Disclosures

An initial confirmation of sexual abuse is only the beginning of the work needed to come to terms with these childhood experiences. Subsequent disclosures of particular incidents and details of the abuse are also very important. An incest survivor should be encouraged to talk about the details of being abused; the helper's task here is to facilitate disclosure in a non-threatening and safe way, and to monitor carefully the woman's reactions during disclosure.

A disclosure can be made in a number of different ways — through writing and artwork, verbally, in face-to-face contact with the helper or over the telephone. Table 6.6. examines the advantages, disadvantages and implications for the helper of each of these contexts and methods. It is useful to discuss each of them with an incest survivor so that she can choose those with which she feels most comfortable at different points. In addition to making decisions about the method of disclosure, incest survivors can be helped by:

– the use of the analogy that everyone has a child within her. A woman should be reassured that 'her' child was abused and needs to tell a safe and trusted adult. The feelings which emerge during this process are those that belong to the child, and the little girl needs to be reassured that she is now safe and was not to blame for what happened.
– being given the choice and control over how, when and how much to disclose. The helper's task is to monitor whether a woman wishes to continue and to respect her right to stop when she feels that she has told enough. If she does not wish to share a particular memory, her right to silence must be respected, though the reasons for not disclosing should be explored with her. Examples of such reasons and subsequent appropriate action to be taken by the helper are given in Table 6.7.

Table 6.6: Methods of Disclosure

	Writing done at home	Writing done with the helper	Drawing and Artwork	Talking face-to-face	Talking on the phone
Advantages	Details of the abuse can be described without having to say the words. Writing can be done in own time and at own pace. Writing can be kept as a record, compared over time	Woman can write what she cannot say. She can be helped and prompted by the helper	Memories are those of a child, who often find it easier to draw than to use language. Has an immediate impact that can be lost in verbal explanations. Helper can guide the drawings	Lessens the power of the secret of the abuse. May be more possible for helper to comfort the woman. Enables woman to use words which may have been avoided	Woman not faced with a person and may therefore disclose more easily. Can be anonymous (e.g. Rape Crisis Line). Fewer distractions present
Disadvantages	Woman may not remember what she has written. Woman has never *said* the words describing the abuse. Woman may have to be told what she has written. She may not want to talk about the writing. She may fear someone else reading the material	Woman may still need to *say* what happened. Poor writing skills may inhibit her	It may be difficult to draw the details of the abuse. Woman may feel silly or incompetent at drawing. Words still needed to clarify the drawings. Simplicity of drawings may limit their usefulness	Woman may be too frightened to say much. She can see the helper's reactions and is wary of this. Can provoke very strong and uncontrolled emotional reactions	May still have to face the helper. Silences may be more difficult to handle. Difficulties with putting a time limit on phone-calls. Non-verbal communication is largely absent. No physical comfort available to the woman
Implications for the helper	There may be a lot to read. Helper can read and react to the material without woman being present, so protecting her a little. Needs to be kept in a safe place	May be very time-consuming	Helper may not feel competent in interpreting the drawings	Helper can monitor woman's emotional reactions. Helper has to maintain careful control over own reactions	Uncertainty about woman's reactions after disclosure. May be difficult to hear the woman, especially if she is softly spoken

Table 6.7: Difficulties with Disclosure and Action of the Helper

Reasons for not disclosing a particular memory	*Helper action*
The memory is too horrific or upsetting	Reassurance that nothing worse can happen to her now by telling. The worst happened at the time of the abuse
She is not sure the helper will believe her	Reassurance that the helper does believe her
She does not want to believe it herself, and telling will make it 'real'	Remind her that the memory is already real to her. Not wanting to believe it does not mean it did not happen
She is not sure it really happened	Comment that the main issue is that this memory/thought is bothering her and that she needs to discuss it in order to decide whether it did happen
She is scared of her own reaction later e.g., suicide attempt, self-mutilation, rage	Offer of more support perhaps, if appropriate, arranging an admission to a psychiatric unit, or other place of safety
She is scared that the abuser's threats will come to pass (even if he is dead) if she tells	Assure her of confidentiality. She is only telling the helper. If the abuser is dead, remind her that he can do nothing further to harm her
Her current life is so full of problems that she does not wish to add to her difficulties	This may be realistic, but the memories are likely to cause more problems as long as they remain undisclosed
She has some important event in her life that she does not wish to upset e.g., exams, marriage, start of a new job	This is realistic, and she should not be pressurized to disclose. It can be useful to set a time after the 'event' to do the disclosing
She has no support at home, and feels unable to cope with being by herself after she has disclosed	Offer more support. Perhaps arrange an admission to hospital or enlist support of other community agencies
She wants to protect the helper from her memories	Remind her that these memories need to be disclosed if she is to get over them, and that the helper's reactions to her disclosures are not her responsibility
She feels pressurized to tell	Remind her she has choice and she will not be forced to tell

Table 6.7: (Continued)

Reasons for not disclosing a particular memory	Helper action
She fears that if she tells about a particular memory, she will remember more unpleasant incidents	Encourage her to disclose and reassure her that any other memories will be dealt with as they appear
She feels ashamed or guilty about the memory and fears the helper will pass judgment on her	Reassure her that these are normal feelings and that the abuser was responsible for creating the situation in which these feelings arose

She should be encouraged, rather than pressurized, to disclose and reminded that only by breaking the silence about her memories will they lose some of their pain. Where she has already disclosed memories, it is useful to remind her of the benefits of that process, and she will need to be constantly reassured that it is safe to tell, and that she will be believed. However, her feelings about making the disclosure may have to be considered first; this allows exploration of any concerns she may have about the helper. Two examples of such pre-disclosure work now follow. In the first, the helper deals with a woman who is disclosing detailed memories for the first time. In the second example, the woman has already experienced the benefits of disclosing details of her abuse.

Example 1

Pre-disclosure work

Jane	I have been having horrible thoughts about what happened to me with my stepfather. I am scared to tell.
Helper	What are you scared of?
Jane	It'll get worse, and then I'll never be able to cope again.
Helper	In my experience of working with women who were abused as children, telling someone about what happened when they were abused is the beginning of being able to get over it.
Jane	But doesn't it get worse?
Helper	Yes, women often feel more upset for a little while, and may need a lot of extra support while they are telling the memories. And that's what will happen for you.
Jane	But why does it get worse?
Helper	I like to think of it like the healing of a wound. Think about having a cut on your hand, and covering it up for weeks and weeks with a bandage.

The cut won't heal properly and might go septic. If you take the bandage off, it will hurt a lot but once it's cleaned it can begin to heal.

Now, image that what your stepfather did to you was like a deep wound inside you, and it's been hidden and covered for years. It has been going bad and causing problems. What we'll be doing is gradually peeling the bandages off until the wound is exposed. It will hurt a lot more but then it will have a chance to heal. Do you understand what I mean?

Jane   Yes.

Helper   Part of exposing that wound will be telling someone you feel you can trust with the details of the memories and flashbacks — then they will start to lose some of the pain, and the panic you feel will gradually get less until you can cope with the memories. Do you feel you want to tell me about these horrible memories today?

Helper   That is fine. You can let me know when you feel ready. Some women do find it easier to write about what happened to them when they were abused. You may want to do that. If you want me to see what you've written I'll be happy to read it, but if you decide you don't want me to read it, that's all right too. It's up to you.

In this example the woman is given choices about disclosing, and the helper respects her right not to disclose on this occasion. Explanations about the benefits of disclosing and the suggestion about writing the memories down whilst leaving her with choices are also given. The helper is realistic about Jane's fears that she may feel 'worse' before she feels better but through the use of the 'wound' analogy helps her to understand the process of coming to terms with being abused.

Example 2

Pre-disclosure work

Anne   I have been thinking about something that happened with my father.

Helper   Do you want to talk about it?

Anne   If I tell you, you won't believe me because it's so horrible.

Helper   I know that these memories are horrible for you, but that doesn't mean they didn't happen.

Anne   But I feel so horrible about what happened.

Helper   I get the feeling that you would like to tell, but are worried about whether I will believe you and how you'll feel afterwards.

Anne   I know in the past it has helped to tell you but this incident is much worse.

Helper	How has it helped?
Anne	Well, remember the last time, I stopped being bothered by those memories, and although I was upset it got much better. It was a relief to find out that someone believed me.
Helper	Do you think the same will happen this time?
Anne	Probably. Maybe I should tell you and then perhaps I won't have to think about it any more.
Helper	Do you want to tell me today?
Anne	Yes I think so.
Helper	How would you like to tell me? Sometimes you like to write it and sometimes you just tell me.
Anne	I think I could manage to tell you, but I might get upset.
Helper	It is all right to get upset. The memories are upsetting and it is quite normal to be upset.

In this example, the helper gradually prepares the ground for a new disclosure. Anne is given choices about whether she wants to tell, and how, is reminded of the benefits of disclosing previous memories and reassured that being upset is normal and acceptable.

There are several situations in which disclosure about a particular incident of abuse becomes essential:

- if the woman is having flashbacks or nightmares about a particular incident which are causing considerable distress;
- where she has become so anxious about making the disclosure that she is unable to cope with her normal life;
- where certain memories continually intrude into and spoil her relationships with her partner and children.

The helper should encourage her to disclose in these situations. Flashbacks, nightmares and related perceptual disturbances will decrease in frequency once all the important details of the incident have been revealed and discussed. Avoidance of disclosure intensifies the emotional reactions and is therefore usually much worse than revealing the details of the incident. The helper should reassure the woman that the worst happened at the time of the incident, nothing worse can happen now and that it is safe for her to tell.

Once a woman had decided to tell the helper it is useful to remind her again of the analogy that everyone has a child inside him or her and it is her 'child' who needs to be encouraged to tell about her bad experiences, knowing that she will be believed. Helping the adult part of her stay in touch with her current life situation and in control of it can be achieved in a number of ways:

- she can be asked to hold firmly onto the arms of her chair, or to some other piece of furniture near her chair;

- the helper might hold the woman's hand whilst she makes her disclosure;
- in a group situation, two group members (perhaps one of the facilitators and one other incest survivor) might hold on to her, one at each side;
- at the end of the disclosure, she could be asked where she is now, how old she is and encouraged to look around the room to establish that she is still the adult.

As we have already seen, disclosure can be made in a number of different ways (see Table 6.6). If the woman has decided to disclose verbally, the helper should also be aware of her non-verbal communication. It is often possible to facilitate the telling through the use of her body language.

Example: Irene was trying to disclose about an incident when her uncle attempted to rape her. It was obvious to the helper that she was experiencing discomfort in the genital area and was writhing about on the chair as if she was being hurt in that part of her body. The helper was able to feed this back to Irene, thus enabling her to begin disclosing.

In addition, some women have memories of the abuse that are triggered entirely by the physical sensation of pain and discomfort in particular parts of their bodies. It is as if the body rather than the mind is remembering the childhood abuse. Such 'body memories' can be used to begin the disclosure.

Example:

Anne   I keep feeling shooting pains in my legs. I haven't fallen or anything. They just hurt especially round my thighs.

Helper Does this pain remind you of any particular time when you were a child.

Anne   (Look of surprise) Well, yes, I used to get these pains in my legs especially after my father had finished with me.

Helper What caused the pains?

Anne   He was a big man and I was quite a small child. He used to sprawl across my legs. It was heavy, like a dead weight, and I think my legs got numb.

This then led into a detailed disclosure of a particular incident of sexual abuse that she had previously forgotten. It involved oral sex and intercourse, but ended with her father falling asleep across the lower part of her body. She was too small and frightened to move him and her legs became numb and then very sore. Following the disclosure, she was very distressed and frightened, but the pains in her legs subsequently stopped.

During disclosure, it is quite common for the woman's behaviour, language and gestures to regress to the age she was when the particular incident of abuse happened. It is as if the 'child within' the woman is actually doing the disclosing. It is essential that the helper's language and behaviour changes accordingly otherwise the woman will not be able to understand what is being said to her.

Example:

The initial part of this disclosure is as the adult, then the woman regresses before returning to being an adult.

Suzanne	I can remember my father's face — leering — the look in his face.
Helper	What did this look say to you?
Suzanne	Lust. I don't know why this is so bad. He was only touching my breasts — no I didn't have any then.
Helper	Do you want to talk about it?
Suzanne	I can see it so clearly, even the shade over the light. It was pink. The strange thing is that I keep thinking that Mummy is in the next room.
Helper	How is that strange?
Suzanne	I never called her Mummy, at least I don't remember ever doing so.
Helper	What did you call her?
Suzanne	Mum, mother but never Mummy.
Helper	I wonder if you called her Mummy when you were very little.
Suzanne	I don't know. I can't remember that far back.
Helper	Sometimes very small children call their mothers Mummy but when they start school, they start to call her Mum.
Suzanne	(Head down, holding and wringing hands. Fighting tears)
	Regression (voice rises in pitch)
	Mummy's in the next room. She's feeding the new baby. She wouldn't do anything anyway. She had just bought the baby at the hospital. We wanted a boy, but she said boys were too expensive. We didn't want another little girl. Daddies make little girls sore (Tears).
Helper	So you didn't want a baby sister?
Suzanne	No, Daddies hurt little girls.
Helper	Does your Daddy hurt you?
Suzanne	(Nod) (tears)
Helper	Where does he hurt you? (Too confusing a question as she had regressed to being a pre-school child)
Suzanne	(Shake of the head)
Helper	Can you point to where he hurts you?
Suzanne	(Gesture towards the top of her legs and genital area)
Helper	So Daddy hurts you in places that he shouldn't touch little girls?
Suzanne	(Nod) (Sobbing)
	But where was Mummy . . . she didn't come . . . I cried . . . she was too busy with the baby.
Helper	What was the baby's name?
Suzanne	Margaret (more sobbing)
	Poor little girl . . .

She changed her position in the chair and obviously reverted to being an adult. Suzanne then realised that the sexual abuse had already started when she was four and a half — the age she was when her youngest sister, Margaret, was born. Previously she had thought that it started at the age of seven.

It is noticeable that in this example, the woman's language becomes simpler, child-like and in the present tense during the regression phase. The helper's language similarly has to match hers or lack of understanding results.

When a woman has experienced severe painful sexual and/or physical abuse that has induced a state of terror, she may regress to such an extent that the methods she used to cope as a child are in evidence during the disclosure. For example, singing songs to herself, reciting poems or nursery rhymes, overbreathing or breath-holding, trying to run out of the room or becoming detached from what is going on around her may have been used to block out the worst of the abuse. These may re-emerge during the disclosure. She is, after all, recalling an incident that consisted not only of the abuse but also the behaviour she used to cope with it.

An incest survivor's reactions after a disclosure should be explored, to assess both her psychological state and the methods used to facilitate the disclosure. Common responses are relief, anger/rage, extreme distress and panic, fear, guilt, physical pain, and sometimes a desire to retract the disclosure because the associated emotions are so strong. Some of these reactions are the result of her childhood fears of her abuser, and his threats to maintain her silence. For example, she may suddenly fear retribution from her abuser for breaking the secret, especially if he threatened to hurt her physically if she ever told anyone.

It is essential, therefore, that the helper is very flexible about offering her extra support and time during periods of continuous disclosure. It may be necessary or appropriate to enlist support for her from other community or health agencies (e.g., rape crisis group, community psychiatric nursing team, health visitors, or voluntary counsellors) or if she wishes, the support of friends or members of her family. If any members of her family are involved in supporting her, they may need support themselves. Not all disclosures require this level of support, but it must be recognised that even a small disclosure can produce a very significant reaction in the woman.

For an incest survivor who was subjected to severe physical and/or sadistic abuse as well as sexual abuse, any disclosure may induce intense terror and continuing fears that the helper will not be able to believe her. These fears may prevent her from disclosing further until she is again reassured that she is believed. The demands on the helper therefore are high, and frequent contact, reassurance and careful management of the disclosures are essential.

This chapter has reviewed the methods for facilitating disclosure together with problems which can arise during periods of disclosure. The helper may need to enlist support for her or himself during periods of disclosure, particularly if the woman is reacting in a highly emotional way to the memories. Ultimately, however, the key to coming to terms with the abuse is breaking the secrets of childhood. Through disclosure, memories lose their power and pain. A woman can then be enabled to begin to shift the burden of responsibility from herself to the abuser. She has to take the risk of disclosing and begin to understand that the pain of her childhood can be significantly reduced by sharing her secrets with adults whom she trusts.

7   Themes in Therapeutic Work

Chapter 5 examined the overall guidelines and aims for therapeutic work with incest survivors. Beyond the general guidelines, there are a number of specific and recurrent themes which arise in the work. These include:

- being believed;
- the nature of the abuse;
- responsibility for the abuse;
- current relationships within the family;
- trust;
- loss;
- flashbacks and memories;
- getting in touch with feelings;
- confrontation and forgiveness;
- living in the present: from victim to survivor.

Being Believed

The issue of being believed is central to all work with an incest survivor. It is particularly important at the beginning, when the establishment of a working relationship between helper and an incest survivor is made. Any suggestion, however slight, that the helper does not believe the woman, will make it extremely difficult to engage her in therapeutic work. The problems relating to being believed originate in the woman's childhood. She may have experienced one or more of the following situations:

- She may have tried to tell other adults about the abuse, but was not believed. She may have behaved in a sexualized way with other children, written about it in her school work, resisted being left alone with the abuser or shown concern or anxiety if one of her siblings had to stay with the abuser. Adults frequently deny or ignore these verbal and non-verbal messages. If this is the case the child is led to believe that sexual abuse is not a subject which can be safely raised with adults.

- She may have told someone, her mother, a neighbour, a teacher or relative for example who did believe her, and who then confronted the abuser. If the abuser denied the accusations the child may have been accused of lying or 'making it all up'. As a result she continued to expect adults not to believe her or tell her that the abuse did not happen.
- Sometimes the child is told by the abuser that if she tells someone, she will not be believed. This threat is used to maintain her silence.
- If the abuser is seen by others to be a 'good person', 'a thoughtful neighbour' or 'doing a responsible job', the child may have, or feels she will have, even greater difficulties in making other adults believe her.

These experiences can continue to colour the woman's expectations of others when she reaches adulthood. It is important therefore for the helper to understand the significance for a woman of being believed. Any hint of disbelief on the part of the helper can be very distressing for an incest survivor. She is often so hyper-sensitive about being believed that questions asking for clarification, changes in voice tone and expressions of surprise on the part of the helper can easily be misconstrued as disbelief.

Frequent testing of the helper's capacity to believe may represent a more fundamental conflict about an incest survivor's desire to be believed; this was summed up by one woman who said,

'I want you to believe because these terrible things really did happen to me, but if you believe, I will have to face up to them and that might be even worse for me.'

Further questioning of the helper's level of belief can occur in relation to the sexual abuse itself. A woman may describe what she thinks is a less serious incident before moving on to discuss her more painful experiences. The woman may wonder how anyone could believe that such experiences could happen to a child. In these situations the helper should reassure her simply and directly by saying:

'Yes, I believe you. I have no reason to doubt what you are saying.'

This should be sufficient to allow the woman to continue, and it is important for the helper to do this regularly and without prompting.

A woman who has experienced physical and sexual abuse of a particularly horrifying or sadistic type, may need constant reassurance about being believed. She may find it difficult to disclose new memories for fear that the helper will not believe her and will then disbelieve everything else that she has disclosed. It may then be necessary for the helper to state clearly the reasons for believing the incest survivor. These might include:

– an incident of abuse may be horrifying, sadistic or terrible, but that does not mean that it did not happen;
– there is no reason to doubt what the woman is saying;
– the helper knows that children are sometimes abused in a very brutal/violent way;
– if the woman has disclosed previous incidents of abuse, the helper should remind her that she was believed on those occasions, and that she will be believed now.

The helper should check regularly with an incest survivor whether she is concerned about being believed. A survivor may constantly ask 'Do you believe me?' needing repeated reassurance from her helper. It is a mark of progress when she asks the question less frequently, knowing and trusting that the helper believes her.

The Nature of the Abuse

An obvious theme in working with incest survivors is the nature of the abuse itself. It can be difficult to encourage a woman to talk about the details of these experiences, but it is essential to do so. It is only by sharing them with an 'accepting' adult that they lose some of their power to hurt. It has been recognized (Lister, 1982) that enforced silence about traumatic events is likely to contribute to the development of psychological problems later. Once a woman feels she can trust her helper with the details of the abuse, it is likely that a history of increasingly upsetting experiences will be revealed. The helper must be prepared for this so that she/he can remain calm and not show reactions of shock, disbelief or disgust. These reactions are likely to prevent an incest survivor from disclosing further information.

Children frequently learn to cope with being sexually abused by dissociating themselves from all or part of the experience (see Chapter 6 for a full discussion of dissociation). This dissociation is likely to continue into adulthood. As a result, a survivor's memories of the abuse are often partial, vague or absent altogether. This has clear implications for her therapeutic work, as it is easy to assume that a woman has disclosed everything about a particular incident. The helper should therefore be aware that:

– The incest survivor may not remember the first incident of abuse. This reflects the insidious onset of sexual abuse. It often begins with a look, or a touch that may be only slightly different from normal behaviour. It may then start to happen more often and include a wider range of sexually abusive behaviour. It is not unusual for a woman to remember that the abuse began at a much earlier age than she had previously recalled. This can be understandably alarming and upsetting for her;

- She may have a clear memory of a particular incident, and initially be fairly certain that it took place at a certain age. Later memory work may reveal that she was mistaken about her age at the time of this incident. This does not mean that she was lying, but that she made an error, just as we might all do if we tried to recall a series of childhood events;
- She may have a clear memory of an incident of abuse which may have been 'condensed' from a number of incidents, or moved in time or place. It might also involve a less threatening abuser (e.g., a stranger rather than her father). The helper should be aware that this may happen;
- Particular memories of the abuse can act like a dam, preventing the woman from remembering other incidents. In this situation, once the 'blocking' incident is disclosed and dealt with, other memories will be released.

Example: Kathy remembered that her father sexually abused her in a particularly frightening way when she was nine years old. She discussed this incident with her helper and no longer felt bad about it. However she began to have flash-backs to previously forgotten incidents from the age of five.

- Talking about the details of the abuse is important since they have caused great distress. Not only was the woman abused by a trusted adult, but the context in which the abuse was carried out can have alarming effects. For example, a woman who was abused in the bath may, in adulthood, find it impossible to feel safe in the bath. A woman who as a child was forced to have oral sex with her father, may never be able to initiate this sort of sexual contact as an adult because of her intense feelings of guilt about her early experiences. Discussing these sorts of details can lead to an increase in fear, pain, distress and despair in the woman. She is therefore likely to need a higher level of support from the helper at this point.
- A woman may not remember all the details of a particular incident of abuse. Chapter 6 outlined some methods for facilitating disclosure. The helper's aim here is to enable the woman to talk about the sexual abuse within a safe, calm and accepting environment.

Responsibility for the Abuse

The issue of responsibility, often expressed in terms of blame and guilt, should be addressed in the early stages of therapeutic work. It is not uncommon for a woman to come for help with guilt feelings about having allowed the sexual abuse to have happened in the first place and for allowing it to continue. As a child she may have known what was happening to her was in some way wrong for a number of reasons including:

- she had feelings of pain, discomfort or shame;
- she was told by her abuser not to tell anyone about what he was doing, otherwise he would go to prison or the family would be split up;
- she realised that the sexual abuse was at odds with her family's attitudes towards physical contact, nudity and basic bodily functions.

Part of her distress has arisen because she was abused by an adult whom she trusted and whom she assumed cared about her. Furthermore, the abuse was not usually an isolated incident, but may have continued over months or years. The question asked by many women is,

'How could he do that to me for so long when he was supposed to love me?'

The only answer which initially seems to make any sense for her is that the abuser must have been disturbed. He could not have known what he was doing and was not responsible for his actions, therefore the logical conclusion for the woman is that she was in some way to blame. Self-blame is often compounded by the reactions of others whom she tried to tell, and by feelings of guilt and shame. These feelings are expressed by the woman in the explanations she gives for the abuse occurring. These are summarized in Table 7.1.

Table 7.1:   Incest Survivors' Explanations for the Abuse

Childhood explanations
> I was a naughty girl so I deserved to be punished
> I never stopped him
> I never told anyone so it must have been my fault
> I told my Mum and she said it was my fault
> There is something about me which made him do it
> I asked him to do it because that way he wouldn't hit me

Adult explanations
> I am a slut so of course he knew it was all right for him to do what he liked
> I used to run around in my nightie so it was my fault — I must have asked for it
> I must have been a very seductive little girl

These explanations ignore the fact that she was a child when the abuse occurred, and that the abuser was in a position of trust, power and responsibility in relation to her. Such explanations need to be gently challenged by the helper, so that the woman can be helped to understand that:

- she was a child when the abuse occurred;
- as a child she was expected to respect and obey trusted adults;

– as a young child she did not have sexual knowledge prior to being abused;

– the only obvious factor which made her abuser 'choose' her was that she was too young to complain;

– her inability to break the secret was because of her fear of the reactions of others, of breaking up the family, or of threats made by the abuser, not because she was in any way responsible for the abuse;

– in families where the woman was not the only child who was abused, she was not responsible for failing to protect her siblings. That was the responsibility of other adults in the family;

– the adult abused his position of power and responsibility by sexually abusing her. He should have been protecting her from, rather than exposing her to, harm;

– the abuse was done *to* her. This can be difficult for an incest survivor to understand if she has been forced to masturbate the abuser or have oral sex with him. Similar difficulties arise if she has been sexually aroused by the abuser's actions;

– it was the adult's responsibility for interpreting any of her behaviour as sexual. Young children who have been sexually abused sometimes learn that by using sexualized behaviour, they can get adult attention which may be absent in their lives. It remains, however, the adult's responsibility for reinforcing that behaviour with sexual attention.

Re-entering the world of her childhood

The therapeutic task here is to help the woman to become more objective about the issue of responsibility by re-entering the world of her childhood. This approach acknowledges that she had the physical size, powerlessness, sexual knowledge and understanding of a child when the abuse took place. This needs to be contrasted with the responsibilities of the abuser. Relevant methods for doing this are described in Chapter 9.

One important aspect of being a child is the expectation that a child will respect and obey trusted adults, particularly family members. The sexually abused child is in an extremely difficult position, since part of that obedience involves complying with the abuser. Incest survivors often forget this feature of their childhood, and should be reminded of it. It is helpful if the helper can include it in any summarizing remarks she/he makes about the survivor as a child. For example,

'As a child you were small and expected to obey the adults around you . . . '

This enables the woman to become aware that compliance cannot be equated with complicity in the abuse. Incest survivors frequently question whether there was 'something' about them that made the abuser single them out for his sexual attention. This may need to be tackled directly, particularly with the use of photographs of the woman as a child.

Her childhood knowledge of sexual matters should be explored in detail to help her to understand her level of sexual awareness and knowledge before the start of the sexual abuse. This can also enable her to see that she was not in any position to question the abuser's wishes or desires. In this context the woman will often berate herself for 'being stupid' for allowing the sexual abuse to have occurred, and it is vital for the helper to again remind her:

'You were only a child of . . . (age)'

Her confusion about her sexuality may have been compounded by physical reactions to the abuse.

Example: Jane described the experience of feeling a 'tingling sensation' when her father touched her 'down below'. She subsequently associated these sensations with feelings of sexual arousal as an adult.

It is essential that a woman understands that a child can and does have sexual feelings which she cannot control when she is touched in certain ways. It is the adult abuser however, who has sole responsibility for creating the situations which produce these sensations.

Incest survivors often feel excluded or isolate themselves from peer group discussions about sexuality and sexual relationships because they become conscious of the fact that their early sexual experiences are similar to those described by their peers during adolescence. This contributes to their feelings of shame and guilt.

Finally, incest survivors often mention the prevailing attitudes which existed in their families about sexuality in its widest sense (e.g., about nudity, bodily functions, physical contact). It is not unusual for them to describe extremely repressed and constrained attitudes in the family. Not only does this create difficulties for a woman in comprehending how the abuse could take place in this atmosphere, but it also makes it harder for her to tell anyone about it. By giving the woman permission to think of herself as a child again in a fairly non-threatening way, she can gain new understanding of her life at that time. She can then begin to shift the burden of responsibility for the sexual abuse from herself to the abuser.

The child's inability to stop the abuse

An incest survivor's inability to stop the abuse when she was a child remains a source of guilt even when she has gained some insight into the fact that she was not responsible for starting it. It may be necessary to help a woman to acknowledge that she was powerless and small as a child and that the abuser was powerful and big. This can help her to understand that any attempt to withstand sexual abuse would have been to little or no avail. In addition, frequent threats or bribes may have been used to maintain her powerlessness and silence (see Table 7.2).

Table 7.2:   Threats and Bribes Used by an Abuser to Maintain Silence

Physical threats	*Threats to split family*
Threat to kill or injure child	The child will be put into a home
Threat to kill or injure mother	The child will be taken away
Threat to kill or injure siblings	The abuser will be put into prison
Threat to kill or injure pets	The abuser will be taken away
Actual injury to child	The child will be sent to prison
Actual injury to others	
Actual injury to pets	
Verbal threats	*Bribes*
'No one will believe you'	Special presents
'You will be called a liar'	Special treats
'You are a slut'	Special outings
Frequent criticism	'You are my special little girl'
Ridicule	

With hindsight, an incest survivor may wonder why she failed to tell anyone about the abuse when it was happening. She usually underestimates the difficulties involved in doing this. The question of who she told and with what result should be explored. There is a general reluctance on the part of an abused child to disclose that she is being abused. There are a number of reasons for this:

- she has a sense of loyalty and/or love for the abuser that makes it impossible for her to speak out against someone who is supposed to be protecting and caring for her;
- she fears the reactions of others, or has had unhelpful responses from people she has already told;
- she is passive because she believes the abuser when he says that the sexual abuse is acceptable;
- threats and bribes are used by the abuser (see Table 7.2) to maintain her silence;
- she feels too much guilt and shame to tell anyone;
- she fears breaking up the family;
- she fears that she will be blamed.

It is important to help an incest survivor to understand that her reasons for not breaking the secret were because of her fears of the reaction of others, or because she felt responsible for the potential break-up of her family. It is vital to recognise that these fears do not imply responsibility. Only by encouraging a woman to challenge her childhood beliefs about these areas of responsibility will she be able to make this distinction.

Sometimes women persist in asking 'Why didn't I stop him?'. In this case a brainstorming exercise may be useful; she could, for example, be asked to think of as many ways as possible she might have used to try and stop the abuse.

Example: Annette produced a list which included telling her father to stop; fighting him off; telling him she didn't like it or that it hurt; running away from home. She was then able to recognise that none of these alternatives were possible. She had tried telling him to stop and that it hurt but to no avail; he was too strong for her to fight him off. She had run away on one occasion but a neighbour had brought her home. As a result of doing this exercise Annette remembered for the first time that her father used to start abusing her in the middle of the night when she was asleep. In reality there was nothing she could do, but for years she had believed that she should have been able to stop him.

It can also help to explore with a woman whether she can recall any ways in which, as a child, she tried to 'break the secret' of the sexual abuse. Many incest survivors recall incidents such as running away from home, taking tablets, doing drawings which indicated the abuse, pretending they were ill, saying that they were sore and so on. By remembering these signals, a woman can be enabled to see that she did not passively accept what was happening to her. It also helps her to realise that she was asking for help but that adults did not recognise the signs or chose to ignore them.

The child's responsibility towards her siblings

This is of particular concern for incest survivors who know or suspect that their siblings were also sexually abused. The oldest child in a family is likely to feel responsible for failing to protect her younger siblings from the abuser. The woman needs to acknowledge that, even though she was bigger and older than her siblings, she was still a child and there was little she could do to protect them. Paradoxically, when incest survivors come from families where several children have been sexually abused, they can usually deal with the issue of responsibility for the abuse more effectively, recognising that the abuser was guilty of initiating and perpetrating it.

Abusers and the issue of responsibility

When an incest survivor begins to resolve her feelings of guilt for aspects of the sexual abuse, she will be able to shift responsibility for the abuse from herself to the abuser.

This is a positive achievement for her but it can have unforeseen consequences; for example, she may have built up a positive picture of the abuser; she might have been ignored by all the adults in her life apart from him; she may care about and love him. This leaves her with a confusing sense of loyalty towards him. Even when the abuse is disclosed, she may continue to defend and idealize the abuser. She might find herself saying, 'He was a nice man' 'He was a good father' or 'He wouldn't hurt anyone'. This can blind the incest survivor to the harm which the abuse has caused her.

If a woman can acknowledge the abuser's responsibilities for sexually abusing her, she will have to reassess her view of him, often with painful consequences. She will also have to face emotional reactions, especially anger, which have been submerged under her guilt feelings. A starting point for examining an abuser's responsibilities is to build up a picture of the abuser with the incest survivor. She could be asked to describe:

- what he looked like;
- how he related to other adults and children in the family;
- what made him angry and how he expressed his anger;
- how he disciplined children in the family;
- what others thought or said about him.

It is useful to ask her to list all the responsibilities an adult, particularly a parent, has towards a child in their care. This list could then be compared with the picture of the abuser already drawn up. In this way the woman can discover how the abuser met and abdicated his responsibilities. She may also find that the picture of the abuser which she has held over the years can be challenged and dismantled, allowing her to gain a more realistic and probably ambivalent view of him. In this way, some of her suppressed negative feelings towards him can be allowed to surface.

A reminder of the abuser's responsibilities should be made when a woman lapses into self-blame. An incest survivor should be enabled to see that the abuser was an adult with particular responsibilities towards her, including protecting her from harm, caring for her and allowing her to mature in a safe environment. If the abuser was her father or in a father's role, e.g., stepfather, foster father or her mother's boyfriend, these responsibilities were important.

Another difficult area for an incest survivor involves the interpretation of her behaviour by the abuser. His excuse for abusing her may have been that her behaviour was sexual or provocative. The woman herself may believe this too. There are two tasks here for the helper: the first is to remind the woman that she is interpreting her childhood behaviour from an adult's perspective and giving it a sexual meaning which it did not have for her as a child; secondly, she should be helped to understand that it was the adult's responsibility for interpreting her behaviour in this way.

A problem can arise if the woman has learnt, as a child, that sexualized behaviour earned some adult attention. This produces a major conflict for her, expressed as: 'If I behave in a particular way I can get some affection and attention but I don't like the nature of the attention.' Abusers are often well aware of the emotional needs of a child. They fail as a responsible adult by using this awareness to manipulate a child into sexual activity. They may give or withhold treats or love as a way of obtaining a child's involvement in sexual abuse. The resulting confusion between physical affection and sexual attention often continues into adulthood.

Mothers and the issue of reponsibility

A recurring theme for incest survivors involves the extent of their mother's knowledge about the sexual abuse when it was happening. Equally vexing is the question of a mother's response to any suspicions or disclosure about the abuse. The main task for helpers in relation to both issues, is to enable an incest survivor to distinguish between responsibility for protecting a child and responsibility for or involvement in the abuse itself. This is also one of the most difficult areas for helpers themselves to address. It raises questions about a mother's competence and responsibilities, and can be particularly difficult if the helper is a mother herself. There are five possibilities which relate to a mother's responsibilities towards her daughter. These are when:

Her mother definitely did not know about the abuse: an incest survivor often knows, without question, that her mother had no knowledge of the abuse. She may know from her mother's reaction to disclosure or from the circumstances in which the abuse took place. As a child, she may have told her mother about the abuse and her mother's response was to confront the abuser, to seek help from a welfare agency or to inform the police. If she has been told about the abuse by her daughter in adulthood, her response may be one of shock followed by acceptance or complete denial of what she has been told. A mother may have known nothing about the abuse because:

- she was not in the house when it was taking place;
- she was doing housework or tending to other children or dependents;
- the abuser had ensured silence by saying 'it would kill your mother if she knew about this';
- the abuse occurred in normal family situations, e.g., putting to bed, bathing;
- each incident lasted a very short time and no-one else could possibly have known about it.

If a woman can accept that her mother did not know about the abuse, she will also accept that her mother was in no way responsible for it. She may, however, continue to wonder what prevented her from telling her mother; fear of not being believed, or of upsetting her mother are two of the most common reasons.

Her mother suspected that sexual abuse was taking place but could not acknowledge it: some mothers pick up signals from their daughters that something is amiss, only to block or disregard the information. Sometimes a mother can doubt her perceptions; she may be convinced that she was crazy to believe that such a thing could happen to her own daughter, or that she was reading too much into an innocent situation. A mother can respond in this way for a number of reasons:

- she finds it impossible to accept that a family member, especially if it is her partner, is capable of sexually abusing her daughter;
- it causes her to question her own judgment in choosing a partner who could sexually abuse a child. If she is forced to accept that possibility, she may blame herself for making this choice. As a result, her guilt prevents her from acknowledging the information;
- she may have been sexually abused herself in childhood and cannot face up to the possibility of this happening to her daughter;
- there may be difficulties in her adult relationship with her partner which she blames herself for.

If a woman has tried to disclose the abuse to her mother only to have the information ignored, she is likely to conclude that her mother failed to protect her from further abuse. The helper should enable her to examine the reasons for this so that she may be more able to understand her mother's reaction and position. This experience may make her feel ignored or invalidated by her mother. The helper should examine all aspects of her relationship with her mother, to see if these feelings have been repeated in other situations. The incest survivor may want to re-establish a more positive relationship with her mother, and some of the related feelings should be worked through first. Joint work between mother and daughter can be helpful in this context.

Her mother knew about the sexual abuse but did nothing to stop it: an incest survivor may have told her mother about the abuse on more than one occasion, and she responded with:

- disbelief, saying that her daughter was lying or that she must have dreamt/imagined it;
- anger at her daughter for making such allegations;
- acceptance, saying that there was nothing she could do to stop it.

A woman with this experience is likely to feel intense anger towards her mother. She will again ask why her mother failed to protect her. Her mother's response might be explained by:

- her own fear of the abuser, especially if he was violent or sexually abusive towards her too;

- feeling forced to choose between her daughter and her partner. If she chooses her daughter she is likely to lose her partner, particularly if the police and social services department become involved. If she chooses her partner, her daughter will still be with her, but the abuse is likely to continue. The choice is therefore very difficult;
- mixed feelings towards the abuser. Despite the abuse her mother may still feel that she loves him and this makes her daughter doubly confused about her mother's reactions;
- she may fear the shame and public disgrace of a disclosure that sexual abuse is occurring in her family;
- she may have been financially dependent on the abuser and cannot contemplate breaking up the family.

The task for the helper is to explore the possible reasons for her mother's inaction in order to help the incest survivor to make sense of it, and to help her to express her feelings about it.

Her mother knew about the abuse and condoned it: this is likely to be very difficult for an incest survivor to admit at all. Her mother may have 'set up' her daughter to be abused by putting her into situations where she would be alone with the abuser, or making her available for child prostitution or pornography. If this is the case the incest survivor is likely to feel intense rage, anger and disgust towards her mother. She should be reassured that these are all valid and justified emotions. She should be encouraged to express them, so that she can come to terms with the fact that her mother did not protect her, thus increasing her sense of isolation and vulnerability. In addition, she may have great difficulty in understanding her mother's behaviour.

Her mother sexually abused her: research to date indicates that this only happens to a very small number of women (Bass and Davis, 1988), and our own experience confirms this. The feelings experienced by an incest survivor in this situation will probably be more intense than those felt towards a male abuser. She will feel doubly isolated and there will be an added sense of betrayal that her mother, of all people, misused her authority and trust in this way. It is likely that the incest survivor will have difficulty in understanding how a mother could abdicate her maternal role completely in this way. She may have much clearer expectations of her mother's role in the family than she does about the role of male family members. The helper's task is to help her to understand that not all mothers can fulfil their expected roles, and that her mother, in particular, left her in an impossible position.

Disclosing that her mother abused her sexually can be even more difficult for a woman than if the abuser was a male family member. Society's rules and expectations in relation to mothers are so strong that she is at even greater risk of being disbelieved.

Current Relationships Within the Family

An incest survivor often has conflicting loyalties when it comes to questions of family relationships, in particular her relationships with the abuser, her mother and her siblings.

Relationship with the abuser

Where the abuser was her father, or was in the role of father, the incest survivor lived with the man who abused her. She was expected to love, obey and respect him, and could reasonably have expected from him a measure of parental care and protection. His parental role meant that he had the opportunity to carry out the sexual abuse behind the closed doors of the family home. Where the abuser was a grandfather, uncle or trusted male adult, the abuse may have occurred less frequently and in locations other than the family home. If this was the case the child may have felt safe enough in her own home to tell other adults about the abuse.

Some of the issues which preoccupy incest suvivors in relation to their abusers include:

- his level of disturbance or 'madness';
- his treatment of the family as a whole;
- his use of subtle manipulation to gain control over herself and other family members;
- his use of physical abuse;
- any pleasure he gained from the abuse;
- his understanding of, or explanations for the abuse.

For some women, gaining an understanding of the balance between the 'good' and 'bad' in the abuser is her aim. This can be very difficult when the evidence points to physical and sexual abuse on a huge scale. It is not uncommon to hear a woman say, 'But I loved him. He was a good person. I just didn't like what he was doing to me and I wanted it to stop.'

A woman may start therapeutic work by blaming herself for the abuse in order to protect the abuser. As her protective excuses diminish, her anger is likely to increase and she may go through a period of intense dislike and hatred for him. Finally, she may be able to come to some understanding of him, although she may never be able to protect or like him again. If a woman is still in contact with the abuser while she is seeking help she may become more vigilant about him, especially in relation to her own children. She may also express fears of meeting him. On the other hand, an incest survivor may feel the need to confront her abuser. The helper should encourage her to consider the benefits and costs of this course of action, together with the methods she proposes to use. It is important not to underestimate the level of fear experienced by an incest survivor if she is determined to face the abuser alone. The helper's task is to help her to look at the situation realistically, and to offer support for whatever course of action she decides upon. Even if the abuser has died, the use of letter-writing or other techniques can facilitate the emotional reactions associated with confrontation. This can be particularly important in enabling an incest survivor to discover the depth of her feelings towards the abuser.

Relationship with her mother

Examination of an incest survivor's relationship with her mother almost always begins with the extent of her mother's knowledge about the abuse. Exploration of feelings associated with this issue, together with some understanding of her mother's position within the family is also necessary. An important aspect of the work is to examine her mother's ability to protect her at the time of the abuse. A woman may assume that her mother should have been perpetually vigilant and always available, with the implication that if this had been so, the abuse would not have happened.

It can be helpful to ask an incest survivor to:

– describe the role of her mother within the family;
– describe the situations, time of day and presence of other people when the abuse took place;
– describe a typical day in her mother's life when she (the survivor) was a child.

She may find that her mother did try to protect her or that she was not around when the abuse took place.

For an incest survivor who was abused by her father, key questions about her mother's loyalty to the abuser are often asked. She may say:

> 'How could she continue to live with him knowing that he was abusing me?'
>
> or
>
> 'How could she love a man who was the type of person who abused his daughter?' (Regardless of whether her mother knew or not.)
>
> or
>
> 'How could she sacrifice me to him?'

These questions are often unanswerable. It is important, however, for the survivor to gain a more realistic view of her mother's concern for her and to remember that her mother may genuinely not have known about the abuse.

Throughout all of these discussions, it is vital to acknowledge feelings of rage and disbelief. An incest survivor should also be helped to see that, following the discovery or disclosure of sexual abuse, her mother may experience a range of emotions:

- anger at her daughter for not telling her sooner;
- guilt that she failed to protect her child. She may also feel that she is responsible for the abuse occurring;
- betrayal by her partner for abusing her daughter;
- anger and hate towards her partner for the consequences of his action, the damage to her daughter, the damage to the relationship between her daughter and herself and the damage to her relationship with her partner;
- revulsion when she thinks about him abusing her daughter;
- confusion about her own feelings in relation to her partner;
- failure as a parent and a partner.

With this may come the need for confrontation if her mother is still alive. Again, this should be considered carefully and adequate preparation time allowed for it. If her mother has died, it can be very beneficial for a survivor to write her thoughts and feelings into a letter.

Relationships with siblings

Questions about an incest survivor's siblings usually revolve around whether she was the only child in the family to be abused. Sometimes she already knows or has suspicions that her siblings were also abused, and she may begin to search for clues to confirm or deny her suspicions. She may see similar long-term effects to her own in her siblings, or may remember situations from her childhood which now suggest to her that another child in the family was being abused. Confirmation of these suspicions can only be made by discussing them with her siblings. Many incest survivors are reluctant to do this for fear of causing extra pain or distress to their brothers and sisters. This is particularly the case when their father is still held in high esteem by other family members. A woman who shatters the myth of 'the perfect father' can easily blame herself for the subsequent pain experienced by her siblings.

Where there is confirmation that others were abused, a survivor is likely to feel relief, but also guilt and responsibility for breaking the secret and causing more pain. Where several children in a family have been abused, it is often easier for them to deal with the issue of responsibility. They may have gained support from each other as children, but it is particularly difficult if one or more of them feels they have coped with the experiences better or suffered less abuse than their siblings. If the incest survivor is the oldest child in the family she is likely to feel an extra burden of responsibility for caring and protecting younger members of her family. For her, the discovery that they too were abused can be devastating, and can contribute to her poor self-esteem and sense of failure. For the woman who discovers that she was the only child of the family to be abused, many questions remain about why she alone was selected by the abuser. A woman will need help to talk about feelings where she was not the only sibling to be abused, but was treated as the 'bad' child by one or both parents, receiving less material comforts and affection and more punishment.

Trust

The betrayal of a child's trust is a central feature of child sexual abuse. Problems with trust continue into adulthood. At the beginning of any therapeutic relationship with an incest survivor, trust is of crucial importance. It may represent a woman's first real attempt to trust someone, particularly with her childhood secrets. The helper should therefore be alert to the fact that an incest survivor may expect to have her trust betrayed again. For example, she may:

- expect the helper to tell her 'secrets' to other colleagues without her permission;
- not expect the helper to keep appointments with her;
- assume that the helper will tell her doctor all the details of their sessions;
- assume that if the helper met any of her family, the helper would automatically believe them, and not her.

With some survivors, the helper may have to work hard at proving and demonstrating her/his trustworthiness. Reliability, confidentiality, punctuality and respecting her rights not to have certain information about her history transmitted to other helpers are all important issues here.

Incest survivors tend to believe that trust is an all-or-nothing concept. As a result, if somone betrays a survivor's trust in a small way, she is likely to stop trusting that person completely. In reality, trust is built up gradually through the discovery that a person's behaviour, words and actions can be relied on; trust is therefore earned. For a woman who has difficulty in trusting, it can be useful to encourage her to begin to trust certain people in small ways or in simple situations. These situations should be specified and should not include broad generalizations, for example, 'I don't expect you to ever betray me', 'I want you never to be cross with me!' Examples of situations include:

- asking her partner to do some shopping for her;
- asking a friend to come and spend a short amount of time with her when she's feeling low;
- asking a friend to baby-sit for her.

In this way, she can learn that some people can be trusted. If a situation fails in some way, she should be asked to reflect on what went wrong. For example she might ask herself:

- Whom did I pick to trust?
- How long have I known the person?
- Has this person let me down in the past?
- What did I trust him/her with?
- Did I communicate my wishes clearly?
- Was it a good time to ask this person to do this 'task' for me?

Gradually, however, she can discover that she can begin to trust again, and this will lead to the possibility of more positive social relationships.

Loss

An incest survivor will need to acknowledge and grieve for the childhood and adult losses she has experienced as a result of being sexually abused. These losses relate to her lack of a normal childhood and its opportunities for normal development. For many incest survivors, the fear and negative feelings associated with the sexual abuse will have coloured normal childhood experiences. For example play, peer group relationships, educational achievements and participation in a whole range of childhood activities may have been severely curtailed by the abuser for fear that a child might talk about the abuse. The consequences of these sorts of restrictions are far-reaching. For example, fun and enjoyment may be difficult to attain in adulthood, and many survivors find it difficult to allow their own children to play freely. Poor peer group relationships, educational and employment underachievement are also very common.

For some incest survivors, the feeling of loss of their childhood resulted from having the responsibility for running the household.

Example: Anne was the eldest of five children. At the age of 9 she was expected to get the younger children up and ready for school. She had to make breakfast, and take all the children to and from school. She was expected to do the washing and cleaning with some help from her younger siblings. She cooked the evening meal, then put the little children to bed, hoping to protect them from their father.

Losses are also described in terms of the lack of normal relationships with parents and siblings. Acknowledging that sexual abuse and its associated secrecy can spread its effects so widely is a painful process. Many incest survivors have little ongoing contact with their families and, even after the death of their parents, find it hard to have normal relationships with brothers and sisters.

Loss may also be experienced through the death of family members. An incest survivor often finds it particularly difficult to come to terms with the death of the abuser. She expects to be relieved but discovers to her dismay that his death releases many of the feelings, flashbacks and memories associated with the sexual abuse. She will often feel cheated that 'he got away with it' and that she is denied the opportunity for confrontation and revenge. She may also feel that the manner in which he died was too peaceful, given the suffering and pain which he inflicted on others. Birthdays and the anniversary of his death can be stressful in this respect.

Coming to terms with the death of her mother can also present problems. Questions about her mother's knowledge of the abuse have to remain unanswered if an incest survivor has never had the opportunity to raise this with her. A woman may also mourn the lack of opportunity for forming a normal adult relationship with her mother.

A bereavement counselling approach can be very helpful in establishing the extent of these losses. It can also focus on the tasks of the mourning process. The features of this approach are described in Chapter 9.

Flashbacks and Memories

Throughout any therapeutic work with an incest survivor, recall of childhood incidents occurs frequently. Sometimes these memories have been repressed or blocked, or they are shadowy or poorly defined. Other memories of childhood incidents return in the form of flashbacks (see Chapter 3).

A flashback is different from normal memories which return or are facilitated during therapeutic work. It is an alarming experience and often leads to fears of ensuing 'madness' for the woman. It is important, therefore, for her to know that flashbacks are to be expected and that they happen frequently to women who have been sexually abused as children. The helper's task is to explain that the memories and flashbacks will lose their pain and associated emotional intensity once she is able to disclose details of them. If the woman chooses to remain silent, however, the helper should draw her attention to the fact that she will probably remain distressed or continue to have similar flashbacks until she is able to talk about them.

Disclosing individual memories can be as painful for the incest survivor as her original disclosure of sexual abuse. Her language and behaviour may become that of a young child, her voice may rise in pitch, she may use words appropriate to the particular age that the memory relates to, and her mannerisms and non-verbal behaviour may revert to those of a child.

Example: Pauline was discussing the effects of being raped by her father at the age of seven, and suddenly said, 'But Mummy, it hurts, it stings'. Her voice became that of a little girl and she began to sob. She was writhing in her seat, experiencing what she later described as a physical pain and burning sensation in the genital area.

The helper should be alert to the possibility that an incest survivor is experiencing flashbacks during a therapeutic session. Common signs that this is occuring include:

- a sudden silence from the woman, sometimes in the middle of a sentence;
- a sudden increase in distress, anxiety or general tension;
- the woman suddenly begins to look into the middle-distance, often with a glazed expression on her face;
- a sudden increase in body movement, indicating increased discomfort.

She may be unable to speak during the flashback and may need help to regain control when it is over. Discussing details of the flashback is likely to be impossible at this stage because of the incapacitating nature of the woman's fear. The helper should therefore:

- reassure her that she is safe and that the flashback is over;
- remind her that the events in the flashback happened when she was a child;
- help to calm her breathing, which often becomes shallow and quick during a flashback;
- reassure her that flashbacks are normal experiences for any woman who has been sexually abused as a child.

Female helpers should be aware that physical comfort can be very useful to an incest survivor during a flashback. Male helpers should be extremely cautious and careful about offering physical comfort at this stage as it may be misconstrued as abusive. When a woman has calmed down sufficiently, she should be encouraged to discuss details of the flashback.

During a flashback and subsequent discussion about it, it is normal for an incest survivor to feel intense physical pain. Thus usually relates to the incident being recalled.

Example: Katherine recalled a particular incident of abuse when her foster father forced her to have sexual intercourse with him, and then beat her around the head and body for crying. During this recall, she experienced deep vaginal pain, soreness and a heavy feeling around her ribs. This latter pain reminded her of being crushed by the weight of her foster father. She also experienced a severe pain on the side of her head which enabled her to recall the pain associated with the incident.

After experiencing a flashback and discussing it with her helper, a woman should be encouraged to look after herself as if she had had a recent injury. This could involve going to bed, having a warm bath, taking mild pain-killers but most of all giving herself permission to comfort and take care of herself. For many incest survivors, this is a totally new experience and can lead to better self-care.

For some women, recalling memories of the abuse can lead to an increase in the number of perceptual disturbances and nightmares. Where visual images occur, the use of visualization techniques (see Chapter 9) can help the woman gain some control of the disturbing images.

Example: Joanne recalled an incident of physical and sexual abuse that occurred when she was 8. For some weeks after, she kept getting an image of her naked father coming towards her, laughing at her. Through the use of visualization techniques, she discovered that she could gain control of this image, and send him out of the room. Initially she had to imagine two large policemen handcuffing him and taking him away, but she quickly discovered she could send him away herself.

The way in which a woman feels about herself when she was a child can also prevent her from disclosing details of her abuse. If this attitude is unduly negative, hostile, or critical, she may not allow herself to remember specific details. A woman can be encouraged to disclose if the helper reminds her, as one might with a child, that part of her/his job is to protect children and make them feel safe enough to talk about the abuse. It can be helpful to remind her, if appropriate, of previous occasions when she has told of particular memories and of the positive consequences for her of telling.

The question of whether the helper can believe details of a woman's sexual abuse is tested to its limits when flashbacks occur. It is easier for a helper to accept general statements about sexual abuse but the actual details can be extremely unpleasant and horrifying to hear, especially where the sexual abuse is combined with physical violence, threats, or pornographic use of the child. However, a helper's inability to picture the sexual abuse should not be equated with a denial by her/him of its occurrence. It is vital for the incest survivor to know that her memories can be accepted by her helper in a non-judgmental and calm atmosphere.

Regression

We have already discussed the tendency of incest survivors to use child-like behaviour and language during disclosure of memories of sexual abuse. Some women cannot properly disclose their memories of sexual abuse without regressing to being a child again. In this situation, the concept of 'the child within' becomes very important, as it is that child who emerges during the regression. The helper should:

- be prepared to allow enough time for the regression to occur and for the woman to return to her adult state;
- remember that the 'child' is most likely to be quite young having regressed to an age that the 'adult' cannot remember;
- use the opportunity to help the woman/child disclose as many of the incidents of abuse as she can;

– remember that the woman is behaving as a small child, and will therefore have concepts, language and behaviour appropriate to the age of the child. This includes methods that the woman used as a child to survive the abuse (e.g., counting, reciting poems, overbreathing and blanking off);

– be aware of the 'child's' vulnerability and not inadvertently misuse it;

– be prepared for the woman to be extremely tired after the regression is over;

– spend some time after the regression helping her, the adult woman, to remember the incidents that the 'child' has disclosed. This may involve telling her directly what has been disclosed or helping her to piece together the incidents from half-memories she already has.

Bringing the woman back to her adult state may involve the use of photographs, objects or concepts that only the adult knows. This can only occur once the 'child' has been told that she is now safe, that she has done well to tell, and that the abuser is no longer here.

Example: Following a period of regression during which Anne had disclosed a number of incidents of sexual abuse that occurred when she was four, the helper reassured her that she was safe, that her father (the abuser) was not there and could not do any harm to her. Anne was then shown a photograph of her daughter aged 11 who was in her school uniform. She was asked questions about the photograph, including what was the girl in the photo doing, what she was wearing, what her name was. Gradually Anne began to talk of her daughter going to a new school and was able to give her daughter's name and state she was her daughter's mother. This allowed the helper to check that Anne had now returned to her adult state.

Regression can be alarming for both woman and helper when it occurs for the first time, but can also be an extremely useful way of enabling the woman to understand how she coped as a child. Chapter 9 gives further information on how to deal with regression.

Getting in Touch with Feelings

A recurring theme for incest survivors is the emergence of well-defined feelings and emotional reactions. These are characterized not only by their range and intensity but also by their unpredictability and newness for the woman. Many incest survivors have restricted emotional responses, especially in relation to the sexual abuse. They talk about their emotions in general terms such as guilt, fear, depression, or 'good' and 'bad' feelings. As a young girl, a woman may have learnt that her emotions were too painful and frightening to show to others and this may have led to a complete blocking of all feelings. Once she begins to feel a range of emotions she will need to learn different ways of describing her range of emotional states.

Initially, feelings of guilt and shame are predominant. These are usually associated with the issue of responsibility, discussed earlier in this chapter. Challenging guilt can be a complex task as an incest survivor will often have a range of self-blaming statements that have to be challenged before she is able to relinquish her guilt. Guilty feelings will usually give way to underlying anger and rage.

Work with an incest survivor often involves extremes of emotional reaction. Complete lack of emotion may be seen at the beginning of the therapeutic work, with descriptions of upsetting experiences being given in a detached and impassive manner. Any attempt by the helper to elicit feelings is met with a lack of understanding on the part of the woman. In this context, it is important to gradually show her that the expression of feelings is acceptable. The helper might say:

> 'Many women in that situation might have felt a bit . . . (name the emotion e.g. angry, guilty, upset) I wonder if you felt like that?'

or

> 'There are lots of different ways women might have felt in this situation. For example, they might have felt angry, sad, guilty, frightened, scared (give appropriate examples). I wonder if you are feeling any of these emotions.'

It is likely that a woman will gradually become able to name and differentiate her emotions. The emotional detachment and dissociation should progressively disappear, to be replaced by more intense emotional reactions. These can be alarming for the incest survivor and are likely to be at their most difficult when she experiences flashbacks or new memories. They can amount to deep sobbing, acute pain reactions and distress of such power that the survivor can become catatonic, agitated or intensely angry. In these situations, the helper must remain calm in spite of feeling very concerned or even frightened by the intensity of emotion being experienced. Feelings of such intensity do pass for the woman once the memories or flashbacks have been discussed.

During work on emotional reactions, the helper needs to facilitate the survivor's awareness of the ways in which they link with her past, particularly with the abuse that she has experienced. Making these connections can be achieved by taking a fairly non-threatening line of enquiry (see Figure 7.1). By following the flow-chart, it can be seen that potential links between past and present experiences and emotions can be clarified by the helper, and the emergence of new emotions can be noted. Where emotional blocking appears to have taken place, it is useful to remind an incest survivor that it is quite normal for women who have been abused to have these feelings in the present and during childhood. This sometimes enables a woman to trust the helper with her feelings, if not at the time, then on a later occasion.

Figure 7.1: Pathway to Disclosure: Helper and Incest Survivor's Responses

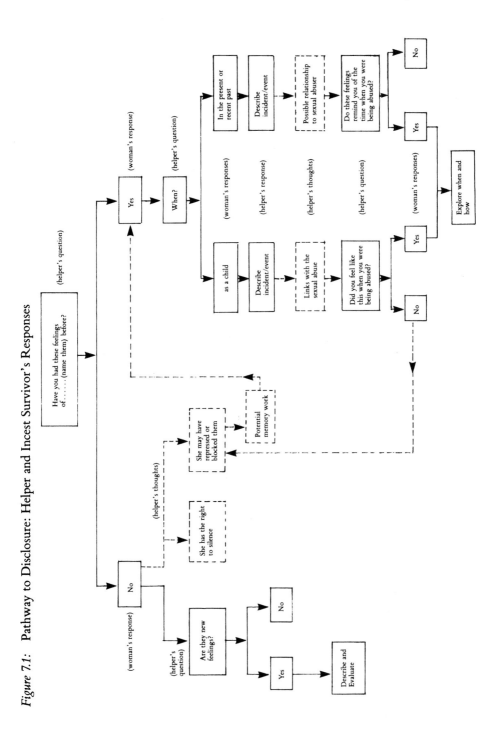

Table 7.3: Emotional Reactions and Consequences

Feeling	Consequence for women	Helper's action
Shock	Like any normal severe shock reaction with both physical and emotional reactions	Reassurance that this is normal
Numbness	Increased self-mutilation (I know I should feel pain but I don't, so I'm just making sure I can)	Reassurance that it is a normal experience for an incest survivor
Guilt	Increased self-blame, depression and helplessness	Reality-testing of guilt — leading to discovery that she is not helpless, or to blame
Shame	Feels dirty. Increased self-blame	Reassurance that this is normal
Fear/Anxiety/ Panic Attacks	At times paralyzed by fear, extreme shaking, withdrawal from supports, and avoidance of any situation where physical symptoms of anxiety are experienced	Anxiety management techniques. Giving understanding of anxiety — physical, behavioural, cognitive components
Terror	Perceptual disturbances and nightmares become more frequent	Acceptance of these consequences as normal. Discussion of perceptual disturbances and nightmares in detail and establishing any links with the sexual abuse
Hurt	Intense pain sometimes experienced as physical pain. Leads to suicide attempts and self-mutilation	Explanations of association of the pain with the abuse. Assessment of suicide risk with aid of appropriate professional agency. Increased support
Anger/rage	Murderous thoughts, increased guilt, and fears of loss of control. Projection of anger on to others and consequent guilt	Reassurance that this is normal for an incest survivor. Detailed discussion of the murderous thoughts. Methods for dealing with and understanding anger, e.g., writing, drawing, physical activities
Disgust	Fears of rejection by any helper who hears her secret, but also too frightened to face that person. Over-concern with cleanliness	Reassurance that the helper is not disgusted by her. What was done to her was dreadful but she is not disgusting. Over-concern with cleanliness sometimes needs to be dealt with if it has obsessional and compulsive qualities

Table 7.3: (Continued)

Feeling	Consequence for women	Helper's action
Grief	Confused feelings, deep sadness, anger, guilt	Bereavement counselling methods
Pleasure	Increased guilt	Help incest survivor to accept that pleasure and enjoyment are reasonable and normal emotions

Experiencing these new emotions can also cause problems. For example, intense emotional states can lead to an increase in self-mutilation or suicide attempts, and the emergence of rage can produce murderous thoughts and fear that she might lose control.

It is likely that an incest survivor will eventually be able to experience a wide range of emotions without linking them all to her experience of being sexually abused. Eventually she will be capable of reacting emotionally, without fear of losing control. She will also be able to allow herself to feel conflicting emotions about people and situations. Table 7.3 summarizes these problems, and indicates possible courses of action open to the helper.

Confrontation and Forgiveness

The issues of confronting the abuser and other family members often occurs in working with incest survivors. It is an extremely problematic issue and should be considered carefully before an incest survivor embarks on it. She may have totally unrealistic expectations about the benefits of confronting. For example, she may believe that confrontation will enable her family relationships to become positive and for her to totally wipe away the past.

The helper's task is to consider her expectations and hopes, prepare her in detail for possible reactions of the family member concerned (e.g., denial, accusations of lying, extreme apology, shock) and to consider how she is going to say what she wants to say. Role-play of the situation is a useful technique here (see Chapter 9). Even if the family member concerned has died or is absent, it is possible to use role-play to enact the confrontation and gain some understanding of the survivor's emotional reactions.

Use of letter-writing is also beneficial (see Chapter 9). Here, the incest survivor is encouraged to write a letter that will probably never be sent, saying all she wants to say. This has some advantages over more direct confrontation in that she does not have to contend with the recipient's reactions.

Forgiveness is an area of considerable difficulty for the incest survivor. Establishing the survivor's understanding of the concept of forgiveness is important, and will be influenced by any religious beliefs she holds. The helper's task is to facilitate some better understanding of forgiveness, making clear that forgiving is not excusing. Hancock and Mains (1987) state:

> A good definition of forgiveness is 'to give up all claim to punish or to exact penalty for the offense' (sic). As long as we are unforgiving, we hold the person who hurt us responsible for us. We demand an account.

By forgiving, therefore, the survivor learns to give up her desire for revenge and deal with the associated resentment and anger.

Living in the Present: From Victim to Survivor

So far we have been concerned with themes which relate directly to a woman's sexual abuse and her childhood experiences. In this section, we consider the very real difficulties which an incest survivor experiences in adulthood. She may have concerns about relationships, sexual difficulties or have considerable anxiety symptoms. Therapeutic work should acknowledge these problems and, where necessary, help a woman to deal with them. This may require referral to an appropriate professional helper such as a sex therapist or marriage guidance counsellor.

Many incest survivors come for help feeling victimized, helpless and unable to make positive changes in their lives. The therapeutic work will hopefully enable them to take more control of their lives and to stop seeing themselves as victims. The boundary between victim and survivor is by no means clear, and it can be very upsetting for a woman to feel that she has made progress, only to suffer a setback which puts her in the role of victim or abused person once more.

Being a victim

Being a victim relates almost entirely to an incest survivor's childhood experiences and the ways which she learnt to survive them. Statements which arise in therapeutic work include:

– 'I cannot say no.' This affects all relationships, and is a particular problem in sexual relationships. A woman may find herself being taken advantage of by friends or colleagues, becoming resentful but unable to assert herself enough to break out of the circle;

– 'I get myself into situations where I am taken advantage of. I know it to be so but I can't do anything about it.' This mirrors the experience of being sexually abused as a child;

- 'I have no rights or choice.' This is often reflected in an incest survivor's inability to ask for anything for herself. It can create a problem when she feels that she has no right to take up the helper's time or says that she does not know why anyone should spend time helping her;
- 'I have no control over what happens to me.' Again, this mirrors the experience of sexual abuse;
- 'I am not able to speak for myself. No-one will listen to or believe me.' The origins of this lie in her childhood experiences;
- 'I am totally passive — it's easier that way.' Extreme passivity is one way in which an incest survivor learns to cope with the experience of being sexually abused. It also allows her to believe that by being passive she will not provoke further abuse or exploitation.

All of these issues have considerable implications for relationships in adulthood. Incest survivors frequently find themselves in abusive relationships and explain this by saying that they do not expect anything better for themselves. It is possible that members of her current family find it difficult to acknowledge that she has needs, opinions and rights, and they may therefore resist her attempts to introduce some choice into her life. It is also probable that she puts everyone else's needs first and is unable to accept that she is a person in her own right.

The therapeutic task is to begin to increase the woman's awareness of her 'victim behaviour' and to gently challenge her assertions that she has no needs, rights or choices in her life. This can be done in small ways, initially by pointing out occasions in which she is able to make choices or state her own needs. Ultimately she may need to learn how to say 'No', to be assertive and to deal with situations in which she is taken advantage of. Further discussion of assertiveness training is to be found in Chapter 9.

Low self-esteem

An incest survivor's extremely low self-esteem is at the root of many of her difficulties. During therapeutic work, it is essential to help her gradually see herself in a better light, and to begin to like herself and the helper's task is to help her examine and challenge her misperceptions and negative thinking about herself. For some women, being accepted and heard by the helper is sufficient, but many women require active work, constant feedback and challenge from the helper when they belittle themselves. Many incest survivors cannot understand why anyone should want to help them or spend time with them. Improvements in self-esteem usually come very gradually, but a lessening of victim behaviour and increased assertiveness both produce significant gains in self-esteem.

Sexuality

As we have seen in Chapter 3, the experience of sexual abuse as a child has major implications for and effects on sexuality. This can result in:

- poor body image;
- fears of her own attractiveness;
- difficulties with choosing or wearing clothes (colours, styles and fabrics);
- uncertainty about nudity and modesty;
- acute embarrassment about words/discussions relating to sex or bodily functions;
- lack of knowledge about sexual functioning;
- confusion between sex and affection;
- problems in sexual relationships;
- fears of abnormality in sexual organs;
- flashbacks in sexual situations;
- avoidance of sexual encounters.

These issues should be discussed so that the woman can begin to change her view of herself as a sexual and physical person. The helper should not be surprised if the woman has relatively little knowledge about the functioning of her body in sexual situations, and they may have to embark together on a course of sex education. Revising a woman's views about her sexuality where appropriate is a gradual process, and requires sensitivity, honesty and patience on the part of the helper. Ultimately, it is hoped that she will be able to accept herself as a sexual person and be free to give affection in a physical way.

Other long-term effects

Incest survivors include women who know that the sexual abuse is contributing to their present difficulties and those who have denied or repressed the abuse and its effects. The latter group has not understood the influence of the past on the present. The helper's task here is to help make these links explicit and to enable a woman to begin to accept that past abusive experiences do continue to have an effect into adulthood.

The long-term effects of child sexual abuse have been described in Chapter 3 and at the outset it is likely that an incest survivor will believe that all or none of her reactions and behaviour are due to the abuse. It is important, therefore, for the helper to clearly state the long-term effects of sexual abuse and to draw the woman's attention to them whenever possible. This is obviously much easier in a group setting, where other incest survivors will confirm that they too have suffered similar effects. In individual work, it can be useful to use material written by other incest survivors to show that a woman is experiencing similar problems to others. Considerable relief is usually felt once she knows that her symptoms and suffering are normal responses to sexual abuse.

Much therapeutic work with an incest survivor will involve undoing many of the long-term effects of being abused. This will necessarily involve careful examination of these effects and encouragement for the woman to try and change them. Many changes come gradually as she begins to understand the relationship between past events and present feelings. The nature of this work varies from woman to woman but could involve work on anxiety, depression and its related negative thinking, alcohol abuse, sexual difficulties, and parenting problems (see Chapter 9).

Apart from the major psychological and relationship difficulties which result from being sexually abused as a child, there are many small effects which contribute to the problems of an incest survivor. It is important to draw a woman's attention to these because they may be easily changed. This gives her opportunities for taking control of her life, and can give her confidence for the future.

Example: Susan discovered that she did not like to sleep in a bed against a wall because she was abused in a bed which was in this position. Her own bed was against the wall; once she made the connection she decided to change the positioning of her bedroom furniture and slept properly for the first time in years. This encouraged her to recognise and change other behaviour. She decided that she did not need to sleep with the light on or to wear pyjamas rather than a nightie. She also discovered that she could safely have a bath when someone else was in the house.

Incest survivors frequently minimize and deny the effects of childhood sexual abuse. It is the helper's task to challenge this, reflecting the discrepancy between consequences of the abuse which a woman has already described and any ways in which she minimizes or denies its severity. A helper might say:

You have already told me that being abused has left you with problems in your relationships, especially sexually, has made you feel very bad about yourself and still gives you bad dreams and nightmares, and yet you are now telling me that it doesn't have much effect on your life any more. It sounds as if it still has quite a big effect.

Helpers and incest survivors alike often assume that all of an incest survivor's problems originate in the sexual abuse. A distinction should be made between problems which are a result of being abused as a child and those which are a result of other life experiences.

Example: Jane was extremely frightened of men and had not recognised the links between her fears and her experience of being sexually abused. It was clear that these fears originated in the sexual abuse.

Example: Andrea believed that her anxiety about starting a new job was because she had been abused by her father when she was a child. It was obvious however, that she was experiencing normal anxiety in this situation. The helper was able to use self-disclosure to help her to understand this.

Why now?

A persistent concern for an incest survivor is understanding why she needs to seek help at a particular point in time. She is likely to see her action as a necessary step and also as a failure to cope. She may feel that she has coped with the effects of being abused for years, and cannot understand why she can no longer deal with them. Fears of 'going crazy' or of having a 'nervous breakdown' are common. Exploration of the possible reasons for the timing of her request for help (see Table 6.1) is valuable and is likely to reduce some of these fears. It can also alert an incest survivor to potentially difficult situations she may have to face in the future; the anticipation of difficult situations helps an incest survivor to be realistic about coming to terms with her past. She learns that it is possible to become a survivor, and to take control of her life in a more effective way.

Becoming a survivor

Becoming an incest survivor entails an acceptance of the past, a recognition of feelings associated with childhood sexual abuse and learning to take control of and make choices in life. It also involves gradually leaving any intensive sources of help and, for some, helping others who have suffered in a similar way.

Resolution of the effects of early abuse can be a daunting task, and it is not unusual for a woman and her helper to become overwhelmed from time to time with feelings of hopelessness and helplessness. However, for the majority of women, a considerable improvement in mental health and general well-being can be achieved with time and appropriate help. There are several factors which govern both the degree of improvement and the amount of time and help needed. These include:

- the personality and resources of the survivor, including her motivation to involve herself in therapeutic work;
- the frequency and severity of the abuse;
- the closeness of the relationship between the survivor and the abuser;
- her adult life experiences. Where these have been or continue to be problematic, resolution of her earlier experiences can be more difficult.

Given that many women who seek help are managing to cope with life in the community, it is important to confirm the strengths and resources which they manifestly possess. In spite of acute distress, they often show great courage and persistence in working on their difficulties. Many are holding down jobs, supporting their families, and helping others in a variety of contexts. Confirming that she has survived her childhood experiences to get to this stage can be very reassuring. Detailed exploration of the methods she has used as an adult to cope with the sexual abuse also enables a woman to see that she does have personal resources which have been useful to her. Table 7.4 gives an illustration of some of the methods which women use in this context.

Table 7.4: Methods used by women to cope with the experience of sexual abuse

Method of coping	*Explanation*
Denial of the abuse	– I imagined it – It didn't happen – I had a good childhood
Denial of the frequency of the abuse	– It only happened once or twice – I forgot about it after each time, so each time became the first time
Denial of the severity of the abuse	– He only touched me – He never had intercourse with me
Protection of the abuser	– He was a nice man – He didn't know what he was doing – He wouldn't hurt a fly – He was a good father
Rationalization	– I deserved it – It was my fault – There are people far worse off than me
Repression/Blocking	– I don't remember the abuse – I don't remember things that occurred at a very young age
Dissociation	– It didn't hurt me – It doesn't matter any more – I learnt as a child not to feel anything, and I don't now

Learning to live in the present without the spectre of the past haunting her may involve learning new skills. It could involve a woman in further education, occupational training or retraining. Many incest survivors write about their experiences before and during therapeutic work, and may want to publish these to help others in a similar position. Some want to become involved in media campaigns about sexual abuse, in training professionals to recognise and identify the long-term effects of abuse and particularly in supporting and counselling other incest survivors. All these activities are very important and valid activities because they can represent the first opportunity for an incest survivor to use her experiences in a positive way.

8   Incest Survivors' Groups

Some women feel more comfortable in a one-to-one therapeutic relationship, whilst others welcome the opportunity to share their experiences and get support from other incest survivors. There are also women who join an incest survivors' group whilst they are receiving individual help, and women who decide to seek one-to-one support in addition to becoming members of an incest survivors' group. Attending a group and receiving individual help have a number of advantages and problems for both the helper and incest survivor.

The advantages include:

- achievements can be shared;
- new feelings or emotional reactions experienced in one setting can be acknowledged or explored further in the other;
- individual work can ensure that a women is committed to working on her problems before she joins a group.

The problems include:

- the question of discussing a woman's progress between helpers;
- a woman may receive contradictory messages in each setting;
- limitations on resources may mean that the individual helper and a group facilitator are the same person.

This chapter examines issues which arise in the process of starting and maintaining an incest survivors' group. These issues include:

- models for incest survivors' groups;
- open and closed groups;
- facilitating an incest survivors' group;
- starting an incest survivors' group;
- setting boundaries;
- joining an incest survivors' group;

- planning group meetings;
- structure of group meetings;
- responding to specific issues;
- ending a group;
- evaluating a group.

Many of the themes which arise in groups have already been discussed in Chapter 7. It is, however, the experience of sharing them with other survivors which enables a woman to feel that,

> for the first time her incestuous experience makes her one of a group rather than the deviant she usually perceives herself as being. She identifies with others the same guilt, anger, shame, fear and grief, needs and hopes.
>
> (Blake-White and Kline, 1985).

Models for Incest Survivors' Groups

There are three types of group:

1   self-help groups, formed by incest survivors themselves, without the help or support of professionals or volunteers. These groups usually operate without a formal leader, or they may rotate leadership between group members. The main issue for self-help groups is their difficulty in maintaining continuity

2   mutual support groups, which usually operate under the auspices of a voluntary organization e.g. Women's Aid, Rape Crisis. They can include one or more facilitators or helpers who may or may not themselves have been sexually abused. Facilitators help to maintain continuity and they also allow group members to take as much responsibility for the group as they are willing or able to do;

3   professionally-led groups, which are most commonly located in residential, day-patient or in-patient hospital settings. These groups are more likely to be time-limited, more tightly structured, and potential members may be screened or assessed for their suitability to join.

All three models offer a useful source of help for women, and the presence of facilitators in mutual support groups and professionally-led groups has some added advantages. Firstly, they make the group easier to sustain through periods of low energy or conflict between group members. Secondly, facilitators have an enabling role in which power and control within the group are shared with group members. This chapter concentrates on groups with facilitators though many of the same issues will emerge in self-help groups.

Table 8.1: Open and Closed groups: Advantages and Disadvantages

OPEN GROUPS

Advantages	*Disadvantages*
Access available when women want it	New members may feel excluded from group culture
New members can prevent group becoming stagnant	Newer members may not know group information which is important to aid their understanding of another member's problems
Members may find it easier to leave the group when they want	Older members may not want to repeatedly share the same information with new members
Reduces the 'secretive' nature of an incest survivors' group and may contribute to breaking silence about sexual abuse	Possibly greater risk of breaches in confidentiality
Repeated sharing of information lessens the power of the secret of sexual abuse	Group may find it hard to resolve conflicts between group members with arrival of new members and uncertain attendance
Members at different stages can give each other encouragement and support	
Not dependent on 'viable' number of members. Allows women control over how they use the group in terms of attendance and input	

CLOSED GROUPS

Advantages	*Disadvantages*
Members can get to know each other well over a period of time	Women may find it hard to leave if group is not meeting their needs
Group can move on together from one issue to the next	Women may be discouraged if they have to wait to join
Easier to plan group activities together	A limited number of sessions may not be enough for some women to trust, feel safe
Easier to establish and maintain group rituals and rules	Women may not feel committed to the group because of its short time-scale
Trust may be more easily established because no new members join	More formalized structure may result in feelings of less control by members

Open and Closed Groups

A key feature of incest survivor groups is whether they are run as open or closed groups. An open group has two major characteristics:

- members are free to join, leave and re-join at any time;
- the group is unlikely to be time-limited.

Open groups are more likely to be found in community-based settings and provide a continuing, long-term resource for incest survivors. Survivors themselves tend to have a strong preference for open access groups. They point to the importance of being able to join a group as soon as possible after making the decision to talk about the past with other survivors. Having to wait until there are sufficient members to start a new group can feel like a rejection at a time when acceptance is of vital importance. Group facilitators, by contrast, appear to have stronger reservations about the admission of new members fearing disruption to the development of the group (Gordy, 1983).

A closed group has the following characteristics:

- membership of the group is fixed at the outset;
- the group is more likely to be time-limited;
- it is also more likely to be found in a hospital or other professional setting, and will have at least one leader who is professionally employed in that setting.

Closed groups often have a limited number of meetings whose overall structure and general content may have been pre-determined by the facilitators or leaders (Gordy, 1983; Davenport and Sheldon, 1987; Tsai and Wagner, 1978).

The main advantages and disadvantages of open and closed groups for incest survivors are summarized in Table 8.1. Whilst groups may prefer to be either totally open or closed to new members after their first meeting, consideration of a third alternative may be helpful. A group may start as a closed group, thus enabling the development of trust and rapport between members, and remain closed for a limited number of sessions. Once the group is established, it then reviews its policy for admitting new members and may become an open group for a period, before closing again.

Facilitating an Incest Survivors' Group

The experience of facilitating an incest survivors' group can be exhausting, exhilerating, sad, exciting, angry, infuriating, and energizing. There are a number of important issues to consider for anyone planning to undertake the work. In the first place, it is our belief that, wherever possible, there should be two facilitators for groups because:

- the material expressed and exchanged is often stressful and painful, and is more easily coped with on a shared basis;
- it helps to reflect on the content and process of the group afterwards;
- if a woman is in distress, one facilitator can attend to the distress while the other pays attention to other group members;
- it is easier for two people to follow all the group interactions, particularly when some of the material is expressed non-verbally;
- mutual support and feedback is more readily available when there are two facilitators;
- cover for the group is maintained during holidays, sickness and in time of personal difficulties,
- ideas can be shared on how to plan future sessions.

Co-facilitating an incest survivors' group

The choice of co-facilitators should be made on the basis of the particular skills and attributes of the facilitators in relation to the group's aims. However, sometimes an *ad hoc* or pressurized decision is made to facilitate a group in response to the constraints of limited resources or the personal interests of facilitators themselves. Whatever the means by which facilitators embark on their work, they need to:

- have the capacity to work together. They may have already worked successfully together in the past. If not, they will need to check out their feelings about working together on this occasion. Discussing and planning the first session of the group can give an indication of their compatibility;
- trust each other and collaborate during the group sessions. Co-facilitators will provide a role-model during the meetings and they need to test their ability to do this;
- be clear about their roles and responsibilities during and between meetings. They will need to agree to share the facilitator role equally, or to work as a leader and assistant, with the former clearly taking overall responsibility. In the early stages of the group, it can be helpful to know who has responsibility for starting and ending the meeting, who takes special note of members' feelings, who introduces different themes or activities and so on. Some pairs split the group task and group process roles fairly explicitly; others prefer to wait and see how it develops naturally;
- be able to examine their working relationship. This is not always easy, but it is important and can be done in supervision. Areas of conflict or collusion can often be more easily identified by a third party who can encourage frank dialogue and a sharing of difficulties.

Gender of facilitators

There are strong arguments for ensuring that facilitators for incest survivors' groups are female. These include:

- women who have been sexually abused find it very difficult to trust male helpers, particularly during the early stages of disclosure;
- they may see male facilitators as potential abusers;
- they may have learnt to 'perform' for men and this could seriously affect the expression of honest feelings in the group;
- their early experiences have disempowered them and the presence of a male facilitator could perpetuate feelings of powerlessness and loss of control;
- female facilitators provide a role model to show that women can be in control of their lives;
- facilitators who have not been abused can share their own more 'normal' experiences of being women.

A male facilitator may present a number of difficulties for a group of incest survivors, not least of which is simply being in close proximity to a male (See Chapter 2). However, if some of these problems can be overcome, a male facilitator can provide a positive role-model of male behaviour, and may enable the woman to learn to trust a man again. If the group is to be short-term or time-limited in some way, it is unlikely that the incest survivors will be able to trust a male facilitator in the time available. The process of learning to trust and be in the company of a man can take some women months and even years.

There is some danger that female facilitators can be seen as 'superwomen', who are in complete control of their lives and are immune from the normal pressures of living. Appropriate self-disclosure can be useful to show that this is not always so. It enables group members to acknowledge that facilitators can feel powerless too, and that they have lapses of self-confidence. Facilitators should choose what they disclose with care, being careful not to allow the group to become a vehicle for their own problems.

Personal qualities of facilitators

The qualities needed to lead an incest survivors' group include consistency, honesty, calm, warmth and reliability, empathy and understanding, the ability to confront constructively and deal with conflicts which arise between group members, to stick to the boundaries set and to be able to cope with distress in others. Facilitators are often placed in a parenting role by the group. Many incest survivors have had 'impoverished' early relationships with adult women, especially their mothers. Facilitators can provide the opportunity for group members to work through feelings relating to these early experiences – feelings of abandonment and not being cared for, and to experience some much-needed mothering.

Overall, facilitators should be able to respond flexibly and with sensitivity to whatever the women bring to the group. This helps to ensure that the power invested in them does not perpetuate the powerlessness felt by the group members.

Attitudes and feelings about sexual abuse

Group facilitators are unlikely to be helpful unless they have explored their own feelings about sexual abuse in some depth. This may involve a painful journey through their own childhood and an exploration of their sexuality (See Chapters 2 and 10). It has been suggested (Gordy, 1983) that having an incest survivor to facilitate the group can accelerate feelings of mutual trust among group members. It is our view, however, that one of the facilitators should not have suffered sexual abuse. This enables the group to be provided with a yardstick of more 'normal' childhood experiences and enables the facilitators to acknowledge the pain of individual group members without triggering off their own pain. In groups where an incest survivor has been a facilitator, it has been reported that experiences in the group evoked repressed feelings which were difficult to manage (Gordy, 1983). This led the facilitator to seek help for herself and withdraw from the group. If one of the facilitators is an incest survivor herself, she should have confronted and resolved her own past before starting with the group.

Support and supervision for facilitators

In addition to the support which co-facilitators are able to give each other, it is helpful to enlist the help of another person for support and supervision. This person should be someone who has had experience of working with incest survivors. Regular meetings with a supervisor should:

- review the group content and process;
- give feedback on the work of each facilitator;
- pick up any potential problem areas for individual members at the next meeting;
- undertake some advance planning;
- explore any personal issues for the facilitators which have arisen during a session.

Facilitators should decide if and how to inform the group about their arrangements for support and supervision. It is important to reassure them about the confidentiality of these meetings and to give an indication of their content and frequency.

Time commitment for incest survivors' groups

Facilitators should be aware of the time they will have to commit to an incest survivors' group. Time-limited groups with an obvious terminating date are less demanding in terms of resources. Open-ended groups on the other hand are by definition less easy to plan ahead. They can be very time-consuming for facilitators and are sometimes difficult to sustain through periods of low energy. Facilitators in open-ended groups should build into supervision a regular review of their time commitment to the group, noting any areas of difficulty and discussing possible solutions.

Starting an Incest Survivors' Group

The impetus for starting an incest survivors' group can come from incest survivors themselves, with or without the support of organizations such as Rape Crisis or Women's Aid, from voluntary organizations or from professionals working in a hospital or community setting. If the group is started by incest survivors, it will probably be open to any woman who was sexually abused as a child. If, on the other hand, a group is started by professional workers, members may have to undergo some form of assessment or screening to determine their suitability for the group. The criteria for assessment might include:

- ability to work in a group setting;
- current support network;
- access to one-to-one help while attending the group;
- level of day-to-day pressures and how these are being managed.

An advantage of screening is that it gives some prior indication to facilitators of the stage which potential group members have reached in coming to terms with their childhood experiences. Its main disadvantage is that women can feel excluded and their sense of isolation is maintained if they are assessed and fail to be included in a group.

Resources and finance

There are a number of issues relating to resources and finance to be considered:

1   the meeting place for the group should be easily accessible, reasonably sound-proof, safe, warm, comfortable and free from interruption. The premises of a sympathetic voluntary organization, e.g., family centre, rape crisis centre, women's centre might be suitable. It is not advisable to hold meetings in a

member's home since it can create problems if the member wants to miss a meeting or if there are constant interruptions from visitors, telephone callers or her family. Access to the same meeting place for all meetings of the group is important for continuity;

2   facilities for making tea and coffee should be available;

3   good quality childcare and/or care for dependents should be investigated whether meetings take place during the day or evening;

4   initial funding for booking a room, providing refreshments and childcare should be investigated. Once established, the group may want to embark on its own fundraising activities;

5   naming the group: women who join a group may be worried about being identified as an incest survivor. Anonymity can be achieved by using a 'neutral' name when booking the room for meetings e.g. Tuesday Group, Self-help Group, Women's Group. The group can decide its permanent name once it becomes established.

Starting a community-based group

In addition to finding a suitable meeting-place, the group will need to be advertised, and the frequency of meetings agreed.

Advertising the group: posters, leaflets, letters to potential referral sources and press statements are all useful and easy to compile. They should contain clear information about:

– the purpose of the group;
– proposed frequency of meetings;
– membership of the group;
– where/how to find out more details about the first meeting.

Details of the first meeting should be kept to a minimum in any publicity. Interested women will take the trouble to ring a contact telephone number (e.g., local rape crisis centre) for further details. This can represent an important first step in encouraging them to acknowledge their past and take control of their lives.

Letters and posters can be circulated to community centres, health centres, libraries, community mental health resources, social work departments and psychiatric hospitals several weeks before the first meeting. Press statements can be sent to local radio stations and newspapers. If an incest survivor is involved at the planning stage, she should have the opportunity to say whether she wishes to be named as a contact person in publicity material, and if she is available for interview with the local media.

Example of Press Statement for first meeting

A new support group for women is to be formed in..............within the next few weeks. The group aims to bring together any women who have experienced sexual abuse by a trusted adult during their childhood.

The effects of such abuse can be long lasting, and it is hoped that the group will enable incest survivors to share their experiences and begin to come to terms with their past.

Further information about the group can be obtained by writing to or telephoning...

....

Example of Poster advertising initial meeting

Are you	a woman who has been sexually abused in childhood by a trusted adult?
Would you	like to meet other women with similar experiences for mutual support?
An Incest Survivors' Group	will have its first meeting in a few weeks
If you would like to know more	Contact ....
	....

Frequency of Meetings: The frequency of meetings should be agreed by the group, but facilitators must also be clear about the limits of their commitment. It is helpful to hold meetings on the same day of the week e.g., alternate Thursdays, so that women who have missed meetings know when the group will meet again. Our experience indicates that fortnightly meetings allow enough time for members to reflect on issues raised in the group and, if a crisis arises, they have access to each other before the next meeting. When a woman joins an incest survivors' group she may find the time between meetings too long. This is understandable but, as time goes on, she will be better able to hold on to her feelings between meetings.

A group for women who
have been sexually abused
by a trusted adult.

IS IT TIME TO TALK?

If you would like to share
your experiences with other
women who are in the same position

CONTACT US!

By phoning **Anytown 12345**
We meet fortnightly in the evenings.

Starting a professionally-run group

Although many of the issues are similar to starting a community-based group, there are some important additional factors to be considered:

Referrals: referrals can be obtained by circulating colleagues with details of the group and asking them to refer women. Posters can also be displayed in the organization, allowing potential members to self-select for referral to the group. Group facilitators may also wish to assess potential members for their suitability.

Location of meetings: where possible, group meetings should be located in the community. This helps to allay fears of identification or stigma which might occur if the group met in a hospital setting.

Frequency and length of meetings: published accounts of professionally led groups indicate that they are more likely to be closed and time-limited (Davenport and Sheldon, 1987; Gordy, 1983; Herman and Schatzow, 1984; Tsai and Wagner, 1978). The number of members averages between eight and twelve, and they usually meet weekly, over six to twelve weeks for an hour and a half to two hours. Evaluation of the groups shows that members would have welcomed more sessions, and there is also some preference for an open-ended group. The rationale for time-limiting the groups is that it helps to establish early bonding between members. One writer does acknowledge, however, that a ten-week time limit was a reflection of the expected tolerance of the group facilitators rather than that of its members (Herman and Schatzow, 1984).

Setting Boundaries

An important activity for an incest survivors' group is the establishment of boundaries for the group's operation. The setting of boundaries allows members some control over one aspect of their lives and it can provide a positive framework for women whose childhood boundaries have been repeatedly violated. As one study puts it:

> Repeated violation in childhood fragments ego boundaries and therefore consistent limits such as punctual timekeeping, and the same physical setting each week were of enormous importance. (Davenport and Sheldon, 1987).

The boundaries which are helpful to a group's functioning include the length of meetings, confidentiality, record-keeping and contact between meetings.

Length of meetings: it is important for the group to agree on a length of time for meetings, whilst acknowledging that it may be difficult to adhere to strict time limits. Two hours should be sufficient. If someone is in distress, or a woman is particularly needy during a session, it can be difficult for the facilitators to resist the pressure for more time. Asking each group member to take some responsibility for ensuring that the group ends on time helps to alleviate this problem. Repeatedly extending the agreed time limit can;

- limit the effective work undertaken during the session;
- tire the group members and facilitators;
- impose additional stress on everyone present.

Confidentiality: every new member should be reminded about the boundaries of confidentiality. The group will need to decide:

- with whom group meetings can be discussed;
- how confidentiality within the group is to be maintained.

There are two ways in which confidentiality can be a problem in groups. The first, particularly in a professionally-led group, concerns information the facilitators pass on to colleagues about the group. The second concerns what individual group members do with information about other members. Both of these issues should be discussed in the group as they may affect members' freedom to trust, take risks and share personal information.

Confidentiality may pose additional problems if:

- group members' families are known to each other outside the group. This may leave some women feeling particularly vulnerable;
- facilitators have made arrangements for support and supervision from someone outside the group. Members will need to be reassured that their confidentiality will be maintained.

Record Keeping also has important implications for confidentiality. The group will need to decide:

- whether to keep records of each meeting;
- what records will be kept (e.g., a historical record of the group, an account of issues covered, exercises undertaken);
- the form of records (e.g., individual diaries which women could decide whether or not to share, a group 'diary' which could be written by each member in rotation or by the facilitators);
- who will keep the records and where they will be kept;
- what will happen to records when the group finishes.

If facilitators are also planning to keep their own records for supervision purposes, the group should be informed.

Contact between meetings: once trust is established between members, they are likely to develop strong friendships and support networks. It is important that individuals have the choice of whether they can be contacted between meetings. They can then exchange addresses, or telephone numbers, opting out if they want to. Facilitators also need to decide whether they are available to group members between meetings. Availability can pose problems, particularly when a women discloses information to the facilitator which she would rather not share in the group. Contact between meetings also extends the boundaries of the availability of facilitators. They may find it difficult to sustain regular contact between meetings even if only one or two members contact them for additional support.

Group rules: The establishment of group rules can be usefully undertaken at the first meeting and reviewed regularly. Agreed rules could be made into a poster, to be displayed on the wall at each meeting, and amended as necessary. They might cover:

- membership of the group (e.g., a clear statement that the group is open to female incest survivors, arrangements for joining, if the group is open or closed);
- financial arrangements (e.g., bank account, money for tea and coffee etc.);
- confidentiality of the group (including record keeping);
- frequency and length of meetings;
- arrangements (if any) for follow-up if a woman misses one or more meetings.

Establishing group rules at the outset can be useful in promoting trust, group cohesion and participation.

Joining an Incest Survivors' Group

Coming to an incest survivors' group for the first time can be a harrowing experience. A woman may get enormous relief from sharing her past with others, but it may also be the first time that she has publicly acknowledged her abuse. She may feel very apprehensive about meeting other incest survivors or worried that she will encounter someone known to herself or her abuser at a group meeting. It is important to acknowledge all of these issues with her at any pre-group meeting and, if appropriate, when she comes to a group for the first time.

Every woman who decides to join an incest survivors' group is bound to feel some anxiety. This is sometimes increased because she does not feel ready to join the group but it has been suggested to her by well-meaning professionals or friends. Difficulties in asserting herself and saying 'No', may lead her to feel that she is obliged to attend the group. It is important to check, therefore, that she feels ready to join.

In open groups at least one meeting with a prospective new member should be arranged before she joins the group. She should meet one of the facilitators and, if she wishes, a group member. At this meeting information about the group can be given, and the woman herself has the chance to ask questions. Arrangements can then be made to accompany her to her first meeting; this gives her time to think over what she has heard before making a final decision about whether to attend. It also allows her to opt out if she wants, without losing face. If she decides to join the group, she knows that she will have the security of being accompanied to her first meeting by a familiar person.

When a woman attends the group for the first time it is important that:

- she is welcomed and introduced to everyone;
- she knows that she has the choice to speak or to listen;

– she knows that no pressure will be put on her to talk about her life experiences until she is ready to do so.

In closed groups, especially if members are assessed before joining it is important to:

- explain the purpose of the group;
- outline the structure of meetings;
- explain the role of facilitators.

Just as group members might be assessed by facilitators it is appropriate that they too have the opportunity to get information and assess what the group proposes to offer to them. This can be done at a preliminary meeting with the facilitators.

The first meeting of a closed group obviously has to begin with introductions. The purpose of the group, the structure of and arrangements for the meetings should be shared before the main discussion of the meeting gets underway.

Introductions: New members should always be introduced to an open group. This will not only break the ice but it can also confirm some of the ground-rules of the group. At a first meeting one of the facilitators might say:

> Welcome to the Incest Survivors' group. My name is ... and I am one of the group facilitators. The other group facilitator is ... Neither of us has been sexually abused by a trusted adult, but we hope that we're able to give support in the group to women who have.

It is also important to explain that women will not be 'put on the spot' in relation to disclosing details of their life experiences.

The women in the group can then be asked to introduce themselves using their first names. If a particular woman finds this too difficult, one of the facilitators could introduce her to the rest of the group. Similar introductions of new members to an open group must be made, with an emphasis placed on a woman's freedom to choose to talk or to remain silent.

Sometimes a woman who has come to the group for the first time may begin to talk at length when she is introduced. Just speaking may cause her such anxiety that she has difficulty limiting what she says. Facilitators should allow her to talk, but bring in other group members at the appropriate time, so that the new member does not monopolize the group's time.

There are alternative methods of introduction which might be considered:

1   Each member could be asked to introduce themselves by their first name. They could also be asked:
- to identify the family member who abused them;
- who they first told or tried to tell about the abuse;
- what were the consequences of telling.

2 Members could be asked to pair with the person sitting next to them and to talk to each other about themselves for a few minutes. Each woman then introduces her 'partner' to the group, saying only what she has been given permission to share.

Planning Group Meetings

The planning of the content and structure of meetings is an important task for group facilitators. The nature of this task depends on whether the group is open, closed or time-limited. If the group is to be time-limited with a pre-determined number of sessions, facilitators may plan the general outline of the content of group meetings in advance; examples of this are described by Davenport and Sheldon (1987), Deighton and McPeek (1985) and Herman and Schatzow (1984). Typically, the first session involves introductions and the sharing of individual and group aims.

In groups that are not time-limited, a more flexible approach is necessary. Planning should be undertaken by the facilitators before each group meeting. The main areas to cover are:

- administrative tasks carried out from the previous meeting;
- planning the introduction to the meeting (including the introduction of new members and feedback of key issues/themes from the last session);
- arrangements for setting aside 'individual time' for any women who want to talk about a specific issue;
- group task or game as a means of exploring an agreed theme.

Structure of group meetings

Planning, starting, facilitating and ending a group meeting are tasks which require thought and co-ordination on the part of facilitators. A consistent structure can promote feelings of 'safety, containment and trust' (Davenport and Sheldon, 1987) although facilitators should be flexible enough to abandon an agreed structure if a woman is in crisis or a more immediate issue is presented.

Starting a group meeting is important in setting the atmosphere for the session. A few minutes to allow everyone to get seated can be followed by an introduction by one of the facilitators. This is a signal to everyone that the group is about to begin. In open groups, new members should be introduced at this point, and there are a number of introductory tasks and exercises that can be used at the start of a meeting. The facilitators should:

- remind the group of the previous meeting's discussion;
- check whether there are any aspects of the previous meeting's discussion that anyone wishes to raise;
- check briefly with each group member how she has been feeling since the previous meeting;
- remind the group of any decision that has been made about the content of the meeting (e.g., topic to be discussed).

In this way, the facilitators can quickly establish which group members may need individual time during the meeting and it also encourages some continuity between meetings. Beyond this, there are several useful introductory exercises that can help the group to begin:

1   Everyone, including the facilitators, could be asked to think about:
    - three hopes;
    - three fears;
    - three expectations
    which they have for attending the group. These can then be shared in the group.
2   Everyone is asked to share something they feel good about having done since the last meeting. In order to set the tone, a facilitator might start by saying something brief. For example:
    'I bought myself a new blouse today'
    'I went for a walk in the park last weekend'
    'I got here tonight!'

The sharing of achievements serves several important purposes:

- it allows women to take credit for things they have done well;
- it reminds them that they can and should do nice things for themselves;
- it helps to reverse the process of self-criticism which may have been with them for years.

In spite of these more positive methods of starting a group, a woman may attend the group in such distress that she may blurt out her problems, hardly pausing for breath. Facilitators will need to exercise great tact in order to enable everyone to contribute. They might say,

> We're trying to get round everyone just now, Jane. You sound very upset, and we'll come back to you in a little while, after everyone has had the chance to say something.

The group in process: after the introductory period, facilitators will have a good idea of what will be useful for the remainder of the session. They may have learnt that:

- a woman is in crisis;
- there are a few women who are so needy that they will use as much group time as is offered;
- whether there is any feedback or follow-up from previous meetings.

The next stage of the group should build on this information, or return to plans already made for the meeting.

Broadly speaking, there are three types of group activities which can be used alone, or in combination, during a group meeting. These are:

- topics for discussion
- exercises
- individual time.

A *topic* has a number of advantages:

- it focuses the attention of group members on a common theme;
- it creates a sense of coming together for a shared purpose;
- it allows women to draw attention to an important aspect of their lives;
- it enables the facilitators to set limits by keeping group members on the topic;
- it enables every woman in the group to contribute.

A range of topics, by no means exclusive, is outlined in Table 8.2.

One of the most important tasks for the facilitator here is to ensure that everyone who

Table 8.2: Topics for Discussion in an Incest Survivors' Group

Trust
Power and control
Expresson of anger, especially towards parents
Difficulties with mothering
Coping with emotions and memories
Problems with relationships
Dealing with feelings of guilt, anger, despair and revenge
Dealing with flashbacks and nightmares
Relationships with men
Feelings towards own children
Experiences with statutory services e.g., hospitals, social work departments
Feelings towards mothers
Coping with anniversaries

wants to gets the chance to speak in the group meetings. Facilitators can draw in other group members by saying,

> 'Jane, you sound very (describe the feeling) about your experience. I wonder if anyone else has had similar experiences.'
>
> or
>
> 'Marion, you've talked about this issue in a previous meeting. Perhaps you could tell Jane how you dealt with it.'

Group exercises may be an appropriate activity when there are more than four women in the group. They can be used to:

- build trust between group members;
- evoke difficult feelings e.g., express anger in a 'safe' environment;
- create childhood experiences from which they were excluded;
- relax and enjoy each others' company.

There are some important guidelines for group exercises:

- the exercises should be kept simple and straightforward;
- they should not make any member feel under pressure to participate;
- time should be set aside for feedback and support if needed.

Detailed examples of group activities and exercises are given in Chapter 9. Table 8.3 gives an indication of their purpose in a group.

Table 8.3: Group Activities and their Purpose

Activity	*Purpose*
Trust games	– building trust – acknowledging trust – taking risks
Touch activities	– building trust – giving support – accepting good feelings from others
Childhood activities/games	– reclaiming lost childhood – having fun – discovering latent skills
Drawing	– expressing feelings – getting feedback from others – working together and building trust
Word plans	– acknowledging common feelings – saying difficult words or phrases
Use of poems (see Appendix 1)	– putting difficult feelings into words – sharing common feelings

Individual time is the time during a meeting which individual women use to talk about pressing problems or issues from their past. It can form the main part of a meeting, or it can be time set aside for individual women to talk after a topic or activity. If the group breaks for coffee during a meeting, individual time could follow the break.

It is useful to remind women of the individual time available by saying:

'We can spend the next hour talking about individual concerns'.

This makes members aware that they are sharing a limited amount of time. It is also helpful to ask a woman if she would like feedback from the group or if she just wants to talk in the knowledge that others understand what she is saying. When she has finished speaking, the facilitators could say:

'I wonder if anyone else has ever felt like that,'

or

'Have you ever faced that problem? What did you do?'

Facilitators can give their ideas and reactions when other group members have spoken.

An important task for facilitators is to maintain their awareness of other group members while listening to a particular woman's experiences. Having two facilitators makes this task easier. One person can pay particular attention to the woman who is talking, while the other takes responsibility for noticing the reactions of group members, e.g., if they are listening, emotionally shut off or showing signs of distress.

Sometimes a woman talks at length and it may be necessary for the facilitators to gently interrupt her in order to re-engage the attention of the group. A facilitator could say:

'You're talking about a lot of very painful things that have happened. I'm sure there are other women who are remembering similar experiences and feelings. Would you like to hear from them?'

or

'You sound very angry/sad/anxious. I'd like to check how everyone else is feeling and we'll come back to you.'

Once other group members have had the opportunity to share some of their feelings, the woman should be allowed to continue. This type of intervention is helpful on a number of counts:

- it breaks some of the tension which might have arisen in the group as a result of what the woman is saying;
- it draws the group together;
- it acknowledges common feelings between group members.

Breaks in the meeting should be agreed beforehand. Breaks can be used to:

- move from topic/exercise/individual time;

– have some refreshments;
– release some of the tension or lighten the atmosphere.

They should last no longer than five or ten minutes.

Ending the meeting: Ending the meeting properly is important, and ensures that the group does not drift to a close. Using the same method of ending each meeting establishes an acceptable ritual for group members. Facilitators should indicate when it is time for the meeting to draw to a close. They could say something like:

'We have fifteen minutes left. It's time to think about ending the meeting.'

It is important to try to end meetings on time, although this may not always be possible, and arrangements for the next meeting should be confirmed. These should include:

– checking that everyone knows the date of the meeting;
– making arrangements for lifts home and to the next group meeting;
– confirming what the group has agreed to do at its next meeting.

Finally, a check should be made to see how everyone is feeling and that they feel safe going home. If someone is feeling distressed she might welcome contact from other group members before the next meeting.

Evaluating the Group

Evaluation can be carried out by:

– asking women directly what they have gained from the group and what they would like to see changed;
– in open groups, noting what more established group members say to newer members about the group;
– undertaking a follow-up of women after they have stopped attending the group.

If more formal evaluation is required, it may be necessary to ask the women to complete questionnaires and other evaluation material before they attend the group and after they leave. In this way, some measure of the changes, problems and benefits of the group can be made. If such an evaluation is to be made, it is essential that permission be sought from the incest survivors themselves.

Responding to Specific Issues

Within incest survivors' groups there are a number of issues which may pose particular problems for members or facilitators. They are listed in Table 8.4.

Table 8.4: Issues which arise in Incest Survivors' Groups

Problems with group membership
Trust
Relationships with men
Lesbian women
Poverty and wealth
Women with multiple problems
Silent women
Anger
Revenge
Not talking about the abuse
Minimizing individual experiences
Going over the same ground
Suicide and self-abuse
Difficulties with touch

Problems with group membership

Sometimes there are unforeseen difficulties which arise as a consequence of group membership. These include:

Previous acquaintances: if a new member discovers that she knows another group member she may express shock, relief or surprise. For some women it is an awkward experience, especially if members of their respective families have an ongoing friendship. If this is the case, there may be questions about the confidentiality of material discussed in the group and trust between the two women may be difficult to establish. The facilitators have a responsibility to help them to confront the issue. This could be done in the context of a general discussion about trust. Alternatively a facilitator could say,

> Karen and Annette, we know that you were upset/dismayed/frightened etc. to meet each other in the group. How do you think that knowing each other might affect/has affected the way you are in the group?

Siblings joining the group: this can pose problems, especially if their experience of the abuse and its consequences has been different. Difficulties can arise if the group spends too great a proportion of its time on their relationship or experiences at the expense of other members. Again, it is important to address the issue openly. A facilitator might say,

> Katrina and Mary, you have spent a lot of time recently in the group discussing your relationship with each other. Perhaps there is no more help that the group can give you with this. What do you think . . . ? What do other women think?

On the other hand the presence of sisters can enable the group to see that sexual abuse can continue for years without other family members being aware of it.

Trust

Trust is a central theme in any incest survivors' group, and it may take a long time to establish. The issue of trust is manifest in a number of different ways:

- women direct their contributions to the group and to each other through the facilitators;
- women find it difficult to show any form of physical affection to each other;
- there are difficulties participating in any trust games;
- women are unable to ask for support from other group members between meetings.

Openly drawing attention to these issues may exacerbate the situation. Facilitators should therefore use every possible opportunity to confirm the achievements made by individual women and the group as a whole in trusting each other enough to share their experiences. Some non-threatening trust games are described in Chapter 9.

Relationships with men

Within an incest survivors' group, women will have had a range of experiences in their adult relationships with men. Some may have supportive or good relationships with their partners or colleagues, some may be in abusive heterosexual relationships and others may have withdrawn totally from all relationships with men.

Women who have rejected relationships with men through fear, are likely to find any discussion of sexuality or heterosexual sexual experiences extremely threatening in a group. They may express nausea or disgust, or withdraw emotionally from the discussion. This can in turn become difficult for women who are in heterosexual relationships, supportive or otherwise. A facilitator faced with this situation might say: 'Martha, it looks as if you are finding this difficult to listen to. How do you feel about what Eileen has been saying?' If Martha can express her negative or distressed feelings, it is important to reassure Eileen that her reaction is due to the general topic under discussion rather than in reaction to the specific events of Eileen's life.

Lesbian women

Many of society's assumptions about female sexuality may be evident in an incest survivors' group, especially in relation to lesbian women. It may be difficult for them to openly acknowledge their sexuality in a group, particularly if other women:

- express anti-lesbian feelings;
- express a fear of being gay themselves.

As a way of opening up the subject, a facilitator might focus on female friendship and support. She could say: 'What sorts of things do you get from a close relationship with a woman friend that aren't always present in a friendship with a man?' This could lead to a discussion about non-sexual friendships and the boundaries between friendship, emotional attachment and sexual attraction.

Poverty and wealth

A variation in income levels and relative standards of living can cause problems in the group in the following ways:

- some women might have difficulty finding money for group outings;
- there may be resentment of members who appear to have a higher income;
- there might be some disbelief that a woman can have an adequate income and still have problems with her children, relationships etc.

A group 'kitty' into which members pay a small amount each week, can help resolve immediate problems with group outings. Otherwise, it is important for facilitators to acknowledge the issue with the group as a whole; they might say,

> Although everyone in the group has a different standard of living, your common bond is your childhood experiences. Money can sometimes dull the pain of the past, and sometimes it also contributes to problems.

This could open up discussion on the issue.

Women with multiple problems

Sometimes women who have had a lifetime of deprivation and abuse join the group. They seem to lurch from one crisis to the next and the group as a whole can easily be overwhelmed by the apparently endless catalogue of disasters which a woman experiences. For some women this is undoubtedly their reality, but the issue for the group to face is whether the woman can realistically get support within it. It is important to help her to focus on one problem but she may need one-to-one help before she can benefit from the support offered in the group context.

Silent women

Sometimes women join an incest survivors' group and for many weeks say nothing at all. They might participate in group activities and come on group outings, but when the group starts to talk about sexual abuse in any detail, these women become silent. Their body language may also show signs of emotional distancing. The reasons for their silence include:

- they are too anxious or nervous to participate in the group;
- they cannot cope yet with the emotional content of the group;
- they do not feel that they have anything worthwhile to say;
- they do not trust the group enough to participate in it.

It is difficult to respond helpfully to a silent group member without her feeling under more pressure; sometimes another group member will address the issue, and a facilitator can follow this up. Asking her direct open questions can also gauge how she is feeling. A group review meeting, when each member takes stock of their experiences, saying how far their expectations of the group have been met, what they like and what they would like to change about the group, can also enable a silent member to participate.

Anger

The expression of anger is often a real difficulty for women who have experienced sexual abuse. Their anger may be associated with or masked by guilt and low self-esteem. Women are sometimes frightened to express their anger for fear that it is not containable or that it will make them go 'mad'. Doing word plans (see Chapter 9) of feelings associated with anger, role-plays of situations in which women feel angry and games which allow the expression of anger will help to release some of these feelings in the safe environment of the group.

Revenge

Incest survivors often express strong feelings of revenge towards their abusers. They want their abusers to feel all the hurt, pain and humiliation which they have suffered themselves. They want to plan a violent or drawn-out death for their abusers, and may spend much time drawing-up a hypothetical scenario for this event.

Sharing these violent thoughts helps women to get some of their deeply held feelings out into the open. Others can acknowledge that they have had similar thoughts and may even have tried to act on them. Reassurance that these feelings of revenge are common, given their childhood ordeal, can remove the sense of 'badness' which they produce. Facilitators should also be ready to point out that feelings of revenge, if held for too long, can sustain a woman's anger and bitterness towards her abuser. It can keep her rooted in her past rather than allowing her to come to terms with it. Too much discussion of revenge can be upsetting for other group members who may not have the confidence to ask for a change of subject.

Example: In an incest survivors' group there were detailed discussions, over a number of meetings, on plans for the form of revenge towards abusers. This was carried out amidst much laughter and even glee. One woman, who left the group at this time, returned some months later to give her reasons for leaving. She said that she had found the prolonged revenge-planning upsetting because she started to have nightmares about her father and now felt that she would 'never be free of him'.

Not talking about the abuse

Incest survivors often avoid talking about the details of their abuse. The reasons for this avoidance include:

- it is still too painful for them to say exactly what happened;
- they have blocked out the details;
- they do not want to give the pain of their feelings to others who are disclosing similar experiences;
- they have never told anyone the details of what happened to them, because they are frightened, disgusted or ashamed;
- they feel they cannot trust other group members with the details;
- they have convinced themselves that they have come to terms with their experiences and they should forget about it all;
- they may still feel they are not believed.

In addition, referring in general terms to being 'bad-used' or 'abused', or talking about when 'it' happened, is all that some women can say about their experiences. The task for facilitators is to encourage individual women to unburden themselves of the details of their abuse, in their own time, under their own control and at their own pace. Facilitators should acknowledge the difficulty of the task and could say,

> 'We have been meeting now for x meetings. We've all shared a lot with each other. Perhaps the time has come for us to talk about what actually happened when you were abused. Unless we all know exactly what happened, we can't help you each to begin to deal with it.'

It has been predicted that the silence following such a statement would not last for long (Tsai and Wagner, 1978). Group members could then be asked about:

- the age at which the abuse began;
- exactly what was done;
- when, and why it stopped.

In order to facilitate explicit detail, specific questions are asked such as

> 'Where did he put his fingers?'
>
> or
>
> 'What did he do next?'

If group members can acknowledge the commonality of their experiences, and talk about them in this way, an atmosphere of safety and trust quickly develops around the common themes of secrecy, isolation, shame, and feelings of hurt, helplessness and fear. They can also build together on their strengths, for example by sharing the methods they used as children to survive the abuse.

Minimizing individual experiences

Sometimes women minimize their experience of being sexually abused because:

- they have not fully acknowledged to themselves its full impact on their lives;
- they compare themselves to other women in the group whom they perceive to have suffered greater pain, humiliation and betrayal of trust;
- they do not want to believe that their experiences really happened.

For these reasons they may not wish to burden other women with their 'lesser' problems. If this is the case facilitators should point out that everyone's experience is equally valid because of its consequences for each woman. Minimizing the experiences may be an extension of the lack of self-worth that incest survivors often feel.

Going over the same ground

Incest survivors sometimes repeat a description of a particular incident of sexual abuse or a sequence of events over and over again. In open groups the newer members may not be aware of this repetition, a signal that it is problematic comes when other group members appear to lose interest as the woman speaks. The issue should be addressed directly by the facilitators by saying: 'Agnes, you have talked several times in the group about (name the incident). Perhaps other group members are finding it difficult to know what to say now.'

The underlying reasons for this repetition may be that the woman has not told all the details of a particular incident, and is waiting for someone to ask the right question, or that she is frightened to move on for fear of uncovering new more unpleasant memories.

Suicide or self-abuse

Incest survivors often talk about harming themselves or of wanting to 'forget about it all — for good'. They may have contemplated or attempted suicide in the past and return to the subject at times when they feel particularly vulnerable. For other women, the reminder of their past attempts stays with them in the form of scars from razor blade cuts. If they talk about self-mutilation it may provoke an angry reaction from other women who might say, 'Haven't you suffered enough pain without putting yourself through this too?' or 'You can't give up now, you're letting him (the abuser) win.'

The urge to self-mutilate or to attempt suicide is a common one and all group members will be able to identify with it. Some group members can be afraid when they are confronted by a woman who is in a self-destructive phase. However, women can be encouraged to support any group member who experiences this sort of stress, and in doing so can learn to acknowledge their own strengths in times of crisis.

Example: Jane arrived at a group meeting one evening in an agitated state. She talked about wanting to die to stop the pain she felt, and half way through the meeting she rushed out of the room. One of the facilitators and another group member, Irene, eventually found her huddled in a corner of her flat. She had made several deep wounds with a blade to both her wrists. Irene immediately took control. She washed and bandaged Jane's wrists tightly and took her to the local hospital. Afterwards Irene was able to recognise that she reacted capably. Jane was able to accept and thank Irene for her concern and practical help.

Difficulties with touch

Many incest survivors have difficulty with giving and receiving touch for comfort or reassurance, because touching had such dangerous and unpleasant connotations in their childhood. Women talk about and show the effects of the problem by:

- having difficulties with expressing themselves in a physical way or responding physically to their children;
- sexual problems with their partners;
- difficulties in comforting another group member who is in distress;
- showing difficulty in participating in group exercises or games which involve touching.

The problem can only be dealt with by slowly building trust and by acknowledging each woman's right to her 'defensible space'. Some of the exercises described in Chapter 9 might also help.

Leaving the Group

Leaving the group, whether it be for all group members in a time-limited group, or for an individual woman in an open group, is a very important issue.

Time-limited groups

In this situation, all group members leave together and know in advance that the group will be ending on a certain date. This allows both facilitators and members to prepare for the end of the group. For some women, the end of the group will represent a big loss. It may also signal the beginning of a new phase of life much less troubled by the history of sexual abuse. Facilitators should therefore:

- prepare the women for the potential feelings of loss (including sadness, anger, emptiness, abandonment);
- look at alternative support networks for the women;
- discuss arrangements for follow-up or further meetings;
- examine the positive achievements made in the group by each member.

Open groups

It is important for women to know that they can leave the group at any time. They should, however, be encouraged to let the group know their intentions, in person or in writing. A woman should also learn that if she decides to leave or to limit her involvement in the group she can maintain a link with the group for support and encouragement. An open group enables members to drop in and report on their progress, or to seek support if they are in a crisis.

Summary

Incest survivors' groups have a great deal to offer women who have been sexually abused. In our view an open group has most to offer these women because it allows them to build trust in a safe atmosphere. It gives them time to feel more secure before disclosing details of the sexual abuse. They also have more control over how they use the group in terms of attendance and what they feel ready to share in this setting.

The words of group members themselves provide ample testimony of the usefulness of incest survivors' groups.

'I don't feel like a victim now, more like a survivor'.

'I no longer feel wholly responsible for everyone and everything.'

'I used to feel like the abuse was happening all over again, every time something or someone triggered a reaction. Now I have a clearer sense of what is unsafe currently and what reminds me of past danger.'

The single most valued experience in incest survivors' groups is the contact with other survivors. One woman wrote,

'Their presence proved ... to negate the message that it only happened to me and that it happened because I *was* me.' (Herman and Schatzow, 1984).

The strength and courage of women who join incest survivors' groups is self-evident in their ability to share, to support others and to carry on with their lives with humour and goodwill. Acknowledging and reinforcing of these qualities can take place in the group.

It is appropriate to end with another quotation, this time from a woman who saw the group in its historical perspective:

'When I look back at the group I see that it confronted me with a choice about whether to go on hating myself or to find a more constructive way to deal with the past.'

In other words, incest survivors' groups can be the means to a new beginning for many women.

9 Therapeutic Techniques

This chapter outlines methods that can be used with incest survivors to help them deal with particular issues and problems. The issues are summarized in Table 9.1. The list is not an exhaustive one, but it offers a range of ideas that helpers may find useful in working with incest survivors. It will be necessary for helpers to adapt these techniques to suit individual women and the helper may need to think about ways to make these adaptations creatively.

A. Re-entering the World of the Child

One of the most important tasks for an incest survivor is to remember what it was like for her as a child. She will refer to her childhood from the perspective of an adult, and may have forgotten her physical size, her feelings of powerlessness and how it felt to be a child in her family. A number of therapeutic methods can be usefully employed to enable an incest survivor to get in touch with herself as a child. The methods described below should be modified to suit particular women.

Photographs

Studying photographs of herself at various ages throughout her childhood and adolescence can facilitate a more accurate perception of herself as a child. Group photographs of family occasions, e.g., birthdays, anniversaries, holidays or excursions are particularly useful, as are photographs of other family members and the abuser. Photographs can be used to:

- elicit memories of significant childhood events;
- compare and contrast photographs of the child and the abuser in order to reinforce the perception of the child as small and powerless in relation to an abusing adult;
- enable an incest survivor to gain a more complete picture of the important people in her childhood.

Sometimes an incest survivor destroys childhood photographs of herself and other family members. She may find the memories which are elicited by photographs too painful. If this is the case, the helper could ask if the woman could obtain photographs from other family members.

Table 9.1:   Themes and Techniques in Working with Incest Survivors

Themes	Techniques
A. Re-entering the world of the child	Photographs Drawings/artwork Remembering key events Constructing a life history Describing places where the abuse took place Visiting places associated with childhood Description of significant adults Description of incest survivor as a child
B. Dealing with flashbacks	Imagery techniques
C. Dealing with regression	Becoming a child again Using images of the incest survivor as a child
D. Dealing with guilt	Challenging beliefs and assumptions about responsibility New strategies for dealing with responsibility
E. Dealing with anger	Awareness and recognition of anger Describing angry feelings Awareness of situations and people that make her angry Validation of angry feelings Expression of angry feelings Expressing anger towards the abuser and other family members Confrontation
F. Dealing with anxiety and fear	Awareness and recognition of feelings Situations and feelings that produce anxiety Dealing with physical signs of anxiety Dealing with avoidance Dealing with anxious thoughts Panic attacks
G. Dealing with loss	Awareness of losses The experience of grief The tasks of grieving Coming to terms with loss
H. Sexuality	Identification of key issues Sex education Dealing with self-image Dealing with sex education Dealing with issue of arousal during the abuse Dealing with sexual problems Dealing with sexuality and sexual development of her own children

Table 9.1: continued

Themes	Techniques
J. Challenging negative thoughts	Types of negative thoughts Methods for challenging negative thoughts
K. Reclaiming childhood	Artwork Play Religious ceremonies Special occasions Shared activities
L. Building trust in a group	Trust exercises Sentence completion exercises Confirming progress already made
M. Building self-esteem	Negative self-image Building self-esteem
N. Assertiveness	Defining assertiveness Identifying basic rights Assertiveness and aggression Role-play Sexuality and assertiveness Ways of being assertive
O. Role-play	
P. Writing	Letter writing Diaries and Journals Personal writing Using other writers work
Q. Brainstorming	
R. Word pictures	
S. Sentence completion exercises	
T. Empty chair technique	
U. Dealing with other areas of difficulty	

Drawings/artwork

Artwork can be used in both individual and group settings. It is helpful for:

- expressing feelings which may be difficult to share verbally;

- getting an immediate response on an issue without allowing too much time to think about it;
- enabling a woman to express herself freely in a medium which is fun to use.

Large sheets of drawing paper, lots of felt tipped pens, crayons or paints are needed for artwork.

Initially a woman may feel inhibited about drawing, especially if she has been told or feels that she is 'not good at art'. Acknowledging that these feelings are widespread can reduce her anxiety and she can then be encouraged to enjoy the experience. Below, we give some examples of the ways in which artwork can be used.

'Me' at different stages: the helper asks the woman to draw a picture of herself and other significant family members at different stages of her childhood e.g., at the age of two, four, eight and twelve. The pictures may indicate:

- how the woman perceives herself in relation to other family members at different times;
- who were the significant adults in her life at various stages.

She could also be asked to draw pictures of:

- her relationship with other family members;
- where the sexual abuse took place;
- her current relationships with adults and/or children.

Drawings can also be used in a group setting as a means of looking at self-image.

Remembering key events

The helper asks an incest survivor to recall key events from her childhood. These might include:

- moving house;
- school days (including teachers, friends, buildings, behaviour at school);
- hospital admissions (especially any connected with the sexual abuse);
- birth of siblings;
- deaths of important people;
- pets;
- hobbies;
- leaving home;
- birthdays, Christmas and other celebrations.

The helper can discuss these in the context of the woman's memories. The discussion can build up an overall picture of her childhood including some of its less painful aspects.

172

Constructing a life history

The helper asks the woman to write down the years since her birth and, where she can, to note one or more significant events in each year.

Example

1952 Born at . . . hospital on . . .
1953
1954 Sister born
1955 Father got new job
1956 Moved house
1957 Started school
1958 Brother born
1959 Sexual abuse started
1960 Grandmother died

This exercise can:

- trigger memories about specific events and incidents;
- lead to the triggering of new memories through discussion;
- identify 'gaps' in a woman's early history and begin to work out reasons for the existence of these gaps (e.g., dissociating herself from the events because of the abuse, chaotic family background where the family were constantly on the move etc.).

Describing places where the abuse took place

The helper asks the woman to describe or draw the places where the abuse took place. She can be asked:

- whether it was indoors, out of doors or some other place e.g., car, shed;
- if it took place in a variety of locations or always in the same place;
- about any colours, smell, fabrics which she associates with the location;
- whether other adults or children were nearby when the abuse occurred;
- the time/s of the day when the abuse took place.

If the abuse took place in the family home, she can be asked to describe the house, inside and out. It is important to ask for descriptions of her bedroom (layout, furniture, bedding, ornaments and toys) and any room in which the sexual abuse took place.

If a woman finds if difficult to give a verbal description, drawings can be very useful. She can be asked to draw a plan of the house and details of its rooms. A picture of the exterior of the house might be drawn, together with a description of the street or neighbourhood in which it was situated. This exercise often triggers new memories.

Visiting places associated with childhood

Taking or encouraging a woman to visit places which were important in her childhood is likely to induce memories of previously forgotten events. Once a woman begins to identify herself as a survivor by coming to terms with her past, she may feel ready and stronger to visit places where the abuse took place. She can be encouraged to visit:

– her school/s;
– the house she lived in;
– places where she played with other children;
– places where she felt safe as a child;
– the graves of dead family members;
– other important childhood places, e.g., houses of other family members.

Description of significant adults

The helper should ask the woman to identify significant adults in her life by compiling lists of 'people with whom I felt safe/trusted' and 'people with whom I did not feel safe as a child'. The lists can be examined together, with the helper asking questions such as:

'What made you trust/distrust these people?'
'How did they show you that they cared for you?'
'How much time did you spend with them?'
'Where did they live?'
'For how long were they significant in your life?'
'Did you ever try to tell them about the abuse?'
'If so, what were their reactions?'

By exploring these areas, a woman can begin to discover:

– that she may/may not have had significant adults in early life;
– the difficulties of talking about the sexual abuse with people whom she trusted as a child;
– that feeling frightened and upset because of the abuse affected her relationships with potentially safe and trustworthy adults.

Description of the incest survivor as a child

In addition to looking at photographs of herself as a child, it is helpful to get a description from an incest survivor of her physical size at various ages, her clothes, hobbies, toys, pets and so on. If it is too difficult or painful for her to remember herself as a child, she can be asked to describe children of relevant ages known to her. This enables her to gain a more realistic view of the size and situation of children in relation to adults around them. It may seem surprising that an incest survivor needs to be reminded of the relative size of children and adults, but many assume that in childhood they had the power and strength of an adult.

B.   Dealing with Flashbacks

Flashbacks have already been discussed in Chapters 3, 6 and 7. Some points to note include:

1   Flashbacks can be used as a vehicle for disclosure about the abuse, and about aspects of an incest survivor's childhood.

2   If the woman is experiencing significant flashbacks in the presence of the helper, it may be possible to facilitate disclosure by close observation of her body language.

3   Once the flashback has subsided, the woman should be encouraged to disclose the memory so that she can take control of the memory contained in the flashback. The following information should be gathered:

   – the age she was at the time of the incident recalled in the flashback;
   – the situation/place in which the incident took place;
   – the adults involved;
   – any other children who were present.

In doing this, it becomes easier for a woman to disclose the difficult details relating to the sexual abuse.

4   If she uses the language and behaviour of a child during a flashback, the helper's language and behaviour should change accordingly.

5   It is essential that the woman should be made to feel safe before she leaves the session. This can be achieved through physical comfort, checking that she is totally in touch with her adult world and that support is available to her if necessary.

6   If the same flashback recurs frequently, imagery techniques can be used to enable her to take control of it.

Imagery techniques

These are particularly useful for helping a woman take control of flashbacks and perceptual disturbances. Incest survivors frequently experience images of the abuse, the abuser(s) and the situation in which incidents of abuse took place. As these are images, it is possible to substitute alternative images which are less distressing.

Method

1 Clarify with the incest survivor the nature of these recurring images (e.g., her abuser is about to abuse her).
2 Explain that these are *images* that frighten her, and because they are images, they can be replaced with less frightening images.
3 Examine alternative images that would allow her to remove the frightening or distressing elements of the images (e.g., making the abuser leave the room before he attempts to abuse her). Table 9.2 outlines some of the alternative images.
4 Help the woman to find a safe place for the 'child' in her image e.g., holding her mother's hand, putting her to bed in a 'safe' house.

These imagery substitutes can be used within a session with an incest survivor, or be recorded onto a cassette so that the woman can deal with the frightening images at home. If a cassette is to be used, the following sequence of events is helpful:

– ask the woman to think about the frightening images;
– substitue others that help her deal with the negative images;
– ask her to imagine going to a safe house/place where there are adults who will take care of her;
– relaxation exercises can be useful at the end of the tape with a suggestion that she rest or go to sleep for a while.

A cassette may have to be re-recorded regularly as the images and perceptual disturbances change with the recall of new memories.

Example: Helen was sexually abused by her father who used spiders and beetles to frighten her. He put them in her bed and clothes, and used them during the abuse. As an adult, she often had visual images of large numbers of spiders coming towards her and her father's voice gloating in the background.

The rationale for changing these images was explained to her.

She was asked to bring the frightening images to mind. She became agitated as she saw the insects coming towards her, and was then asked to imagine them all turning round and going back out of the door of the room.

She was able to do this and her fear subsided but remained until her father's voice was dealt with. This was achieved by imagining him standing in the room, and two policemen coming in and taking him away.

Helen then became calm and was able to use these simple substitute images as a way of dealing with the images at home. A cassette repeating these instructions was made to help her at home, and concluded with relaxation exercises.

This procedure was repeated with other images.

Table 9.2: Imagery Techniques: Images and Substitutes

Image	*Possible Substitute Images*
The child is alone	Add a safe adult (e.g., the helper, the mother)
	Get her to go to another place/room where there are safe people
The child is injured	Get a safe adult (e.g., the helper) to take her to a hospital/doctor's clinic where she will be looked after and her injuries dealt with. Then return her to safe place where adults care for her
The child is crying	Get a safe adult to hold and comfort her
The child is running away	Imagine running to a safe place (real or fictitious) where she will be cared for by adults who do not abuse her
The abuser is present	Make him leave the room
The abuser is violent	Introduce other adults (e.g., policemen) to remove him
The abuser sexually abuses her	Introduce other adults (e.g., policemen) to remove him
Weapons (e.g. knife, broken glass) used during abuse	Ask the woman or another adult to pick them up and throw them away
Insects, especially if used to frighten her during the abuse	Introduce another adult (or the woman herself) into the scene to remove the insects or to kill them with insecticide
Particularly frightening situations where she was abused	Get the woman to take herself to a pleasant place/safe house
	Go to an imaginary safe place away from harm and danger
	Have another adult (e.g., the helper) take her to a safe place

C. Dealing with Regression

Some incest survivors use regression as a means of disclosing painful details about the sexual abuse and other childhood events. The term 'regression' can be defined as 'becoming a child again'. Incest survivors do this in two main ways:

- by reverting to being a child in behaviour, feelings, thinking, language and comprehension. At the time the woman is out of touch with her adult world. The woman will therefore talk as if she is a child e.g. '*I* am frightened' 'he is hurting *me*';
- by becoming aware of the child within herself, and beginning to listen to and report back on what the child is telling her. She is likely to talk about the child in the third person e.g., 'she is telling me that . . . ', 'she is doing . . . ', 'she is frightened because . . . '

The reasons for the occurrence of regression are by no means clear although they may be related to:

- the extent of the memory gaps and dissociation about the abuse;
- the terror engendered by the abuse;
- the age at which the abuse started;
- prolonged, violent or sadistic abuse (Gil, 1988).

Becoming a child again

A good description of this type of regression is contained in 'When You're Ready' by Evert and Bijkerk (1987). The survivor behaves as if she has become a child again, she may show behaviour that is typical of a sexually abused child, for example:

- she may withdraw and be uncommunicative;
- she may expect the helper to hurt or abuse her;
- she may try to run away (e.g., to places where she hid as a child);
- she may roam the streets, unaware of potential dangers such as roads and traffic;
- she may have temper tantrums, with breath-holding, head-banging and other self-injury;
- she may start cutting herself;
- she may become verbally or physically aggressive;
- she may not have words to describe the abuse, and may be able to disclose only through play or drawings.

It is essential that the regression should occur in a safe place, preferably with comfortable furniture and a supply of cushions. The helper must prevent self-injury by holding the woman, and by removing any sharp instruments (broken glass, razor blades or knife) or tablets.

The start of the regression can be detected in a number of ways:

- the woman's tone and pitch of voice changes;
- her breathing quickens and she shows signs of extreme fear;
- she begins to use simple sentences and vocabulary consistent with that of a child;
- she appears to become distant and seems to be unable to maintain her usual eye-contact with the helper;
- her behaviour suddenly changes to that of a frightened/distressed/hurt child.

The helper's presence may be a trigger for the woman to regress, or it may result from direct questions about any memories/flashbacks or from the woman's sudden awareness of pain in her body (Evert and Bijkerk, 1987).

Disclosure:

1 The helper should facilitate the disclosure using methods and language appropriate to work with an abused child. These might include drawings, use of books, play, anatomically correct dolls.
2 The language of the helper will also have to be modified to suit the age of the child that the woman has regressed to.

Post-disclosure:

1 The 'child' should be congratulated on telling.
2 Any question from the 'child' about the abuse, the abuser's behaviour, or any other aspects of the 'child's' life should be elicited and answered.
3 The 'child' should be made to feel safe, perhaps through physical comfort and telling her that she is now safe and will not be going back to live with her abuser.
4 It may be necessary to do some re-parenting or re-educating. For example, correcting misconceptions about sex, or giving the 'child' some pleasant experiences e.g., reading children's stories, listening to nursery rhymes and children's songs.

Bringing the woman back to reality:

1 This may happen spontaneously after the disclosure is ended.
2 If it does not occur spontaneously, the following methods are useful:
    - use of a photograph of a person or people known only to the adult (see Chapter 7). The 'child' is asked questions about the photograph until gradually she can identify the picture;

– getting her to walk round the room and examine its contents in detail until she gradually recognises the environment in which she lives as an adult.

3   The disclosure should be discussed with the woman once she has returned to her adult state. She may have some or no recollection of the events during the regression.

4   At the end of the regression, which may have lasted for a couple of hours, she will be exhausted, and should be encouraged to rest.

Example: Ruth was violently sexually abused by her father. She started to experience pain in her ribs, and on questioning from the helper, regressed to being herself when she was six. The pain intensified and she became very fearful that the helper would hit her. She started to bang her head against the chair and had to be restrained. Gradually, in very simple language, with drawings and her doll, she was able to disclose a particularly brutal incident of abuse involving being beaten around her rib-cage before being raped by her father. Once the disclosure was over, she was noticeably calmer, was physically comforted by the helper and told she was now safe. She and the helper then looked at some children's books, before being asked to focus on furniture, ornaments and pictures in the room. Gradually she returned to her adult state, and discussed the disclosure. She was by then exhausted.

Regression: using image of the incest survivor as a child

In this type of regression, the survivor remains in touch with the reality of her adult world, and may act as a parent or protector of the young girl she once was.

Disclosure:

1   In this situation, the helper encourages the adult part of the woman to act as a spokeswoman for the child. She therefore listens to the child and reports the child's disclosures to the helper.

2   Once the 'child' has disclosed, the helper should enable the incest survivor to make sense of the information.

Post-disclosure:

1   The incest survivor may require comfort as she may be distressed.

2   It is vital that the survivor should make the 'child' safe. She should be asked what would make the 'child' feel safe. This may involve:

– taking her to a safe place (real or imagined);

- checking the 'child' has all she needs to feel safe and warm e.g., a safe place that her abuser(s) cannot come to, a warm and welcoming place/room/house with all the necessary equipment to make a child feel comfortable;
- giving the 'child' a cuddle;
- getting someone else e.g., the helper, another safe adult to cuddle the 'child';

3 Before the survivor leaves to go home, the helper should check that she feels safe to leave.

Example: Sue was sexually abused by her stepfather, and had a clear image of herself as a child of eight. She was asked to watch the little girl, and ask her a number of questions about the events in the little girl's life. She told her helper that the little girl was frightened because her stepfather had just come home. The little girl then told Sue what had taken place the previous day. This incident of sexual abuse was one that she had not previously recalled. Once the disclosure was over, she was encouraged to make the little girl feel safe, and in her imagination, Sue took the little girl to a room which no-one could enter and played with her. The helper then had to help Sue to deal with her feelings about this incident of abuse, before checking that she felt safe to leave.

D. Dealing with Guilt

Guilt is the predominant emotion that an incest survivor carries when she decides to seek help. The guilt may not just relate to the sexual abuse but is also present in many other areas of her life. It is as if she has learnt to blame herself for everything that happened to her as a child and has never stopped feeling guilty since. She therefore needs to learn to test her feelings of guilt in a realistic and rational way, instead of automatically believing herself to be guilty for everything that happens to herself and others.

Challenging thoughts and beliefs about responsibility for the sexual abuse

It is important to examine issues of responsibility rather than blame. Blame is an emotive word that tends to allow the survivor's feelings of loyalty towards her family to interfere with her ability realistically to challenge her feelings of guilt.

The survivor should be helped to understand that:

- a child is never responsible for being sexually abused;

- a child is not responsible for experiencing sexual arousal or orgasm during the abuse;
- a child is not responsible for being unable to stop the abuse;
- a child cannot be held responsible for remaining silent about the abuse (she may have been too frightened or did not know how to tell);
- a child is not responsible for failing to protect her siblings or other children from the abuser;
- a child needs attention and affection and is not to blame if she takes whatever attention she is offered even if it is unhealthy unwanted sexual attention;
- even if the abuse continued through adolescence and adulthood, the survivor is still not responsible for it as as she is still in a powerless position in relation to the abuser.

Specific Methods

1   There are a number of useful questions that can be asked to help an incest survivor to challenge her beliefs and thoughts about the guilt (see Table 9.3).

2   Use of photographs of herself as a child (see Section A) to correct her misconceptions about the strength and size of herself as a child. These can be contrasted with photographs of the abuser.

3   Suggest she looks at other children of an age close to the age she was when the abuse was occurring. This will enable her to get a more objective perspective on the powerlessness of a child.

4   She should be asked to examine the responsibilities of the abuser, her mother and other important adults in relation to her as a child. This should include protection, care, facilitating normal development, education.

5   A useful imagery technique is to ask the survivor to imagine her case of sexual abuse being brought before a court of law. She should be asked to imagine a court with judge, jury, prosecuting and defending laywers, a witness stand, and the defendant's box. She should be asked to place the abuser in the defendant's box as he has been charged with the sexual abuse. Then she is to imagine herself as a child, and imagine herself in various places in the courtroom — first in the witness stand telling the court what the abuser did to her, then alongside the abuser to justify her feelings of guilt about the abuse.

Key points to stress are that:

- a child cannot be tried for a crime against herself;
- a child is not considered to be legally responsible for her actions;
- she is not charged with sexual offences against a child: the abuser is;
- no judge would allow her to be placed in the defendant's box.

This imagery technique enables her to recognise that feeling guilty is not the same as being guilty, and that is is always an adult's responsibility if he acts in a sexual way towards a child.

Table 9.3: Useful Questions to Challenge Guilt Feelings

The occurrence of the sexual abuse

Whose idea was it to start the abuse?
How old were you when it started?
Do you know a child of that age now? If so, would she be guilty/responsible?
Did you know what the abuser was doing the first time?
When did you realise that what he was doing was wrong?
What told you that it was wrong?

Stopping the sexual abuse

What could you have done to stop it?
What would have happened (This should be asked about every response produced to first question).
Who could you have told?
How might they have reacted?
What prevented you from telling someone?

Inability to protect siblings

In what way should you have protected your sister(s)?
In what way could you have protected her/them (remembering you were a child too)?
Whose idea was it that she/they should be abused?
When did it happen to her/them?
Who should have been protecting her/them?

Learning new strategies for examining issues of responsibility

This involves examining situations in a realistic way. The following are useful:

1 Careful analysis of the sequence of events and the involvement of the incest survivor and other people.

2 A closer look at the responsibilities of all the individuals involved (including herself).

3 Awareness of her feelings, which may include a number of differing or conflicting emotions.

4 Effects of her emotional reactions on her actions and vice versa.

5 Acknowledgement of emotions that are justified and normal e.g.,
 – guilt when she has done something wrong, hurtful or thoughtless;
 – anger with others for their part in the situation;
 – anxiety/fear that other people may take some action against her;
 – disgust with someone's behaviour.

6   Any action that may need to be taken. For example:
  – she may need to confront someone with his/her behaviour;
  – she might want to apologize;
  – she might have to make a decision about the situation;
  – she may decide to do nothing.

E. Dealing with Anger

Many women find anger an extremely difficult emotion to deal with because they have been brought up to believe that:

  – anger should never be shown;
  – anger is a dangerous emotion;
  – as a woman they must be polite, peace-making, understanding and forgiving at all times;
  – anger is associated with aggression and violence.

Anger can be expressed constructively and released in a safe way, and is an important part of recovering from being abused as a child. Bass and Davis (1988) have called anger 'the backbone of healing'. It is a natural and normal response to abuse and violation. For many incest survivors, anger is an emotion that has been hidden behind feelings of guilt and depression. Anger has probably been denied or turned in on themselves in a self-destructive way. For others, anger and rage have been experienced indiscriminately and without control, so that people around them have borne the brunt of it.

The aim in dealing with an incest survivor's anger is not only to become aware of it, but to learn to direct the anger where it belongs in a safe and non-destructive way. Without this, anger can remain suppressed and can eat away at the survivor in bitterness and desire for revenge.

Awareness and Recognition of Anger

The task here is to help the incest survivor to recognise her angry feelings. Not only may she have little or no awareness of her reactions when she is angry, but she may have no words to describe these feelings.

1   Anger is an emotion that can be detected through awareness of body language. Common signs are tension, particularly in the jaw and hands, clenched fists, gritted teeth, feelings of nausea, quickened heart-beat and shallow breathing.

2   It can be recognised through tone of voice and behaviour e.g., shouting, door slamming, stamping feet, swearing.

3   It can be detected through thought patterns e.g., thoughts of doing harm to someone, rudeness, or never wanting to be in a particular person's company again.

Describing angry feelings

1   The woman should be helped to find ways of describing angry feelings. 'Angry' may be too difficult a word to use. The following are alternatives that may be more acceptable: annoyed, irritated, cross, frustrated, wild, furious, put out, cheesed off, narked.

2   It is useful to help a woman describe her angry feelings through the use of phrases and sentences. Suggesting that she completes the sentence 'I was so angry that I . . . ' can be helpful. For example:

I was so angry that I . . .
– felt like slamming the door in his face
– wanted to hit her
– could have exploded
– went over the top
– lost my temper.

Awareness of situations and people that make her angry

This is an important step in dealing with angry feelings as it allows anticipation of and preparation for potentially difficult situations in the future. It involves examination of situations and people in the past and present that have made a woman angry. This will inevitably include the sexual abuse, the abuser and other key adults in her childhood.

Validation of angry feelings

An incest survivor must be allowed to see that her angry feelings are valid emotions, and they are often entirely justified, especially when dealing with her childhood experiences. It is also important that she can distinguish between justifiable feelings of anger and those that are an over-reaction to a situation.

Expression of angry feelings

As we have already noted, anger is a very physical emotion. It is often best expressed in a physical way, but safely, so that this expression does not harm the woman, other people or possessions belonging to her or to other people.

Suggestions for expressing anger safely include:

- finding an isolated place in which to scream loudly;
- screaming in a place where the sound is masked by other sounds, e.g., under a railway bridge when a train goes over, on a stormy beach;
- visiting a beach, river or other open space e.g., field where stones can be thrown with force and abandon;
- visiting a beach where pictures can be drawn in the sand and then scrubbed out;
- punching a pillow/cushion;
- ripping up old newspapers or telephone directories.

Expressing anger towards the abuser and other family members

There are two stages here:

1   Identify specifically and in detail the reasons for her anger. For example:

   In relation to the abuser:
   - he did sexual things to her;
   - he caused her problems (specify) in adulthood;
   - he did not take care of or protect her;
   - he had double standards e.g., don't go near strangers, don't do anything with boys (whilst he was also sexually abusing her).
   In relation to her mother:
   - she should have known what she was trying to tell her;
   - she loved the abuser;
   - she protected the abuser rather than her;
   - she made her do too much in the house.

Similar examples could be generated for other family members. A woman may feel that she is not justified in being angry but at this stage, identifying all the possible reasons why she might feel anger is important.

2   Examining ways of expressing anger include:

   - Methods outlined in the previous section.
   - Writing letters to the abuser or other adults and not sending them. This leaves her free to write whatever she wants in the knowledge that it will

not be seen. The woman does not have to be reasonable, literate or polite in her letter. There will be no response or retaliation to what she writes. Letter-writing is particularly useful if the person has died, or if the incest survivor has lost contact with them.

- A letter could be sent to the person. This is a more difficult letter to write and the incest survivor may need help and support to write what she wants to say.
- Empty chair technique (see Section T).
- Role-play. This is a useful technique for expressing anger. It can be done in a one-to-one situation with the helper taking one role and the survivor taking the other, or in a group setting with two group members or a facilitator and the survivor, taking the roles. (see Section O).

The survivor may wish to role-play herself or another family member, and she should be encouraged to do both if possible. Again, the helper should assist her in her choice of words, responses, tone of voice. The role-play situation also allows her to examine the responses of the other person and her feelings about them.

Confrontation

This requires considerable preparation and use of the techniques described earlier, so that the woman is clear about what she wants to say, can predict the responses of the other person, and how she might react to those responses. Confrontation does not always go according to plan, and can leave the survivor more confused and upset than before. Only if she is determined to confront should she be encouraged to do so, as the responses from the abuser or others can compound her problems e.g., the abuse is denied, its effects minimized, or the survivor is blamed for allowing the abuse to happen.

If she is determined to confront, the following guidelines are useful:

- decide in advance what she will say;
- make her statements specific and straightforward. For example, 'I am very angry because you sexually abused me as a child' is better than 'I am angry with you because of what you did to me';
- consider the other person's responses. For example 'You've made it all up';
- consider how she might respond. For example 'No I did not make it up. I know you abused me. I can remember the details. For example, I can remember the time when you . . . ' (give specific details, time, age, place and what was done);
- consider whether she wants to ask any questions of the person. For example:

To her mother, 'Did you know that he was having sex with me?'
To the abuser, 'What made you abuse me?'

Again careful preparation of how she might ask these questions is important:

- consider how she might deal with her emotions e.g., fear, anger, distress. Ask her what she will do if she gets too frightened/upset/angry to say what she wants to;
- look at alternatives to confronting the person verbally, e.g., writing a letter, telephoning;
- consider what support she needs from the helper or from others before, during and after the confrontation;
- visiting the grave of the abuser/mother/other family member. Here, the woman visits the grave of the person and voices her feelings towards them in that setting. She should do this with the support of others as it can release feelings that may be overwhelming;
- expressing anger physically. This can be very constructive. The woman should be taken to a safe room/place where she can imagine the presence of the abuser/mother/or other family member. She is then encouraged to act out her anger physically. This might be by punching, kicking or screaming at some object e.g., cushion, punch-bag or by throwing objects.

Example: Members of an incest survivors' group went down to a beach. They were encouraged to draw pictures in the sand of their abusers, and then to scrub them out with force. It was suggested that they might get stones and boulders and throw them at a disused break-water (imagining that the post of the break-water represented the people they were angry with). They were encouraged to scream and shout with anger at the waves.

3   Remember that anger may have to be expressed many times before the survivor feels that it is manageable. Letting go of the anger can be both a relief and an extremely exhausting process, but in the end it is a necessary and justifiable part of the work with incest survivors. As one incest survivor said: 'He messed my life up. I have suffered enough because of what he did. Why shouldn't I be angry? I've every right to be.'

F.   Dealing with Anxiety and Fear

Most incest survivors have experienced significant problems with feelings of anxiety and fear. Some may have been prescribed tranquillisers to deal with these problems, and tranquilliser dependency can produce its own difficulties.

Awareness and recognition of feelings

Anxiety develops into a problem in a variety of ways:

- it may have become a habit, and the woman reacts to many situations with anxiety;
- after experiencing unpleasant anxiety feelings, the woman may become very sensitive to any slight physical sign of anxiety. This leads to fear of the symptoms themselves;
- if anxiety has been experienced once in a situation (e.g., in a crowded shop, or social situation), the woman is likely to feel anxious in similar situations;
- if anxiety has been experienced in a particular situation, the woman is likely to anticipate similar situations with anxiety.

Anxiety is, however, a normal emotion experienced by everyone at various times in their lives.

Awareness and recognition of anxiety: Anxiety affects an individual in three main ways (Wyness, 1985):

1   Physical signs: Some of the more common physical signs of anxiety are shown in Figure 9.1.

Figure 9.1:   Some Common Physical Signs of Anxiety

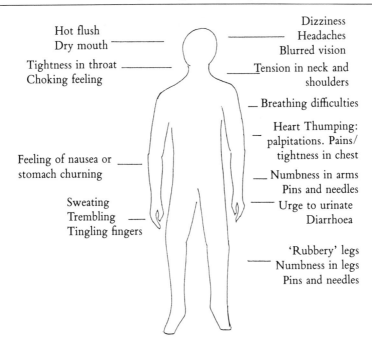

Anxiety also manifests itself in the following ways:

- irritability, quick-temper or easily upset;
- sleeping difficulties;
- fatigue and exhaustion;
- loss of interest, motivation and confidence;
- unreal feelings;
- heightened sensitivity to noise;
- absent-mindedness, forgetfulness and inability to concentrate;
- indecision;
- restlessness;
- clumsiness.

The incest survivor needs to recognise and become aware of these signs of anxiety as this is the first step in beginning to deal with them.

2   Effects on behaviour: If an incest survivor is anxious it is likely that she will be one of the following:

- over-active, rushing from task to task, rarely achieving anything satisfactorily;
- under-active and unable to motivate herself;
- showing signs of avoiding situations in which she fears becoming anxious;
- avoiding situations which she learnt to be frightened of as a child when she was abused.

3   Effects on an individual's thinking processes: Anxious thinking tends to be distorted or biased. The anxious person will interpret events and situations in such a way as to increase her anxiety. A full description of negative thinking patterns in anxiety is to be found in Section J.

Awareness of situations and people that produce anxiety

As a child, the incest survivor may have developed anxiety in a number of situations and towards certain people as a result of the abuse. Common childhood-related situations are:

- being in the presence of men;
- being in places/houses/other situations that remind her of the environment in which the abuse took place;
- situations with authority figures (especially teachers, social workers or police);
- confined spaces which induce feelings of being trapped;
- sexual situations.

These should be distinguished from situations that might cause anyone to feel anxious (e.g., job interviews, driving lessons, starting a new job, having a baby, going into hospital).

Dealing with physical signs of anxiety

Bodily tension and physical signs of anxiety can be reduced through the use of relaxation techniques and deep breathing.

Deep breathing: Deep breathing exercises involves taking two or three slow deep breaths in the following way:

> Breath in very slowly
> Hold the breath for 5–10 seconds
> Breathe out very slowly
> Repeat twice more, then resume normal breathing

This can be particularly useful when actually in an anxiety-provoking situation.

Relaxation exercises: There are a number of different relaxation exercises that can be taught. Relaxation techniques should be practised until the incest survivor feels comfortable with the exercises. The method known as autogenic relaxation is particularly useful for the following resons:

> – it does not take long to do (5–6 minutes) and therefore can be easily and regularly practised;
> – it induces pleasant sensations of heaviness and warmth.

A version of this exercise is described below. It can be recorded by a helper onto a cassette, so that an incest survivor can replay it in a comfortable environment.

The exercise can be taught as a whole or in sections, gradually building up to doing the whole exercise. Suggestions for doing this are given in Table 9.4.

The woman should first be instructed to loosen tight clothing, remove contact lenses and shoes, and to go to the toilet (relaxation is impossible with a full bladder). She should choose a comfortable but well-supporting chair. Although these exercises can be done lying on a bed, a chair is preferable because it means that the woman can use the exercises in situations outside her home e.g., in a friend's house, on public transport, at work or in other situations where she can sit down.

She should be sitting in the following position:

> – feet flat on the floor (or on a footrest if she is not very tall);
> – back firmly against the back of the chair;
> – lower arms resting on thighs;

– hands relaxed;
– fingers loosely resting on thighs;
– head down, chin resting on chest;
– eyes closed (optional). If left open, she should look straight ahead at a point on the floor.

Speaking in a slow, even and calm voice the helper says,

> First of all, I want you to try and forget about any worrying thoughts, and just listen to my voice.
>
> ......PAUSE......

ARMS

> Just think about your arms. I want you to allow them to become heavy, gradually feeling the weight of your arms pulling down from your shoulders. Allow them to become quite heavy.
>
> ......PAUSE......
>
> Keep thinking about your arms. Allow them to become quite heavy. (Repeat as necessary).
>
> ......PAUSE......
>
> At the same time, I want you to allow your arms to become warm. Imagine sitting beside a warm fire. Feel the warmth of that fire on your arms. Allow your arms to become quite heavy and warm.
>
> ......PAUSE......
>
> Keep thinking about your arms. Feel them getting warmer and heavier.
>
> Perhaps you are beginning to be aware that you are feeling a little less tense. Keep allowing your arms to get warmer and heavier.
>
> (This can be repeated several times).
>
> ......PAUSE......

LEGS

> Now, keeping your arms warm and heavy, I want you to think about your legs. I want you to gradually allow your legs to get heavier and heavier. Feel the chair and floor supporting them. (Repeat as necessary).
>
> ......PAUSE......
>
> Just as with your arms, I now want you to imagine that fire again, and allow your legs to become warm. Feel the warmth of the fire on your legs.

Gradually you feel that your legs are getting heavier and warmer.

. . . . . . PAUSE . . . . . .

Keep thinking about your arms and legs. They are gradually getting heavier and warmer, and you are beginning to feel more comfortable and relaxed.

. . . . . . PAUSE . . . . . .

BREATHING

Now, keeping your arms and legs heavy and warm, I want you to think about your breathing.

I want you to allow your breathing to settle into a steady rhythm. Not too fast and not too slow. Not too deep and not too shallow. Let your breathing move along at a steady gentle rhythm.

Gradually you will notice that you are becoming more and more relaxed.

I want you to keep thinking of your breathing, and begin to enjoy the feeling of being more relaxed.

. . . . . . PAUSE . . . . . .

LOWER BODY

Now the last thing I want you to do is to think about the lower part of your body — your tummy — imagine having a hot water bottle on that part of your body, and feel the warmth from the hot water bottle spread across your body.

Allow your tummy to become quite warm and comfortable.

. . . . . . PAUSE . . . . . .

Keep thinking about the hot water bottle — feel the warmth.

. . . . . . PAUSE . . . . . .

Now I want you to keep thinking all these parts of your body in turn — your arms, legs, breathing and tummy. Allow your arms and legs to become heavy and warm, your breathing steady and your tummy warm and comfortable. Notice that you are gradually becoming more and more relaxed.

Now I want you to stay like this for a few minutes until I speak again.

Relaxation period. Up to five minutes silence from the helper.

Now I want you very slowly to open your eyes, put your head up, and gradually
stretch yourself — your arms and legs. Just sit quietly for a few minutes. Don't
get up and rush about. Just allow yourself the full benefit of being relaxed.

If the woman finds any part of the exercise very anxiety-provoking, she should be instructed to leave that section out. However, the breathing stage should ALWAYS be
done.

These exercises can be modified for use in a variety of situations:

1　In public situations, e.g., social situations, public transport, they can be done
without the dropping of the head or closing of the eyes. They can be done for
a very short time, or just by doing the easiest part of the exercises, e.g., just
the arms or breathing;

2　To help encourage sleep. In this case, the woman is told to lie comfortably in
bed and do the exercises, but then to allow herself to drift into sleep than
move on to the final 'waking-up' stage.

Table 9.4:　A Programme for Learning Relaxation

	Instructions	*Length of relaxation period*
Week 1	Arms	2–3 minutes
Week 2	Arms Legs	3–4 minutes
Week 3	Arms Legs Breathing	3–4 minutes
Week 4	Arms Legs Breathing	4–5 minutes
Week 5	Repeat of Week 4 Lower part of body	5 minutes

Dealing with avoidance

Avoiding difficult or anxiety-provoking situations is common, but in the long run
adds to a woman's problems. The most effective way of dealing with avoidance is for
the woman to gradually confront the situations she avoids, so that she learns:

– to cope with her anxious feelings;
– some helpful techniques for coping with difficult situations.

Method

1　Situations which the woman finds difficult should be listed and ranked from
most to least difficult.

2 A situation from the least difficult end of the list should be chosen to work on.

3 A specific task should be set: e.g., to visit a large shop for half an hour, tolerate being in the presence of a male colleague for ten minutes.

4 Feelings of anxiety should be expected.

5 She should stay in the situation for the agreed amount of time in spite of mounting anxiety. These feelings should be tolerated.

6 The task should be repeated several times until the woman learns she can cope with her anxiety.

If the avoidance of situations has reached an unmanageable level, the incest survivor may require to be referred to the local clinical psychology department for specific help with phobic problems. Examples are when she shows symptoms of:

– agoraphobic problems — where she cannot tolerate being out of her home;
– specific phobias — e.g., dogs, birds, insects, that prevent her from leading a normal life;
– phobias about medical procedures — e.g., injections, giving blood, visits to the dentist that prevent her from receiving appropriate treatment.

Dealing with anxious thoughts

Anxious thinking can become established as a habit, and a woman will find herself worrying continually about many things. The first step in dealing with this is to begin to recognise the anxious thoughts as they come to mind (see Section J).

Some examples are:

– I won't be able to cope;
– Everyone will think I'm stupid;
– If I go out, something is bound to go wrong;
– Everything I do is a disaster;
– I'll never be any good at this;
– I shouldn't be worried about it.

The next step is to substitute more reasonable objective thoughts. For example:

Anxious thoughts	*Reasonable thoughts*
I shouldn't be worried about going to the hospital	It is normal to be anxious about a situation like this
I'll make a fool of myself at work if I feel like this	I often feel like this at work but nothing bad happens. I am jumping to conclusions

195

Learning to be more realistic in her thinking about situations takes practice and time. Anxiety is a normal feeling, but if it is too severe, it can be disruptive and prevent rational decision-making. It also affects self-confidence and self-esteem and it often occurs in conjunction with symptoms of depression.

Panic attacks

Panic attacks are different from high levels of anxiety, and consist of a combination of palpitations, shortness of breath, dizziness, nausea, shaking and sweating. A panic attack is a very physical and unpleasant experience. The body is responding as if it had a very severe fright, but without any obvious reason. A panic attack often occurs during a period of stress e.g., when a woman experiences difficulties at home or work, a bereavement or illness, but for incest survivors, it can also occur in response to memories of the sexual abuse. For some survivors, panic attacks can be confused with flashbacks.

A first panic attack is an alarming experience and, as a result, most people misconstrue its nature and consequences. Women can perceive a panic attack as a very dangerous event, leading to serious physical harm, loss of control, mental breakdown or making a fool of oneself in some way. The extreme fear reported in panic attacks is a result not only of the unpleasant physical sensations but also of the way the woman interprets the attack as extremely dangerous. As a result, she becomes extremely sensitive to and fearful of any physical signs reminiscent of the panic attack. This leads to a triggering of further fright responses, and a fear of panic attacks rapidly becomes established. Not surprisingly, this leads to the development of strategies to avoid or escape from any situation where she thinks that panic attacks might occur.

Dealing with panic attacks: The following information about panic attacks should be explained:

- the panic attack is the body's fright response being triggered in the absence of any danger. This makes it difficult to understand;
- the body has a normal response to threat or danger. It can be useful if a woman has experienced a normal fright response to a real threat or danger e.g., being followed at night, a near-miss situation in a car, to explore her physical responses on those occasions;
- it does not last for long;
- it will not do any serious harm or have serious consequences.

This information is often sufficient to relieve a woman's anxiety about panic attacks. However, if her thinking about the panic attacks has led her to avoid situations, she may need to test out the possibility that nothing worse than the panic will occur. This can be achieved by risking going into these situations, allowing a panic attack to occur and discovering that:

- the panic attack itself is the worst that will happen;
- nothing more serious will happen;
- the panic attack passes after some time.

During this stage she will need support to help her take the risk of going into the avoided situations. Gradually, as she becomes less afraid of the panic attacks, they will occur less often (McFadyen, 1989).

G. Dealing with Loss

Any woman who has been sexually abused as a child has suffered many losses. She may be unaware of her losses, or of her need to grieve for them. However, unexpressed or unresolved grief causes problems and leaves the woman emotionally chained to her past. As Bass and Davis (1988) explain to incest survivors:

> Buried grief poisons, limiting your capacity for joy, for spontaneity, for life. An essential part of healing from traumatic experiences is to express and share your feelings . . . To release these painful feelings and to move forward in your life, it is necessary, paradoxically, to go back and to relive the experiences you had as a child — to grieve, this time with the support of a caring person and with the support of your adult self.

There are a number of stages in dealing with loss.

Awareness of loss

The first stage is for the survivor to become aware of the losses that have resulted from the experience of being abused.

Losses in childhood: These are numerous and include loss of innocence, the ability to enjoy and to play, loss of normal peer relationships, loss of safety and protection, of educational opportunities (because of difficulty in concentrating), of normal relationships within the family. The extent of the losses will vary from woman to woman, but each one should be explored in detail.

Losses in adulthood: Again there are many losses including loss of normal sexuality, loss of relationships, freedom, enjoyment, family relationships, friendships, the ability to sleep and to relax, peace of mind and trust.

Loss of normal relationships: Where the abuser, mother or other important person has died, an incest survivor may express the loss of her chance to have a normal relationship with that person or to confront them about issues from her childhood.

The experience of grief

Grief can be experienced in many ways, through emotional reactions, thoughts and behaviour patterns. It is often experienced physically. Table 9.5 outlines the normal reactions to loss.

Table 9.5: Normal Reactions to Loss

Emotional reactions	*Physical Sensations*
Numbness	Anxiety symptoms
Shock	Hollowness in stomach
Sadness	Tightness in Chest/Throat
Anger	Oversensitivity to noise
Guilt/self-reproach	Sensations of unreality
Loneliness	Breathlessness
Apathy	Muscular weakness
Helplessness	Lack of energy
Relief	Loss of appetite
Yearning/pining	Loss of sleep
Emptiness	Dry mouth
Freedom	Panic attacks
	Weight gain/loss

Mental processes	*Behaviour*
Disbelief	Dreams/Nightmares
Denial	Avoiding reminders of loss
Confusion	Searching behaviour
Poor concentration	*Calling out
Loss of memory	Sighing
Preoccupation with thoughts of loss	Restlessness
*Sense of presence of lost person	Over- or under-activity
*Visual/auditory hallucinations	Crying
of lost person	*Carrying reminders of lost
Repetitive thoughts about the	person
events of the loss	Treasuring objects relating to loss
Absent-mindedness	*Refusing to disturb possessions
	of lost person
	*Behaviour like lost person
	e.g. in mannerisms, habits
	Social withdrawal

* Particularly common in situations where there is loss of a person e.g., through death, divorce or separation.

The tasks of grieving

Worden (1983) outlines four tasks of mourning that are useful in determining the process of resolving grief. We have modified his ideas for incest survivors. The tasks are:

- to accept the reality of the loss;
- to experience the pain of grief;
- to adapt to life, bearing in mind the significance of the loss. For example, an incest survivor might have to adjust to the fact that she can never have a normal relationship with the abuser, and therefore learn to stop searching for the hoped-for opportunity to make her relationship with him perfect. In the case of loss of a person (through death, separation or divorce), the task is to adapt to the environment in which the person is missing;
- to withdraw the emotional energy bound up in the loss and to free it for use elsewhere. For example, when an incest survivor is very bitter about the loss of positive childhood experiences, much of her emotional energy is taken up with this bitterness. Once she has worked through the loss, that energy is gradually released for use in other areas of her life.

Coming to terms with loss

This process is similar whatever the loss — whether it be through traumatic experiences, sexual abuse, death, separation or normal life experiences e.g., loss of job, moving house, leaving home. A helper should help:

The woman to become aware of the reality of her loss: This involves detailed exploration of the causes and effects of the loss. This process reduces the denial and minimization of loss. For example, an incest survivor might want to explore the loss of normal childhood experiences of play. Areas to discuss might include:

- what opportunities for play did she have?
- how were they spoiled?
- what effect has her lack of play opportunities had on her as an adult e.g., playing with her children, knowing how to enjoy herself, allowing herself to have fun, missed learning opportunities, not feeling normal or worthwhile.
- what effect has her lack of play opportunities had on her as an adult e.g., playing with her children, knowing how to enjoy herself, allowing herself to have fun, missed learning opportunities, not feeling normal or worthwhile.

In the case of the loss of a person through death, the areas to discuss might include:

- how, when and where the death occurred (including any illness of the person)

- how did she find out about it?
- the days between the death and the funeral;
- the funeral and any other family rituals;
- her relationship with the dead person.

Help the woman identify and express her feelings: This usually occurs in conjunction with a growing awareness of the reality of the loss. Coming to terms with loss is a painful process, and this stage is often highly charged with mixed and confusing emotions. Common reactions include unaccountable periods of crying and sadness, anxiety, rage, anger and guilt. The woman may need to test out her guilty feelings to see if they are rational. She should be encouraged to release these emotions, even if it means spending many hours crying. Crying with a sympathetic friend, partner or helper can bring great relief, particularly if support and comfort are available. Incest survivors often feel that once they start crying, they will never stop, but through crying they release pent-up feelings that have been suppressed. Eventually the crying stops.

Provide time to grieve: This is important, as coming to terms with loss is a gradual process, and incest survivors find it very hard to justify to themselves that they are entitled to time for grieving over events and losses that occurred many years before.

Helping the woman to adapt to the loss: When the loss is of a person through death or separation, it is necessary to examine the various roles which that person played in the woman's life, both as an adult and a child. It is useful to ask her the following questions:

- What will you miss about that person?
- What will you not miss about that person?

Where the person has fulfilled roles in her adult life, she may have to learn new skills or make new arrangements to fill the gap. For example, the loss of a partner may leave her with decisions that she has never had to make before. In the case of losses relating to her childhood, she may have to learn skills and to re-experience childhood activities in order to compensate for the missing parts of her childhood (see Section K).

Normal grief behaviour and reactions should be noted: The woman needs to understand normal reactions during the grieving process. It is useful to help her understand that other incest survivors go through similar periods of grief. This can be achieved by encouraging her to read personal accounts by other survivors, or to join an incest survivors' group.

Help the woman to withdraw her emotional energy from the loss: This involves acceptance that she cannot change what happened to her, and that she may have to leave behind her many of her hopes and aspirations for better relationships within her family. As Gil (1983) suggests, she may have to say good-bye to the parents she never had.

This is a gradual process and can only be achieved successfully once she has experienced the reality and the pain of the loss. Usually, incest survivors find that they move gradually from an intense phase of reliving their childhood to a point when they begin to live for the present and future. The process of grieving can be extremely emotional and the helper may find that she/he needs more support when taking an incest survivor through a particularly intense phase of grief.

H. Sexuality

This is a central issue for many incest survivors and it requires great sensitivity on the part of the helper.

Identification of key issues

For each incest survivor, the issues concerning sexuality will vary and are dependent on her particular circumstances, her family and the nature of the sexual abuse. However, some common problems emerge:

Poor self image: This relates to the generally low levels of self-esteem in the incest survivor, and results from the conflicting messages she received as a child about herself, her body and being female. The following areas should be explored with the woman:

Her perception of herself as female: This will be influenced by:

- her perception of other significant females (mother, aunts, grandmothers, sisters, teachers) in her life;
- the messages she received from the abuser about being female;
- her beliefs about the attitudes towards women's roles in her family and in society generally;
- her perception of her own sex-role within the family and in other areas of her life;
- her feelings about her body, especially as a result of being sexually abused.

Body image: An incest survivor's image of her body is very important. She may see it as unattractive, dirty, ugly or sexual. She may respond to this poor body image in a number of ways:

- she may hide her body with excessive weight, clothes or hairstyles;

- she may neglect her physical appearance and personal hygiene;
- she may harm her body with drugs and alcohol;
- she may frequently injure herself deliberately (e.g., with cutting, burning);
- she may neglect her health and general nutrition;
- she may wish to subject her body to excessive tattoos, or plastic surgery.

Sex education

This involves close examination of childhood and adult perceptions of sexuality. The following areas should be discussed:

Childhood knowledge: knowledge and attitudes about sexual behaviour and physical aspects of being female, the attitudes of key family members, especially her mother and the abuser should be explored. The main issues are:

- the onset of menstruation;
- physical development at puberty;
- sexual behaviour;
- conception, pregnancy and childbirth;
- sexually transmitted disease;
- misconceptions about sexual behaviour as a result of the abuse;
- attitudes in the family towards sexual behaviour;
- attitudes in the family to reports of child sexual abuse in the media.

Through discussion of all of these issues, it is possible to assess the woman's childhood knowledge and attitudes towards sexual behaviour and physical development. It is essential to check how much of her lack of knowledge and misconceptions have continued into adulthood.

Physical arousal during the sexual abuse: This is a very sensitive area and should be tackled very carefully. Discussion might include some of the following:

- Did she experience any physical sensations/arousal during the abuse?
- If so, when, how and to what degree?
- What were her beliefs about these sensations?
- What was the abuser's knowledge, use of language and attitude towards this arousal?
- When did she discover that this physical arousal was the same as that experienced by adult women during sexual activity?

Her adult knowledge and attitudes about physical aspects of being female and sexual relationships: The following should be examined in detail:

- any new knowledge about menstruation, conception, pregnancy, childbirth gained since she became an adult;
- her current understanding of sex, sexual relationships and male and female sexual responses;
- her sexual history during adolescence and adulthood, especially in relation to any further misconceptions about sex;
- cultural and religious influences on her sexuality.

Rules within her family about sexuality: All families have rules surrounding sexuality. In families where sexual abuse has occurred these rules have been broken. It is useful to highlight this conflict through exploration of the rules within the incest survivor's family. The discussion should cover:

- privacy in relation to sexual matters within the family;
- locking the bathroom door during bathing and toileting;
- nudity;
- who broke these rules, and with what result;
- displays of physical affection between family members;
- any other physical contact between family members;
- knowledge of sexual behaviour between the parents;
- any adolescent sexual behaviour;
- parental reactions to sexual behaviour or nudity on television or in films.

Effects of sexual abuse on sexual functioning: the following areas should be addressed:

1 Disclosure of the details of sexual abuse (see Chapter 6).
2 The nature and extent of problems in the woman's adult sexual relationships. Issues to be covered are:
   - occurrence of flashbacks or perceptual disturbances (see Chapter 2);
   - do flashbacks/perceptual disturbances occur at particular times during sexual activity, e.g., if a partner touches her in a certain way, if she becomes sexually aroused, if a male partner attempts penetration of her vagina with his penis;
   - symptoms of anxiety, panic or pain during sexual activity, how and when these occur and with what effect on her sexual behaviour;
   - 'freezing' during sexual activity, how and when it occurs and with what effect on the sexual activity;
   - level of interest in participating in sexual activity;
   - level of arousal and occurrence of orgasm during sexual activity.

Male sexual partner: The following areas should be explored if possible:

- Does he resemble the abuser in any way, physically or in his attitudes?

- Is he coercive during sexual activity?
- Is he violent during sexual activity or violent in order to gain her participation in sex?
- What is his general attitude about sex?
- What is his attitude towards women generally and the survivor in particular?
- What is his knowledge about and attitude towards the sexual abuse?

Relationship between the sexual abuse and the incest survivor's sexual difficulties:

- Do her difficulties match the details of the abuse in any way?
- Is the attitude and behaviour of her sexual partner similar to that of the abuser in any way?

Discussion of the woman's previous sexual relationships, both as an adolescent and adult.

Discussion, where relevant, of the woman's sexual preferences or orientation: Some incest survivors form lesbian relationships for example, whilst others have a great fear of being a lesbian.

The outcome of discussions in all these areas should determine the next steps in dealing with difficulties surrounding the woman's sexuality.

Dealing with self-image

This is associated with the building of self-esteem and self-confidence. In this section we will consider the issues relating to sexuality.

Perception of herself as female: The incest survivor needs to learn more positive attitudes towards herself as a woman, and towards women in general. This may be helped by having a female helper who acts as a positive role-model of a woman. If she joins an incest survivors' group she may find herself making friends with other women for the first time in her life. This enables her to value the friendship of women and to value her femininity (see Chapter 8).

Body image: An incest survivor should gradually be encouraged to develop positive attitudes towards herself physically. For example:

- she can learn about the positive effects of regular exercise, and a balanced diet. The effects of drugs and alcohol on her body can also be explored;
- if necessary, she should be encouraged to take care of herself physically, in terms of hygiene;
- where appropriate, she could be encouraged to seek advice about losing weight

- she should be encouraged to become familiar with her body, (including the genital area) by examining herself in front of or with a mirror;
- she should become familiar with her body by touch. This should include the genital area.

The helper may have to give a more direct lead in this area of work, as women generally and incest survivors in particular, have great difficulty in discussing issues of such personal concern.

Appearance: Incest survivors frequently neglect their appearance. For many women this is closely associated with their wish to be seen as asexual or unfeminine. Other incest survivors dress to attract attention from men — attention which they do not always welcome. Challenging a woman's assumptions about her appearance is important. Her beliefs about her appearance are likely to have arisen as the result of:

- direct comments from the abuser;
- demands or her assumptions of demands made by a partner in adulthood to wear or avoid certain clothes;
- her feelings of depression;
- her feelings of shame.

It is necessary to help the woman understand:

- the effect of her dress and appearance to others;
- that she can choose to wear different styles and colours of clothes because she wants to, rather than because of what someone thinks she ought to do;
- wearing make-up and jewellery can be fun, if that is what she wants to do;
- changing hairstyle, and wearing new or different clothes can increase self-confidence;
- clothes should be comfortable. Incest survivors often feel that they have no right to feel comfortable, and as a result wear clothes that emphasise discomfort.

Any positive changes in clothes and appearance should be noted by the helper as they are usually an indication of increasing self-esteem.

Self-image exercise for use in groups: Each person is asked to lie on a piece of paper six feet long. Another group member draws her outline, and each woman then fills in the outline to show how she perceives herself. When everyone has finished they look at all the drawings, and write on a small piece of paper their immediate thoughts on each person's drawing. These are lodged under each drawing and the artist reclaims them at the end of the exercise. The group members then decide if they want to share the comments, or to talk about their drawings.

This exercise is a useful way of identifying positive aspects of self-image as well as the more negative areas.

Dealing with Sex Education

Information: The woman can be provided with clear information on:

- the sexual functioning of male and female bodies;
- normal male and female development at puberty;
- menstruation, menopause and pre-menstrual tension;
- male and female sexual responses;
- sexual relationships and sexual orientation;
- if relevant, conception, childbirth and contraception.

Menstrual and pre-menstrual problems: For incest survivors with these difficulties, they should be given information about PMT and menstrual problems. The next step is to keep a menstrual chart over several months to determine the extent of these problems (Lever *et al.*, 1980).

If the menstrual chart indicates a clear pattern of problems related to her periods, medical advice should be sought. In severe cases, the woman's family doctor may refer her to a gynaecologist at the local hospital. The helper may have to prepare the woman for these consultations by anticipating likely questions she may be asked, and by considering with her her attitudes and feelings towards having an internal examination.

Menopausal problems: Where relevant, information should be supplied about the menopause and related problems. Again, medical help may need to be sought to deal with more severe symptoms of the menopause e.g., frequent flushing, mood swings and depression.

Dealing with the issue of sexual/physical arousal during the sexual abuse

Some incest survivors disclose that they experienced sensations which they now identify as pleasurable sexual feelings during the sexual abuse. Such disclosures are extremely distressing for an incest survivor, as she can feel that her body's physical reactions may have indicated some enjoyment of the abuse. This is one of the most difficult areas of work with an incest survivor. She may have beliefs about sexual arousal and orgasm that compound her negative feelings about her involvement in the sexual abuse. For example, she may believe that she had control over her arousal level. There are often misconceptions about sexual arousal that need to be clarified.

An incest survivor should be helped to understand that:

- a child can have physical arousal and orgasmic feelings if she is stimulated in the genital area;

- orgasm and physical arousal are simply the body's automatic responses to being touched or stimulated in certain ways;
- she had no control over this arousal;
- it was the abuser who created her arousal through his inappropriate stimulation or sexual behaviour;
- she was not guilty of causing her arousal;
- she may have enjoyed physical sensations of arousal but that does not make her a guilty party in the abuse. It was the adult who created the situation that produced these sensations;
- she may have enjoyed the close physical contact with the adult, of which the sensations of arousal were part;
- she may have sought out the sexual situations in order to get the feelings of arousal. However, it was still the adult's responsibility for creating these situations.

Dealing with sexual problems

Sexual difficulties are common among incest survivors. They may be limited to the occurrence of flashbacks and disturbing visual images during sexual activity, may amount to significant problems with sexual motivation, interest and arousal, or an inability to cope with any sexual activity with a male partner that involves penetration. It is important that a woman's sexual partner is involved in discussing sexual problems at this stage as he or she may be very confused, upset or angry by her reaction to any sexual approaches. The following areas are important:

1   Opening communication about any sexual difficulties with her partner is a crucial first step. This must, however, involve disclosures about the sexual abuse. The woman may need to be prepared for these disclosures by discussing with her helper:
    - how she will tell her partner;
    - what reactions she might expect from the partner;
    - whether the helper should be involved, and if so, how.
2   Flashbacks should be dealt with by encouraging disclosure of the details of the memory. The woman's partner may feel able to hear these disclosures but very often she prefers not to tell him/her the details for fear of hurting or angering him/her.
3   Visual images of the abuser can be very disturbing during sexual activity. These can be dealt with by using imagery techniques (described in Section B).
4   Extreme physical tension during sexual activity can be significantly reduced through the use of relaxation exercises or massage (see Section F).

5   The woman should be encouraged to become familiar with her body and with her sexual response through self-stimulation. This could involve:
- sex education;
- using a mirror to examine herself genitally;
- becoming familiar with her genital area through touch;
- gradual discovery of the process of sexual arousal through masturbation or stimulation by a partner.

6   Beyond these general processes, referral can be sought to a trained sex therapist. They can usually be found in clinical psychology departments and sometimes within marriage guidance organizations. The helper should encourage and facilitate this referral if she/he does not feel qualified to deal with detailed sexual counselling.

    Sexual counselling or therapy is a complex process that examines issues of sexuality and relationships and helps the woman and her partner to learn new ways of relating to each other sexually. It involves learning to give and receive pleasurable sexual touches and pleasure and asserting themselves sexually before moving on to a fuller sexual relationship.

7   Incest survivors should be encouraged to read about women's sexuality. Useful books for doing this are listed in Appendix 2.

Dealing with the sexuality and the sexual development of her children

An incest survivor's experiences of being abused as a child may leave her confused and concerned about the physical and sexual development of her own children.

    The main concerns are:

- difficulties with showing physical affection towards her child or towards other children (key fears are 'Will I be seen as an abuser?', or 'Am I abusing my child?');
- establishing safe boundaries for the child with regard to nakedness, personal hygiene, and toilet-training;
- sex education of her children;
- how to teach her child to reject unwanted physical or sexual advances;
- dealing with puberty;
- dealing with an adolescent child who is having a sexual relationship;
- contraception.

These issues should be discussed openly with the helper so that the incest survivor can begin to come to some resolution of any problem areas. The following are general guidelines for tackling the issues:

1   The age of the child is critical. For example, a small child of four or five should be supervised during bath-time whereas an older child should be allowed to bath him or herself with minimal supervision or help.

2   The child's intellectual capacity is important both in determining how much supervision is necessary and how much information is given. For example, a handicapped child may have limited understanding of the dangers of her/his environment and may not be able to understand much about basic sex education. Similarly, a young child does not have sufficient awareness to understand sexual relationships.

3   A child's questions should be answered when they are asked, but the information should be geared to the age and intellectual capacity of the child. For example, a four year old might point to her mother's breasts and ask 'What are they for?' A simple response, explaining that they are for feeding a baby is sufficient explanation.

4   A child should be given sex education in a straightforward and direct way, involving discussion, reading of age-appropriate books and permission to attend sex education classes at school (Rayner, 1979).

5   Using Michelle Elliott's (1988) book *Keeping Safe* to help children learn about difficult or dangerous situations. This is a practical guide to help parents and other adults help children and young people develop skills which can protect them in difficult or dangerous situations.

Children should be informed in a matter-of-fact way about:

– how their bodies work;
– safe and unsafe touches to their bodies;
– what to do if someone abuses them sexually;
– how to deal with a number of difficult situations (e.g., by playing 'what if x happens' games);
– good and bad secrets.

J.   Challenging Negative Thoughts

Incest survivors often have poor self-esteem, feel extremely guilty and show signs of anxiety and depression when they first come for help. These difficulties are characterized by a considerable number of negative thoughts about themselves, about their past and their present situation. In this section we consider some common negative thoughts and point out how incest survivors might learn to think more objectively and positively about themselves (Jehu *et al.*, 1986).

Types of negative thoughts

The following are common types of negative thinking:

'All or nothing' thinking: This is the tendency to see everything in very black or white terms, e.g., a complete failure or complete success. It is unrealistic, and is likely to lead to poor self-esteem, as one mistake will lead a woman to categorize herself as a total failure. Some examples are:

  – I am a weak person because I can't forget about the abuse;
  – I cannot do anything right (after making one mistake);
  – I am a bad person because I forgot to telephone my mother.

Overgeneralisation: This involves drawing a general rule from a single event. Some examples are:

  – I had a bad day last week. I am never going to get over this;
  – I will never be able to cope with anything because I can't handle the memories of my past;
  – I was turned down for this job. I will never be able to get a job.

Mislabelling: The woman creates a totally negative view of herself because of a single weakness or mistake. For example:

  – I am a useless person because I can't remember what happened to me during the abuse.

Mental filtering: This involves picking out a negative detail in any situation and dwelling on it to the exclusion of everything else. The whole situation becomes negative. Positive aspects are filtered out. For example:

  – I was late for my appointment, and that made the rest of the day bad.

Disqualifying the positive: Another way of filtering out positive aspects is to discount them in some way. For example:

  – I only got the job because they knew me;
  – I had a good day on Tuesday but it won't last.

Jumping to conclusions: This involves drawing a negative conclusion that is not really justified by the facts of the situation. For example:

  – I must have been to blame for the abuse because they took me away from home when I told about it;

- It was my fault that he abused me because he didn't force me;
- I must have enjoyed it because I didn't stop it;
- I got angry with my daughter today so I am a bad mother.

Catastrophizing: This involves exaggerating the importance of mistakes or deficiencies and leads to poor self-esteem. For example:

- I wil never be able to lead a normal life because the damage from the abuse is permanent;
- I made a mistake. I can never show my face there again.

Minimizing: This is the tendency to play down good points or qualities. For example:

- I can sew, but so can most women;
- My kids have turned out all right — but it's in spite of me rather than because of me.

Emotional reasoning: Feelings are taken to be evidence that something is true or real. For example:

- I feel guilty about the abuse, therefore I am guilty.

'Should' statements: These involve beliefs that a woman should behave in ways that are unrealistic and overdemanding. For example:

- I should be able to forget about the abuse. It was in the past;
- I should be able to handle these flashbacks by myself;
- I should do everything for my children.

Personalization: This involves assuming total responsibility for an event that was not her fault. For example:

- It was my fault that he abused me for so long because I didn't tell anyone;
- It was my fault that my sister was abused.

Methods for challenging negative thoughts

1   The woman is asked to recall thoughts about herself, situations and events. This can be done by:

- asking her to keep a record of any thoughts that have made her distressed;
- role-playing a recent or past event so that she can identify any thoughts that provoked distress;

- describing a distressing event in detail so that the negative thoughts can be clarified.
2 She should be helped to identify negative thoughts and distorted beliefs.
3 The final stage is to explore more realistic and accurate thoughts and beliefs. This may be done through:
- the provision of accurate information in order to correct any misconceptions. For example, the helper might provide information about children's reactions to sexual abuse, the long-term effects into adulthood, incidence of sexual abuse as well as information about sexual and physical functioning;
- reviewing the evidence for her belief. This involves examining both her conclusion and any alternative there might be. For example:

Her belief	*Alternative explanation*
I was to blame because I was removed from home.	I was removed for my protection.
I am guilty of the abuse.	The abuser, and not the child, did the abusing. I was only a child who did not know about sexual matters at that age.

- Gaining a more objective perspective on her beliefs. This can be achieved by:
  - asking the woman to assess how others would see the particular situation e.g., if other people knew she had been sexually abused, who would they say was responsible?
  - suggesting she reads the accounts of other incest survivors in order to check out if her experiences as a child and adult match theirs;
  - encouraging her to join a group for incest survivors so that she can recognise that her problems are common amongst women who were abused as children;
  - helping her to gain a wider perspective on events. For example, her perspective might lead her to believe just because she had a bad day she will never get over the abuse. Putting this into a wider context, she can be enabled to see that:
  - she has had lots of good days;
  - everyone has bad days (even the helper!);
  - by coming to talk about the abuse, she has taken the first steps in coming to terms with it;
  - it is a difficult and painful process and she may get worse before she gets better.

- helping the woman to correct her tendency to assume responsibility for the abuse. This can involve examining:
- factors that were beyond her control (e.g., the abuser's wishes, intentions and behaviour);
- responsibilities of others who were involved, especially the abuser.

K. Reclaiming Childhood

For many incest survivors there is an acute sense that they have lost important aspects of childhood. For example, play, sporting activities, friendship and schooling may all have been impaired. This has implications not only for a woman herself, with feelings of loss, but it can also affect her role as a parent. She may have difficulties in playing with her own children, or she may be over-protective of them. One way of enabling a woman to become less anxious is to help her to reclaim her childhood; this can involve doing art work, children's play, religious ceremonies, or re-creating special occasions.

Artwork

Artwork can be used to take women back to different stages in their childhood, and to express their feelings visually. The following exercises are useful.

1   The woman is given paper and crayons and told, 'Imagine that you are eighteen months old, and you have just found paper and crayons under the kitchen table. Play and draw with the crayons and paper.'

This exercise can be repeated for older age groups and the pictures are then compared.

2   The woman is given paper and crayons and told, 'You have just had your first day at school. Before you go home, your teacher asks you to draw a picture about your first day. Try to draw it now.'

This exercise will evoke feelings and memories of an important day in every child's life. Women will be able to draw through a child's eye rather than as an adult.

3   The woman can be taken to a beach, park or into the country and allowed to draw or paint whatever she wants. The freedom of expression gained from dabbling and dipping into paints can be both exhilarating and healing.

Play

Recreating child's play can be fun, but can evoke strong feelings and memories of exclusion, prohibition or spoiling by parents. Some suggestions are given below:

- a doll's/teddy's tea party, complete with food, drink and games;
- pillow fights;
- playing with sand, play-doh or plasticine;
- bicycle rides;
- sports e.g., swimming, horse-riding, hill walking, football;
- collecting stones, shells, twigs or leaves on a walk;
- listening to a children's fairy or adventure story read aloud by the helper;
- building with Lego or other construction toys;
- experimenting in a group with musical instruments;
- singing nursery rhymes or local children's songs;
- playing children's board games.

Religious ceremonies

Many incest survivors have an added confusion resulting from being brought up in a home where religion was practised. This is likely to provide a source of considerable conflict for a woman because:

- she was aware that the abuser went to church and yet at home forced sexual activities on her;
- any religious activities or ceremonies she was involved in were spoiled, desecrated or made unclean by the sexual abuse;
- she may have felt it wrong to take part in special religious events when she felt dirty, unworthy or hypocritical;
- she may have been told that she must forgive people who wronged her.

As a result, key religious occasions, e.g., baptism, confirmation, first communion may have left her feeling guilty and confused. It can be very important for an incest survivor to be given an opportunity to repeat these special religious occasions. The help and cooperation of key members of a relevant religious organization, congregation or church should be sought by the helper and the woman herself.

Many incest survivors return to the roots of their religion later in life, enabling them to gain comfort, hope and a sense of reparation. Forgiveness often remains a difficult problem. A useful book for use with incest survivors with a Christian background is *Child Sexual Abuse* by Hancock and Mains (1987).

Special occasions

Birthdays, anniversaries or other family celebrations may have been absent or spoiled in an incest survivor's childhood. They can be re-created in adulthood, and can be marked by:

- a party, complete with cake, candles and party food;
- party games;
- small gifts to mark 'missed' birthdays and other occasions;
- dressing in clothes reserved for special occasions;
- a visit to a hairdresser, gym, sauna or beauty parlour.

L.   Building Trust in a Group

Chapters 7 and 8 emphasized the importance of trust for incest survivors. Here we describe some exercises which can be used to explore and confirm the issue of trust in a group setting.

Trust exercises

Trust in a circle. Everyone stands in a close circle, and each group member takes it in turn to go into the centre. The woman in the centre stands straight, legs stiff, feet together, eyes closed and body relaxed. She begins to rock herself backwards, forwards and from side to side. She allows others in the group to gently catch her, and to pass her back and forth around the circle. If the woman really allows herself to trust other group members, she will be able to allow her body to go limp as she is passed from person to person. If she feels tense or cannot relax, she should try to be aware of what makes her feel like this. When everyone has had their turn in the centre of the circle, group members can discuss any feelings they had during the exercise.

Blind walk. This exercise is useful for:

- highlighting feelings about trusting another person to care for you;
- experiencing dependency.

The group divides into pairs, one person is blindfolded and the other leads her on a walk around the room or outside. The 'leader' directs the blindfolded woman to a variety of objects, fabrics and textures, allowing her to explore each one for as long as she wishes. After about ten minutes the pairs swop roles. When everyone has completed their 'blind walk', the feelings they had doing the exercise can be discussed in the pairs and then in the whole group.

Group facilitators should be aware that the experience of being blindfolded can be frightening for some women. If this is the case the woman should be reassured and given the opportunity to 'lead' the pair in the first instance.

A range of group trust exercises can be found in:

In Our Own Hands by Ernst and Goodison (1985) and *Gamesters Handbook* by Brandes and Phillips (1977).

Sentence completion exercise

The group facilitator writes the words:

'Trusting someone means . . . '

on a large sheet of paper. Group members complete the sentence, and the facilitator writes down each contribution. When the list is complete, it is discussed in the whole group. The exercise can be repeated with a range of sentences relating to trust e.g., 'I find it difficult to trust people because . . . '; 'The things which help me to trust people are . . . '

Confirming progress already made

In a group setting it is helpful to take stock of progress already made and to plan for the future. This is especially so in relation to the issue of trust. Some methods for doing this, together with exercises for 'taking stock' generally are given below.

1 Ask group members to write down three items in response to the sentence 'Things which have enabled me to trust women in this group are . . . '
2 Group members write a note to every other woman in the group starting
   'Dear —
      I value you as a member of this group because . . .
      from —'
   The notes are distributed, read privately and, if anyone wishes, elaborated further or discussed.
3 Each woman is asked to write down what being in the group has meant to her. These thoughts are shared in the whole group with the facilitator writing them all down on a poster and helping group members to discuss them.
4 If group members identified their personal aims when they joined the group, these can be reassessed regularly.

Shared activities

This is especially relevant to a group setting where members can plan and undertake a range of shared activities. These might include:

- an evening walk;
- a shared meal with food prepared by group members;
- a meal in a pub or restaurant;
- a visit to a swimming pool or other sports centre;
- a residential weekend in the country, planned in advance over a number of weeks;
- a visit to a funfair;
- an evening at the cinema, concert or theatre.

M. Building Self-esteem

From the beginning of any work with an incest survivor the process of building self-esteem and challenging feelings, behaviour and thoughts that lead to a sense of worthlessness, self-doubt and self-hate, are central.

Negative self-image

The abused child grows up with many messages about herself that do not encourage the growth of a positive adult self-image. For example:

- she may have been told directly or indirectly that the abuse was her fault;
- because of the abuse she felt powerless and alone;
- she felt dirty and unloveable;
- she may have been told that she was no good at anything;
- she felt ashamed and guilty because of the sexual abuse.

As an adult, she may live a life which is based on these ideas about herself. A list of negative statements made by incest survivors is provided by Bass and Davis (1988). It emphasises this lack of self-worth (see Table 9.6).

It is important that an incest survivor learns to discover the origin of her negative statements. Many are based on childhood experiences. By learning where these negative messages come from, she can discover that their origins do not lie within herself, but in how others made her feel.

Dealing with her feelings of guilt about her childhood is a vital stage in improving self-esteem (see section D). Once an incest survivor no longer feels guilty for the abuse, she begins to free herself from the negative image she has built of herself. She is then able to evaluate the negative thoughts she has about herself, as well as linking them to her past.

Example: Jane phoned her friend to invite her to supper when her friend refused abruptly, without giving a reason. Jane automatically assumed that her friend did not like her any more, that she had not invited her properly and that she didn't deserve to have any friends anyway. When she re-assessed the situation she recognized that her friend would only have refused if she really couldn't come, and that she might have refused more politely. Jane could also see that a refusal to supper did not mean the end of the friendship, even though she was hurt by it. The incident helped her to make links with her childhood by remembering her father's negative comments about her ability to keep friends.

Table 9.6: The Origins of Negative Self-Images (Adapted from Bass and Davis, 1988)

Negative statement	*Possible origins from childhood*
I hate myself	– I allowed myself to be abused – I did not stop the abuse – I got aroused during the abuse – because the abuser told me it was my fault
I don't deserve it	– pleasant things have never happened to me – I feel so bad about the abuse, – I don't deserve to have anything nice – I don't deserve to be loved because I am guilty
I can't do it	– as a child I could never do anything right – I was always in trouble – my family and teachers told me I was no good (I couldn't concentrate on anything because of the abuse).
It has to be perfect	– the abuser/mother always found fault with everything I did – good was never good enough in my family
Whatever I do, it'll never be enough	– I'll never make up for all the lack of achievements in my childhood – even when I'd done everything he asked, there was always more abuse
It's not worth trying	– I tried to stop him (abuser) but he wouldn't stop – I'll never be normal after that abuse – I feel like damaged goods because of the abuse
What I want doesn't count	– as a child, my wishes and needs were ignored – I was just there to clean up round them – I wanted him to stop but he didn't
I have no right to feel good	– he made me believe that the abuse was my fault
I deserve to feel bad	– he told me that he abused me because I was bad

Building self-esteem is also about learning that she does not have to continue giving herself negative messages. She must learn, therefore, to assess situations in a different way. She might begin by asking herself the following questions when she starts to think badly about herself:

- what started off this train of thought?
- what was I doing when it started?
  - e.g. – was I remembering something that had happened recently?
    - was I remembering something from my childhood?
    - what had happened just before I started thinking like this?
- did something frighten, upset or anger me?
- how would other people (e.g., a friend) react in this situation?
- is there any reason for me to feel particularly vulnerable just now?
- is this a familiar feeling?
- does it remind me of something I learned as a child?

Building self-esteem

Discovering the positive: An incest survivor often finds it extremely difficult to say anything good about herself. Helpers can encourage her to construct a list of all the things she does well. To begin with, she may find it hard to write anything down because she undervalues good qualities, assuming that everyone has them.

1 Helpers can point out the qualities *they* have identified. For example:
   - she manages her household finances even though money is short;
   - she always attends her appointments on time;
   - she is a good listener;
   - she is good at making fruit cakes;
   - she can swim;
   - she is good at her job;
   - she knits her own jumpers.
2 A woman can be helped to construct a list of things she likes about herself. For example:
   - she is concerned about other people;
   - she has a good sense of humour;
   - she can make people feel at ease;
   - she likes helping at the Youth Club;
   - she likes her determination.
3 Help her construct a list of things that other people like about her. This will inevitably involve the helper (or friends and family if she is brave enough to ask) giving her feedback. The list may surprise the woman as she is probably not used to asking for or hearing anything positive about herself.

Positive feedback: Most survivors find it difficult to hear anything positive about themselves, and tend to disqualify compliments and praise with, 'But it was only because of . . .'

- luck;
- someone else feeling sorry for me;
- someone trying to be nice/cheer me up;
- I just happened to be there.

Example: Working as a nurse, Anne was presented with an award naming her as the Best Nurse of the Year. She disqualified the achievement by saying that she only received the award because she was well known to the people who nominated her and other, better nurses were not!

The helper should make use of opportunities to give the woman positive feedback, no matter how small the change or achievement in her life. Positive feedback should:

1   Be very specific. For example it is better to say:
    'You did well when you managed to go to your friend's house last Tuesday' rather than 'You are getting better at visiting your friend'. It is more difficult for the woman to disqualify specific and accurate feedback.
2   Contain a statement about the positive nature of the achievement. Examples are:
    - You did well when . . .
    - A few months ago you wouldn't have been able to do . . . and now you are able to . . .
    - It is good to see you doing . . .
    - You seem pleased that you managed to . . .
    It is better to avoid statements which indicate the helper's approval. For example, 'I am please that . . . ', 'I am delighted that . . .' The woman may then begin to do things just to gain the helper's approval rather than for her own reasons.
3   Do not exaggerate the achievement by repeatedly drawing attention to it e.g., 'I've told you so many times that . . .'

At times when she feels low about herself, it is useful for the incest survivor to find a task that she can do, rather than allowing herself to sink further into self-criticism. For example, she might do a routine task (clean a room, make a meal), read a book/magazine, listen to music she enjoys, phone a friend.

Buying herself something: this may seem a trivial task, but incest survivors have great difficulty in treating themselves to anything that is not strictly necessary. They prefer to buy things for other people. Encouraging a woman to buy herself something small because she wants to is an important first step in helping her see that she is a person of worth and has a right to treat herself. Examples of small things she might buy are: bath oil, earrings, a book, magazine, some favourite food, talc, bunch of flowers, colourful socks, a cassette.

Learning to be assertive: improvements in self-esteem come with learning to be assertive. This is discussed in full in Section N and involves enabling a woman to learn that she has rights to her feelings and opinions and to make decisions and choices in her life. It will also help her to establish limits on the demands of others, and enable her to begin to say 'no' when she wants to.

N. Assertiveness

Many women feel that they lack control over different aspects of their lives, rarely do they feel confident, and they worry about criticism, comparison and security. For incest survivors these feelings can be magnified and they feel powerless in most areas of their lives. Some of the most frequently mentioned examples of lack of assertiveness include:

- not being able to speak to a stranger at the door;
- difficulties with authority figures e.g., teachers, social workers, medical staff;
- difficulties with saying 'no' to friends, family, colleagues, partners and children;
- reluctance to challenge someone who is taking advantage of their goodwill, whether in a home or work situation;
- not being able to challenge a waiter, shop assistant or colleague on issues relating to poor service or standards of work;
- not feeling able to express sexual wishes or preferences;
- allowing others to make decision on her behalf, even when they are not in her best interests.

There are a number of tasks which can be carried out with incest survivors, either in a group or one-to-one setting. These can help women to identify areas where they feel particularly unassertive, where they would like to change their behaviour and to reflect on changes made.

Ann Dickson's books *A Woman in Your Own Right* (1982) and *The Mirror Within: a new look at sexuality* (1985) are excellent handbooks to use when exploring the issue of assertiveness in everyday life and in personal relationships.

Defining assertiveness

An important first step is to understand the meaning of assertiveness. An effective method is to ask women to complete the sentences:

> 'Assertiveness to me means . . .'
> and
> 'Assertiveness is not . . .'

When the lists are complete they can be discussed and any areas of disagreement noted. Once assertiveness has been defined, women can begin to identify situations in which they would like to be more assertive.

Exercises for a group setting. Each woman takes ten to fifteen minutes to make a list of situations in which she would like to be more assertive. These can cover any area or aspect of her life. When the list is complete the women are asked to note beside each situation the way in which they respond to it now. A helpful distinction is:

passive	– opting out of making decisions
	– avoiding taking responsibility for making choices in life
	– avoiding confrontation
	– negative outlook on life
aggressive	– attacking when under threat
	– provokes defensiveness in others
	– engenders resentment from others
	– makes other people feel guilty
indirectly	– manipulates situations to avoid rejection
assertive	– respect for self and others
	– accepts own and others positive and negative qualities
	– believes she is responsible for what happens to her
	– recognises own needs and asks for them to be met openly
	– does not depend on approval of others

Each woman looks at her list again, and tries to arrange or rank the situations in order of difficulty, putting the number one opposite the situation in which they think they would find it easiest to be assertive. They work their way through all the situations until they have identified the one they would find the most difficult to change.

Identifying basic rights

The idea that a woman has basic human rights often comes as a surprise to an incest survivor. Ann Dickson (1982) has produced a set of eleven basic rights which she suggests are fairly straightforward but which can enable women to start changing their behaviour. She suggests that women should remember these basic rights when they feel unsure of themselves. The eleven basic rights are reproduced in Table 9.7.

Women can be asked to consider the rights and to decide how easily they can accept or reject them. They will probably discover that it is easier to accept the rights on an intellectual level than to understand their significance in their lives.

Table 9.7:   The Basic Rights

---

1. I have the right to state my own needs and set my own priorities as a person, independent of any roles that I may assume in my life.

2. I have the right to be treated with respect as an intelligent, capable and equal human being.

3. I have the right to express my feelings.

4. I have the right to express my opinions and values.

5. I have the right to say 'no' or 'yes' for myself.

6. I have the right to make mistakes.

7. I have the right to change my mind.

8. I have the right to say 'I don't understand' and to ask for more information.

9. I have the right to ask for what I want.

10. I have the right to decline responsibility for other people's problems.

11. I have the right to deal with others without being dependent on them for approval.

From Dickson (1982)

Assertiveness and Aggression

It is important to distinguish between assertiveness and aggression. This can be done by defining aggressive behaviour, and comparing it to the earlier list of assertiveness. Alternatively examples of situations can be given, and women asked to identify an aggressive response and an assertive response. For example:

> You have been sold an item which has shrunk on its first wash. When you return it, the sales assistant suggests that it has shrunk because you have not followed the washing instructions.
>
> How would you respond aggressively?
> e.g., Tell her that if she's not careful she might lose her job.
>
> How would you respond assertively?
> e.g., Point out that you followed the instructions carefully and suggest any other explanation.

A relative telephones to say that she will call to see you at a time which is inconvenient. How could you respond in an assertive way?

e.g., Tell her that the time she suggests is inconvenient and ask her to make another time to call.

What would be an aggressive response?

e.g., 'You always ring when it's not convenient — don't you ever listen to what I say?'

Your manager at work has criticised an aspect of your work. You feel that her criticism is unjustified.

What would be an assertive response?

e.g., 'I wonder if we could look a bit more closely at the reasons for your criticism. I feel that they might be a little unjustified!'

What would be an aggressive response?

e.g., 'There's nothing wrong with me — it must be your problem.'

Role-play

Role-playing situations in which a woman feels that she would like to be more assertive can be a very helpful method. Role-play is described in some detail later in this chapter. Role-play situations might include:

- saying 'no' to repeated requests from family, friends or colleagues;
- telling someone that they have hurt your feelings;
- asking for time off at work;
- making an appointment with a schoolteacher to discuss a child's progress or school report;
- telling a partner what your sexual needs are;
- returning shoddy goods to a shop;
- refusing to engage in conversation with doorstep sales personnel;
- refusing to baby-sit for a friend/relative.

Sexuality and assertiveness

Assertiveness in relation to sexual situations is often one of the most difficult areas for women, especially if they have experienced sexual abuse as a child. There are some basic rights which merit consideration and discussion. They are outlined in Table 9.8.

Each of the basic rights should be discussed in relation to a woman's experience of her sexuality and what she would like for herself. One of the likely issues to emerge from this discussion is the way in which women are taught what they 'ought' or

Table 9.8:   Basic rights in relation to sexual situations

1. I have the right to whatever information I want about sexuality.

2. I have the right to choose my own sexuality.

3. I have the right to ask for what I want sexually.

4. I have the right to sexual pleasure.

5. I have the right to choose my sexual pleasure.

6. I have the right to change my mind.

7. I have the right to say no.

'should' enjoy sexually. Ann Dickson (1985) suggests an exercise which challenges these assumptions.

Exercise

Compiling an erotic guide

Ask an incest survivor a list of as many sexual 'turn-ons' and 'turn-offs' that she can think of. Each person's list will be unique and will reflect past experience and the conditions which each woman finds most congenial for sexual enjoyment. If the list is shared in a group setting, some items may be common to everyone, and often one item is pleasurable to one woman and distasteful to another. The important thing is that each list is unique to its author.

This exercise can lead to a discussion of how to communicate the items on the list to a partner, and ways of achieving greater sexual satisfaction.

Ways of being assertive

Once women begin to examine situations in which they would like to become more assertive, they will be able to examine issues such as:

- making clear and specific requests;
- saying 'no' directly and clearly;
- not automatically conceding their own needs and wants as less important than those of other people;
- recognising feelings of anger, hurt and fear and being able to express them assertively;
- not allowing fear of criticism to dominate behaviour;
- finding ways of approaching difficult topics when communication is difficult or has broken down.

All of these issues can be discussed by looking at specific situations in a woman's life and working out how they could be improved. In addition, women can set themselves tasks in relation to the situations they have identified; an example of the way this can be done is given below.

> *Exercise*
> Working in pairs in a group, or with her helper in a one-to-one setting, a woman completes a sheet which asks her to identify situations which at the moment she feels she does not handle assertively (Figure 9.2).

Figure 9.2:   Handling Situations More Assertively

Think of a situation you don't handle assertively, which you would like to change and fill in the sheet below.

Situation/Action/ Words of other person	My response	My feelings	What I wanted to say	How I would have chosen to handle the situation assertively

The woman picks one situation and discusses it in depth with her partner or helper. They might choose to role-play the situation. This can lead to identifying ways in which the woman can become more assertive. It is important that the woman is also encouraged to try out these new approaches in real-life situations. She will need to review her progress and examine any setbacks she encounters. Setbacks can be discouraging but they often provide useful information on a woman's difficulties with being assertive.

O. Role-Play

Talking and thinking about behaviour is a prelude to changing it. Role-play is a useful method for trying out new ideas and ways of doing things. It can be used for:

- rehearsing what might be said and how to act in a particular situation;
- learning new ways of behaving in situations e.g., being more assertive;
- expressing feelings towards someone e.g., anger with a family member;
- understanding why a woman behaves in a particular way in certain situations.

There are usually at least two roles to be played in a role-play. The incest survivor plays herself, and a second person takes the complementary role e.g., shopkeeper, relative, partner, boss.

Many woman initially express reluctance to try out role-play and they may feel embarrassed or self-conscious at the outset. Once the role-play has got under way, however, the pairs can get 'into role' very quickly. The person taking the complementary role can be a helpful source of insight and feedback on non-verbal behaviour such as tone of voice, posture and eye contact. These may not be readily apparent to the woman herself.

Setting up a role-play: there are a number of helpful guidelines which include:

1 Do the role-play with somone you trust, preferably a friend;
2 Be specific about the subject of the role-play, e.g., rather than saying 'I want to try out being assertive', say 'I want to practise taking back a faulty jumper to a shop';
3 Set the scene if this would be helpful e.g., a shop assistant might stand behind a counter, a boss behind a desk;
4 Do not worry about having dramatic ability. The value of role-play lies in its ability to enable someone to practise a situation over and over again until they are reasonably happy with the way it has been handled;
5 Once a situation can be managed in a role-play, there should be no need to try it out 'for real' immediately. This may take a long time.

The importance of role-play is that it allows someone to see how it fee[l] to be in the situation. Any lessons learnt through the exercise should only [b]e put into practice when the person feels ready.

Example: Hannah wanted to role-play a forthcoming meeting between herself and her daughter's teacher. She had received a complaint that her daughter had not been doing her homework. Hannah was very worried about the meeting. Her daughter had always assured her that her homework was done. The teacher frightened them both. Hannah role-played the meeting with a friend, acknowledging her daughter's problem, but pointing out possible reasons for it.

6   The role-play does not need to last for long. Initially short role-plays a[re] better until the individuals feel comfortable with the method.

P.   Writing

Many women resist writing down their thoughts and ideas simply because they disli[ke] writing. They may think that writing is for other people or are worried about the[ir] spelling, grammar or handwriting. Also, women often find it difficult to find time [to] reflect and put their thoughts on paper. A woman should be encouraged to writ[e] without worrying about spelling, grammar and punctuation. She should be offere[d] the opportunity to share her writing with her helper if that is what she wants to d[o].

Writing down thoughts and feelings has a number of very important function[s].

1   Writing makes things concrete. If a woman has conflicting or contradicto[ry] thoughts, writing them will help to clarify them.

2   Writing can make a woman more aware of her thoughts. It is sometim[es] difficult for her to take note of things she tells herself; saying them out lou[d] helps; writing them down can help even more.

Women should be encouraged to make some time to write. Writing can take the for[m] of a diary or journal, a note of feelings at different stages, lists, positive and negati[ve] emotions or reactions to specific situations, prose or poetry.

Bass and Davis (1988) suggest a variety of writing exercises which are summa[r]ized below:

– Ask the women to write down a list of all the ways in which she is still affecte[d] by the abuse.

– Ask her to write down the ways in which she coped with the abuse as a chil[d].

– Suggest she writes down how she feels she has come to terms with the abu[se] since coming for help. The list should include her achievements and successes [as] well as any difficulties she has encountered.

- Suggest that she tries to talk to 'the child within' herself by writing a letter to her or engaging in a written dialogue with her, writing first as the adult and then as a child responding to the adult.
- Ask her to make a list of all the things she did right today.
- Ask her to write down what she did do this week to make things better for other people? e.g.,
  - prepared a meal;
  - controlled her temper with her partner;
  - listened to a neighbour's troubles;
  - kissed her daughter's knee better after a fall.
- Ask her to write what she has done to begin to take control over her life. e.g.,
  - made a decision;
  - found out about local evening classes;
  - found out about driving lessons;
  - asked a welfare rights worker to check up on her benefits;
  - decided to write a letter to her mother.
- Ask her to write down what she has done to make herself feel better e.g.,
  - had a bubble bath;
  - went for a walk all by herself;
  - went to bed early with a magazine;
  - bought herself something.

Women who have been abused often find it very hard to think of anything they have done well. Writing down accomplishments, however small, helps to confront a woman with the fact that she is not a total failure. If she is to begin to feel that she has some control over her life, she has to start giving herself credit for things well done, although this may not mean that a specific objective has been achieved.

In drawing up these sorts of lists, women should note whether they have added any negative qualifiers to their positive statements. Women often qualify a self-compliment with a criticism or they discount its importance, e.g.,

- 'I'm a good mother — but then anybody could do that.'
- 'I'm a fairly placid person — except when I get depressed I get really mean to my family.'

They should be encouraged to cross out any qualifying statements.

Letter writing

Incest survivors can find it very helpful to write letters to significant people from their childhood. It allows them to express feelings which they might never have the courage to express verbally. Letters also have the major advantage of no comeback if a woman chooses not to post or deliver them.

Letter writing is useful when:

- a woman feels that she will not have the confidence to confront someone (usually the abuser or her mother) about the sexual abuse;
- the abuser or other significant adult is dead or she is unable to make contact with them.

Writing a letter can be a very cathartic experience. Feelings and emotions are often easier and more clearly expressed in writing. Women can say what they want to in stages, without feeling the need to modify or camouflage any strong feelings. They need never post the letter, and may choose to destroy it or put it somewhere safe when they have completed it.

An incest survivor should be encouraged to:

- decide who she wants to write to, and why;
- equip herself with plenty of paper and pens;
- wait until she feels ready to put her thoughts on paper before starting;
- find somewhere she feels comfortabe to write the letter. This might be at home sitting in a crowded cafe or somewhere quiet e.g., an art gallery, library, church or park;
- write the letter in stages or in one sitting.

It may be helpful to start the letter with such words as,

'Dear —
I am writing to you because . . .'

or

'Dear —
This letter is important to me because . . .'

Women who have written letters, especially to an abuser, report that their thoughts flow freely and it is often hard to stop. Once complete, the letter can be shared with helper, group members or whoever the woman chooses. Alternatively, she may wish to destroy it or put it somewhere secure. Letters can be written to:

- abusers;
- mothers;
- siblings;
- other family members;
- adults whom the woman tried to tell about the abuse;
- other significant adults e.g., teachers, youth club leaders, family friends.

If the letter's recipient is still alive, the woman may want to personally deliver or post it. If she/he is dead, the incest survivor might wish to place it on their grave. Alternatively she may suggest that the helper accepts it and destroys it at a later date. The helper should encourage the woman to accept responsibility for the letter and decide how to dispose of it herself.

Diaries and journals

A diary or journal of her work with a helper or in a group might be kept. A woman can use it to write down:

- her expectations of a session or meeting;
- her thoughts on how it has gone;
- good and bad experiences during the sessions;
- new memories;
- connections with her past made during sessions;
- reflections on relationships past and present;
- points to follow up;
- her hopes for the future;

She may wish to keep a diary as her private record, or she can use it as a dialogue with her helper, here she asks for feedback from the helper on what she has written.

Keeping a diary is important for the following reasons:

- it is an important part of a woman's self-expression;
- it can be a significant means of acknowledging the process of change in her life;
- it can help to identify issues which are resolved and those which still recur in her life.

Personal writing

Many incest survivors have turned to poetry and prose to express their feelings. They have produced emotional personal writing when it would have been difficult to express their feelings verbally; Appendix 1 gives examples of poems written by incest survivors. Women should be encouraged to write as much poetry or prose relating to their experiences as they can produce. It can be kept privately, shared with a helper or read aloud in a group and if the helper feels that a particular piece of writing may be useful for other incest survivors, permission must be sought to use it with other women. An incest survivor may be surprised that a piece of her writing could be used in this way, and it may be the first time she has felt that anything positive has come from her childhood experiences.

Using other writers' work

Poetry and prose from incest survivors can be used to:

- reflect on and identify with feelings expressed by other incest survivors;
- encourage women to write down their own feelings;
- stimulate discussion on specific issues identified by other writers.

Helpers should try to have a selection of material to hand, so that women can be given appropriate material. The helper might suggest:

- giving material to a woman to take away and read. They could discuss it at future session;
- reading it aloud together, checking out the impact of any particularly emotional passages;
- sharing a reading of the material in a group and discussing its meaning for individual group members;
- giving women a selection of poetry, prose and autobiographical material which they can read at their leisure. Alternatively, a woman could be directed to specific material at particular stages in her therapeutic work.

Q. Brainstorming

The objective of brainstorming is to generate ideas on any subject or topic in a short space of time. It is also useful for producing material for further discussion. All that is needed for brainstorming is a large sheet of paper and a pen.

1   The helper explains the aim of the brainstorming session and asks for ideas on the topic which is written down on the paper or board: e.g.
    - ideas for a group to pursue;
    - ways I could have stopped my abuser;
    - people I could have told about the abuse.
2   There are some basic rules for the helper in a brainstorming session:
    - write down every idea, without comment, and discard nothing;
    - suspend judgement on each idea — they can be discussed individually later;
    - aim for as many ideas as possible — quantity rather than quality;
    - if ideas are slow to come, the helper might put down one or two of their own, but they should wait before doing so.
3   When ideas have stopped flowing, the helper can:
    - go through the list and group the contributions into smaller groups of related ideas;
    - go through the list with a woman or group members pointing to each idea and checking if and how it should be followed up.

Example (taken from a group setting)

Ideas for the group to pursue
Feelings about mothers
Feelings about fathers
Feelings about own children
Feelings about sex
Reading some poems or stories
Playing games
Doing some drawings
Going for a swim together
A night out

R. Word Pictures

Word pictures can be used for:

- saying words which are difficult to say aloud;
- verbalising feelings and thoughts relating to a particular topic;
- acknowledging common feelings and experiences in a group setting.

1   The helper puts a large sheet of paper on the floor or wall. In the centre of the sheet she/he writes the word or phrase which it has been agreed to explore.

Example

2   She asks everyone present to say what they associate with the word or phrase. She writes the words and phrases down, just as they are said.
Example

3   Links between words and phrases can be drawn if they are apparent.
Example

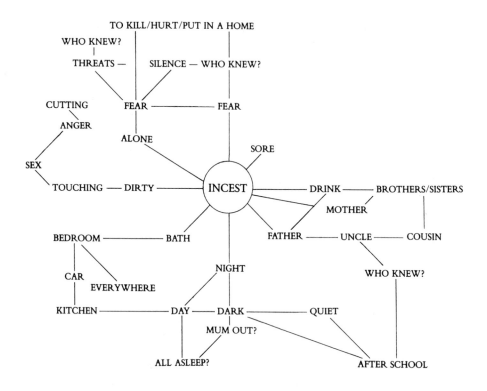

The picture is complete when everyone agrees that there is nothing more they wish to add.

4   Time is allowed for everyone to look at the picture and to ask for explanation or information if they need it. This leads to a general discussion of issues raised.

5   The helper checks how people are feeling and what they have learnt from the exercise.

Topics for a word picture might include:

Sexual abuse is . . .
When I get angry I . . .
Reminders of the past
Feelings about abuser/father/mother/other trusted adults
The thing which frightens me most is . . .
Being a survivor means . . .

The effects of sexual abuse on my life are . . .

The ways I coped when I was young were . . .

Initially participants might feel too inhibited to contribute. Once the picture develops, however, the ice is broken and it becomes easier for people to participate. In a group setting, if one person dominates the construction of a word picture, the facilitator should ensure everyone who wants to contribute, does so. This can be done at intervals during the exercise by asking women directly if they want to add anything.

Sometimes contributions do not directly address the issue or they may be 'safe' thoughts or feelings. The facilitator can help by contributing her/his own ideas, or material changing the emphasis of the input. Finally, participants with poor literacy skills may be inhibited from joining in. The helper can help by repeating each word or phrase and summarizing the picture at regular intervals.

S.   Sentence Completion Exercises

Most relevant in a group setting, sentence completion exercises are useful for:

- getting an immediate response on an issue;
- allowing women to respond individually and then to share their responses;
- focusing thoughts on a specific topic.

1   The helper or group facilitator provides sheets of paper with the beginning of a sentence written on it. These are distributed to group members.

e.g. I find it difficult to trust people because . . .

2   Women take five to ten minutes to complete the sentence, adding as many items as they can think of.

e.g. 'I find it difficult to trust people because . . . '

- I don't expect them to trust me in return;
- I'm afraid they will hurt me;
- I don't usually get to know people well enough to be able to trust them;
- it's better to keep your distance.

Once everyone has completed their individual lists, these can be shared by:

1   members of the group working in pairs;

2   the facilitator asking for one or two contributions from each group member in turn and noting these on a poster. The poster is complete when everyone has exhausted her personal list. Discussion may focus on:

- points of similarity or difference;
- clarification of specific points;
- situations in which women have experienced particular emotions or reactions;

   – situations or conditions which help or hinder women in the area under
     discussion.

A sentence completion exercise can cover almost any topic. Some examples are given
below:

> 'The things which remind me of my past are . . . '
> 'For me, the effects of being sexually abused as a child are . . . '
> 'The feelings I have towards the abuser are . . . '
> 'The feelings I have towards my mother/sisters/brothers etc. are . . . '
> 'The things I like about myself are . . . '
> 'The things I dislike about myself are . . . '
> 'When I get angry I . . . '
> 'When I get angry I would like to be able to . . . '
> 'The things this group avoids talking about are . . . '
> 'The things I find easy to talk about in this group are . . . '
> 'The things I find hard to talk about are . . . '

T. Empty Chair Technique

This technique which is a method derived from Gestalt therapy, can help by preparing
the survivor for an actual confrontation with the abuser or other family member, or if
the person concerned is dead or absent. It can be useful too when the incest survivor
feels it will never be possible to say these things to the person concerned (because of
her fear of their response, fear of violence or denial of the abuse).

   Here an empty chair is placed in the room with the incest survivor. She is told to
imagine that a person she is angry with is sitting in the chair, and cannot say anything
back to her. She is encouraged to be angry with the person — to state the reasons for
her anger and to express the feelings she has in an angry tone of voice. She may need
considerable encouragement to begin, particularly if she is 'talking to' the abuser. She
may be overcome by fear, or embarrassment. She may also get very upset. The helper
can assist by:

   – preparing her for what is to be said;
   – helping her to find the right words;
   – encouraging her to repeat what she has said in an increasingly angry tone. The
     helper may have to say it first in order to let her hear what her words could
     sound like;
   – allowing her to stay with her anger only for as long as *she* can tolerate.

U. Dealing with Other Areas of Difficulty

There are a number of specific problems that are beyond the scope of this book.

Incest survivors with these problems should be encouraged to seek help from appropriate agencies. They include:

Alcohol and drug abuse: These are serious problems that require the guidance of agencies dealing specifically with these problems. There are a number of agencies e.g., Alcoholics Anonymous, Alcohol Advisory and Counselling Services, Drug Abuse projects and professionals working within health and social services with specific expertise in these areas. The woman's G.P. should be able to advise on referral procedures, and it is recommended that helpers have the relevant local information about appropriate sources of help.

Eating disorders (anorexia, bulimia, compulsive over-eating): These are serious problems that require professional help. Some health professionals are trained to deal with these difficulties and referral should be made through a woman's family doctor. Admission to a psychiatric hospital may be required if an eating disorder has reached a life-threatening stage.

Severe suicide attempts: Referral to psychiatric services is appropriate, as the woman may require admission to hospital. The woman's G.P. must be informed so that the referral can be made.

Severe depression: Referral to psychiatric services is appropriate so that admission to hospital can be arranged if necessary. Again the woman's G.P. should be informed so that the appropriate referral can be made.

Significant obsessional problems: Such difficulties e.g., compulsive hand washing, contamination fears, can be dealt with by clinical psychologists and psychiatrists. Sometimes, admission to a psychiatric hospital may be necessary in order to work on the problems.

Tranquillizer dependency: Withdrawal from tranquillizers is a difficult task, and should be done under medical supervision. The woman may require professional help to manage the withdrawal slowly and safely, to deal with the symptoms of withdrawal and any underlying problems that are revealed as the effects of the drugs wear off. Once a woman has begun to break her dependency, she should be informed of any support groups in her area.

Significant marital or relationship problems: Help can be sought from appropriate agencies e.g. marriage guidance agencies (Relate), social work departments, psychiatric and clinical psychology departments which are willing to work with couples. Psychotherapy and other counselling services may also be available.

Problems with children: Children in a family often have difficulties when one or both parents are having problems. Children's difficulties include truanting, school phobia, bed-wetting and soiling, sleep disturbance and eating problems. If an incest survivor's children are experiencing such difficulties, referral to child guidance, child psychiatry or child clinical psychology departments should be encouraged through the woman's G.P. Parenting difficulties may also be dealt with in this way.

10 Training and Support for Work with Incest Survivors

A vital prerequisite to giving help to incest survivors is to explore any issues in the work which are likely to affect the helpers themselves. In Chapter 2 we drew attention to the personal and professional issues which can arise for helpers who are involved in working with incest survivors. Confronting attitudes regarding sexual abuse and sexuality are important, as are examining the issue of responsibility and the relevance of the helper's own life experiences. Training needs will obviously vary from one helper to the next. Some will have already undergone professional training courses, whilst others may have had little preparation for working with incest survivors.

In this chapter, we look at issues which relate to training, supervision and support. These include:

- preparatory work;
- principles of training for work with incest survivors;
- planning a training programme;
- support and supervision;
- making links with other resources.

Training should not be seen as the sole preserve of professional workers. It can range from a one-off discussion for helpers in a voluntary agency, to a detailed programme for helpers from a range of organizations taking place over a number of weeks or months. It can involve two or three people with a similar level of knowledge, all keen to extend the boundaries of their experience or a larger group with different experiences who have come together for a day workshop or longer conference.

The most important qualities of effective training are its ability to:

- meet the needs of its participants;
- extend knowledge and skills;
- challenge assumptions and confirm the existing knowledge base.

Preparatory Work

A minority of helpers are attached to agencies whose main focus is work in the area of sexual violence. For the remainder, they may find that a woman who they have been seeing for some other reason suddenly discloses her history of sexual abuse. It will help if the following aspects are covered before starting to work with incest survivors:

Counselling skills: It is a distinct advantage if the helper can learn basic counselling skills, and if this has not been part of any previous training, helpers should consider taking part in a basic counselling training course. Counselling is an active process that enables the woman to help herself. There are many models of counselling but one that is particularly useful and practical is Egan's three-stage model (1982). His three stages consist of:

- exploration of the individual's problems and feelings from her perspective;
- understanding and gaining new perspectives on her problems;
- action in dealing with them.

The model outlines the skills necessary at each stage and emphasizes the importance of exploring a problem with a woman before moving towards a solution and acting on it. It also involves building a relationship with the client to facilitate this process.

Helpers should examine their attitudes, feelings and beliefs about child sexual abuse. This will certainly involve exploring their attitudes and feelings about relationships between men and women, relationships within families, the concepts of good and evil and sexuality and children. Sarah Nelson's book, *Incest: Fact and Myth* (1987) is very useful in this context.

Helpers should explore their own background for any history of childhood sexual abuse. If a helper discovers that she/he has been abused, and has not resolved these issues, it is not wise to embark on helping other survivors until this has been done.

If they have not been sexually abused, helpers should explore any childhood and adult experiences that come closest to the betrayal, humiliation, sexual violence or violation experienced by a child who has been sexually abused. These experiences might include secrecy in the family, sexual assault or harrassment in adulthood, or situations in which the helper has felt powerless.

Helpers must be willing not only to believe women when they talk about their experiences of sexual abuse but also to accept that some women have experienced sadistic and cruel forms of abuse which challenge the boundaries of human understanding.

Helpers should read personal accounts written by incest survivors in order to de-sensitize themselves to the nature of sexual abuse and its effects on children and adult survivors. It is far better to have had emotional reactions of horror, disgust or sexual arousal to the contents of a book than to an incest survivor as she discloses details of her experiences.

Helpers should be aware that, although the majority of incest survivors are abused by male members of their family, from time to time a woman will disclose sexual abuse by her mother or another female relative. Attitudes and feelings on this issue should be considered by the helper.

Principles of Group Training

There are a number of important principles which underlie any training for working with incest survivors:

1 Trainers should be alert to the needs of course participants. They should be sensitive to the possibility that the training may cause distress. Some participants may have been abused as children; this possibility should be acknowledged at the outset of the training.

2 Training should use a range of learning methods, including large and small discussion groups, examination of personal attitudes and values, videos, and roleplays. It should be enjoyable as well as hard work!

3 Training should provide a theoretical base and practical application of the issues under discussion. This allows the examination of relevant research findings and the challenging of assumptions with evidence.

4 Participants should be actively involved in the training process. In an area of work which relies so much on the expression of feelings, it is vital that helpers learn to express their own feelings and points of view in training. For example, thought should be given before compiling a programme which comprises a series of 'experts' all giving their opinion on selected topics. Whilst there is a place for hearing from people with particular experience or knowledge in this area of work, invited speakers should be chosen for their ability to communicate and to match the level of the audience. 'Experts' who talk in jargon and above the heads of course participants will alienate their audience.

5 Training should encourage participants to explore existing professional roles and responsibilities in relation to sexual abuse. It should, for example, explore the potential for collaborative work between different professional groups and encourage contact between professional and voluntary organizations.

Planning a Training Programme

Careful planning is needed for any programme of training, whether it is a day work-shop, a series of training sessions or a short introductory programme on sexual abuse. There are a number of important factors to bear in mind:

Facilitators for the training: someone who has recent experience of working with incest survivors is preferable. It may be easier for facilitators to work in pairs, provided the members of the pair have worked together before and have confidence in each other.

Venue for the training: the venue should be comfortable, free from interruption and, if possible, located away from 'work' settings.

Sequence for the training: consideration should be given to starting with course partici-pants examining their own sexuality and any issues this raises. It could then look at issues identified by course participants. It may be that the group decides to start with a less 'personal' topic. If this is the case sexuality should still be covered in the training.

Understanding the feelings of an incest survivor: it is essential that helpers gain some under-standing of the feelings of an incest survivor. This can be achieved by using written personal accounts, videos or by the exercises outlined later in this chapter.

Theories about the sexual abuse and abuser: it is important to share what is known about men and women who sexually abuse their children. Training should also explore helpers' feelings in relation to abusers.

The Training Group

Some attention should be paid to membership of the training group. The following should be explored:

Stranger vs familiar group: a group of people who are known to each other may feel more at ease in a training session. They may be more able to challenge each others' assumptions, and to receive and give support if personal material is disclosed. On the other hand, they might find it hard to face each other afterwards if very personal issues emerge.

Single sex vs mixed group: women often feel safer and less inhibited in an all-female group; men should also be given this opportunity of an all-male group. If it is decided to have mixed-sex training, single sex groups should be considered as an option for part of the training.

Size of the group: the group should be small enough to enable everyone to contribute in a safe and supportive environment. We would recommend a maximum group size of twelve, which can be split into smaller groups when appropriate.

Content of Training Sessions

We would recommend that the following areas at least should be covered in training:

- personal childhood experiences of discipline and punishment;
- the helpers' sexuality and its relevance to working with incest survivors;
- the meaning of sexual abuse;
- the long-term effects of sexual abuse;
- feelings about abusers/mothers/other family members;
- personal issues raised in working with incest survivors;
- identification of local and national resources;
- identification of future training needs.

Below we outline some of the ways in which training might deal with these topics.

Starting a training session

It is important to ensure that course participants are put at their ease at the start of a training session, and that their feelings about and expectations of the training are acknowledged — the following exercise can be helpful in this respect.

EXERCISE 1

Ask the whole group to complete each of these two sentences:

My expectations of the training are . . .

and

My feelings about discussing sexual abuse are . . .

The facilitator notes all contributions on a poster, making sure that they are recorded as they are said, without abbreviation or interpretation. When the posters are completed, the facilitator or other group members can ask for explanation or expansion of the items listed in a general discussion.

Personal childhood experiences

Most children know what it is like to feel afraid and we have all experienced being punished. By identifying their experiences of both these situations, helpers can be enabled to identify feelings which were a common part of an incest survivor's childhood. This enables helpers to challenge the assumption that incest survivors are 'different' from other people; what distinguishes their experience of fear and isolation is the intensity and frequency of these feelings. The following exercises are useful in this respect.

EXERCISE 2

Working in pairs, participants are asked to remember and share with their partner how they were disciplined in their childhood. The following questions could be distributed as a guideline:

– What sorts of things were you punished for?
– What form did the punishment take?
– Who was responsible for discipline in the home?
– How did you feel about being disciplined?
– How do you feel now about it?
– How were other members of your family disciplined?

The main themes to emerge are then shared in the whole group. Participants should check with each other about any material which they would prefer not to be shared in the whole group. Facilitators make a poster of the main points.

EXERCISE 3

Participants are divided into two groups. Each group is given large sheets of paper and pens. They are asked to draw a line down the centre of the page, with the words 'discipline' and 'abuse' on either side of the line. They are then asked to note what sort of things they think constitute discipline and what abuse entails. The posters are then shared in the whole group and the main issues to emerge are noted by the facilitator/s. This exercise is useful for examining boundaries between abuse and discipline and for identifying the difficulties in reaching a consensus on the issue.

EXERCISE 4

Ask participants, in pairs, to think of people or situations which made them feel frightened as a child.

Prompts might include:

– How did you feel?

- How did you cope with these feelings?
- Who did you tell about your fears?
- What was their reaction?
- How would you have felt if you hadn't been believed?

In the whole group, facilitators ask for feedback from each pair and make a poster of common feelings, responses and ways of coping. In discussion, facilitators should try to relate these experiences to those of a child who has been sexually abused. In this way, course participants can begin to understand the problems faced by an abused child when she tries to tell about the abuse.

Exploring the helper's own sexuality

Chapter 2 drew attention to the importance of acknowledging personal experiences in working with incest survivors. Nowhere is this more important than in relation to a helper's own sexuality, since much of the therapeutic work with an incest survivor revolves around problems associated with this issue. Ideally, sexuality should be addressed in a day workshop, allowing time for course participants to feel comfortable with one another and with the subject. However it can also be addressed in three or four shorter sessions programmed over a longer period of time. A selection of the following exercises could be used.

EXERCISE 5

On a poster write the words

'Sexuality is . . . '

and ask the group to complete the sentence.

When everyone has made their contribution, follow with a general discussion, noting:

- main areas of agreement and difference;
- importance of seeing sexuality within the context of lifestyles and relationships.

EXERCISE 6

A good exercise for desensitizing participants in relation to their use of sexual language is to ask them, in the whole group, to call out any words which are used to describe any of the following:

- male genitalia
- female genitalia
- sexual intercourse
- homosexuals

– lesbians
– bisexuals

We suggest that no more than four topics are chosen from the list.

When the list is complete the facilitator leads a general discussion which could focus on some of the following issues:

- the meaning and use of words used;
- any feelings of discomfort which participants have about using certain words and the reasons for this;
- words which are used by children and adults and their possible origins.

EXERCISE 7

Working in groups of three, participants are asked to share with one another their memories of being told or of finding out about 'the facts of life'. After about fifteen to twenty minutes, participants return to the larger group, where a general discussion might include:

- childhood knowledge about sexual matters;
- sexual awakening;
- the range of ways in which sexual matters are dealt with in families;
- sexual mores within families and within peer groups, and their influence on subsequent adult behaviour.

Note: this exercise may provoke strong feelings or lead to anxiety among some participants, particularly if a group member has experienced childhood sexual abuse.

In any exploration of sexuality it is important to look at helpers' attitudes and values and to unravel the main influences on them. Exercises 8 and 9 are useful in this respect.

EXERCISE 8

Participants are asked to stand in a group in the centre of the room. Different corners of the room are signposted AGREE / STRONGLY AGREE / DISAGREE / STRONGLY DISAGREE. The facilitator explains that he/she will read out a number of statements, one at a time. On hearing each statement, everyone is asked to move immediately to the signposted part of the room which reflects their response to the statement. When everyone has relocated themselves, the group under each signpost is asked to share with one another the reasons for their response. These are then shared in the whole group in a general discussion before the facilitator calls out the next statement.

Statements which could be used in this exercise include:

- heterosexuality is normal;

- homosexuality is sometimes the result of having a weak father and a domineering mother;
- lesbians do not make good mothers;
- most women sometimes fake orgasms.

This exercise enables helpers to see that attitudes concerning sexuality are often based on a lack of knowledge, social conditioning and unchallenged assumptions.

EXERCISE 9

Large sheets of paper and felt tipped pens are distributed to everyone. Each person is asked to use the paper to draw their sexual development, noting the times, people and events which have been major influences on their development. They are asked to try not to use words in their picture. When they have completed this part of the exercise, they are asked to work in pairs to share and explain their illustrations.

This is followed by a general discussion in the whole group which should note:

- the sort of life events which influenced the development of helpers' own sexuality;
- the way in which individual experiences and events can influence later development;
- how societal, family and peer group pressure can interact in the development of sexuality.

The reality of sexual abuse

There is a general unwillingness to acknowledge what sexual abuse actually entails. A simple and effective way of illustrating the reality for children who have been abused in this way is described in Exercise 10.

EXERCISE 10

Participants are divided into groups of 4–6. Each group is asked to make a list to complete the sentence 'Sexual abuse is . . . '

They are asked to be as specific as possible, avoiding euphemisms or generalizations.

When the lists are complete they are displayed and read out. They are then discussed by the whole group. If they avoid giving specific details, the facilitator could draw attention to the material described in Chapter 1 or to Sgroi's (1982) work, reading out her 'continuum of abuse'. This exercise is a useful way of acknowledging how difficult people find it to come face-to-face with the reality of sexual abuse. It also enables helpers to see how hard it is for incest survivors to say exactly what happened to them.

The effects of sexual abuse

An understanding of the effects of childhood sexual abuse on all aspects of a woman's life is a crucial prerequisite for giving help. Extracts from personal accounts, poetry written by incest survivors and videos of women talking about their experiences provide powerful evidence of the long-term effects of sexual abuse. Helpers should also have some understanding of the possible consequences of sexual abuse at different stages of a woman's life.

EXERCISE 11

Group members are given a short case study of a child's experience of sexual abuse and its effects on her childhood development. They are asked, in small groups, to draw up a list of the potential consequences of the abuse on her sexual and emotional development:

– in adolescence
– in adulthood.

The lists from each group are shared in the large group. They can also be compared with the material outlined in Chapter 3.

EXERCISE 12

The group is asked to brainstorm:

'How children cope with being sexually abused'.

When the list is complete it should reveal the wide variety of ways in which children learn to survive their childhood experiences of sexual abuse. It may also reveal some of their reasons for remaining silent about the abuse.

Facts and myths about sexual abuse

A helpful means of exploring some of the facts and myths about sexual abuse is through the use of a short questionnaire, outlined in Exercise 13.

EXERCISE 13

Participants are asked to work in pairs and complete a short questionnaire with a series of statements which illustrate commonly held assumptions about the nature of sexual abuse. They are asked to say if they think the statements are true or false.

The majority of sexual abusers within the family are men   (TRUE/FALSE)

Sexual abuse usually occurs when girls reach puberty (TRUE/FALSE)

Overcrowding, low intelligence and geographical isolation are all contributory factors in sexual abuse (TRUE/FALSE)

Fathers are often aided and abetted in their incestuous activities by a collusive wife/mother/partner (TRUE/FALSE)

On completion of the exercise, the whole group examines each statement. The facilitator can supply information from the literature e.g., Nelson (1987) and the group might also contribute examples from their own experience.

Knowing local resources

This is an essential part of any training. Information on all the local resources which offer support to incest survivors should be supplied in a handout. Referral methods to all sources of help should also be noted.

Personal accounts

It can be a very powerful experience to hear an incest survivor talking about her childhood experiences with a training group. Obviously the woman must be at a stage of recovery from her experiences that allows her to discuss sexual abuse without undue panic or distress. Videos with incest survivors talking about their past are also very useful in this respect.

Feelings about abusers

It is useful for the training group to address their feelings towards abusers. This can be done by using Exercise 14.

EXERCISE 14

Working in groups of 4–6, participants are asked to complete on a poster the sentence:

'My feelings towards men who sexually abuse their children are . . . '

When each group has made a list, the posters are shared in the whole group.

Personal issues raised

Another important area, which should be addressed at the end of a training session, is the extent to which helpers are aware of the personal issues raised for them in working with incest survivors. Chapter 2 has outlined the main issues, and Exercise 15 can be used as a preliminary exercise in this respect.

EXERCISE 15

The training group is divided into two or more smaller groups. Each group is asked to make a poster of all the personal issues which might be raised for a helper in working with incest survivors. Each poster is read by the other groups and a general discussion in the whole group follows.

Ending a training session

Some of the training exercises which we have outlined may lead to heightened emotions. Group members may be upset, angry, distressed or exhausted by the experience. It is important, therefore, to end each training session by checking how everyone is feeling and what they have learnt from the session.

EXERCISE 16

Everyone takes turn in the group to say what she/he has got from the session and how she/he is feeling now. This gives everyone the chance to express any 'unfinished business' and to end the session giving or receiving support if it is needed. It also enables participants to look ahead to future training sessions by noting issues they would like to raise in further sessions.

Evaluating future training needs

Evaluation and feedback on the training can be made through a short questionnaire or by getting verbal feedback at the end of the session. If a written evaluation is made, group members can be asked to identify topics for future training sessions as outlined in Exercise 17. Another way of getting this information is to display a sheet of paper headed 'Future Training Needs' on the wall throughout the training sessions. Group members are invited to note anything they would like to cover on the sheet, and this is discussed with the whole group at the final session.

A training programme

We have suggested that any programme of training should include issues identified by participants themselves. Below are examples of the structure of a series of day training workshops which allow time for structured input, exercises and small and large group discussions. A programme should be distributed to participants beforehand or displayed on a large poster during the session.

EXERCISE 17

Evaluation

Please complete this short questionnaire before the end of the training course.

1. How useful was the training to you?
   (please circle)
   Not at all useful   Very useful

      1   2   3   4   5

2. What did you like about the training?
3. What did you dislike about the training?
4. What would you have liked more of?
5. Please comment on the training methods.
6. What would you like to cover in future training sessions?
7. Any other comments?

Example 1

DAY WORKSHOP	*Sexuality and sexual abuse*
9.30–10.00	Welcome and introductions
	Exercise 1
10.00–10.30	Our own sexuality (1)
	Exercise 5 or 7
10.30–11.00	Our own sexuality (2)
	Desensitizing exercise
	Exercise 6
11.00–11.30	Coffee
11.30–12.30	Our own sexuality
	Attitudes and values
	Exercise 8
12.30– 1.30	Lunch

Example 1 (Continued)

DAY WORKSHOP   *Sexuality and sexual abuse*

1.30– 3.00	Our own sexuality
	Exercise 9
3.00– 3.30	Coffee
3.30– 4.30	Where do we draw the line?
	Exercise 2 and 4
4.30– 5.00	Evaluation and planning
	Exercise 16 and 17

Example 2

DAY WORKSHOP   *Sexual abuse and its effects*

9.30–10.00	Feelings and expectations
	Exercise 1
10.00–11.00	The meaning of sexual abuse
	Exercise 10
11.00–11.30	Coffee
11.30– 1.00	The effects of sexual abuse
	Exercise 11 and video/personal account
1.00– 2.00	Lunch
2.00– 2.30	Feelings about abusers
	Exercise 13
2.30– 3.30	Personal issues raised
	Exercise 14
3.30– 4.00	Coffee
4.00– 4.30	Evaluation and planning
	Exercises 16 and 17

Support and Supervision for Working With Incest Survivors

There is a need for good support and supervision to be available for anyone who is working, or planning to work with incest survivors. We would define a support person as someone to whom the helper would choose to turn for informal discussion about the work, and for personal reassurance, it could be a colleague, friend or partner. A supervisor, on the other hand, is a colleague, or group of colleagues, who are formally involved in detailed discussions with a helper about the work.

Supervision

The main criteria to be met for good supervision are:

> The supervisor should be someone who is currently involved in helping incest survivors to come to terms with their experiences. Helpers may wish to arrange supervision with someone outside their agency/setting, e.g., facilitators in a small self-help group may arrange supervision from a health or social worker. However, helpers employed by large bureaucratic organizations may experience some difficulty from their managers if they request supervision from outside that setting. This problem might be solved by ensuring confidentiality and stressing inter-professional co-operation.

> Supervision should take place in a safe and supportive climate. Working with incest survivors can raise difficult personal issues and provoke feelings of anger, distress, uncertainty and anxiety in the helper. Creating a climate in which the helper feels safe enough to express these feelings is an important step towards resolving them. It also helps to ensure that concerns and doubts raised by the helper are balanced with recognition by a supervisor of the positive work being done.

> In order for it to be of maximum benefit, supervision should be held on a regular basis (e.g., weekly or fortnightly).

Content of Supervision

Supervision should cover the following areas:

Content and process of work with an incest survivor: detailed feedback on the work should be given by both helper and supervisor. In this way the helper can be encouraged to reflect on what was said or done and to note the successful and problematic aspects of the work. The way in which the work is progressing can also be reviewed at regular intervals. Any parts of a survivor's personal history that are causing difficulties for the helper, in emotional terms or in relation to the helper's personal life should be discussed in supervision.

Help with planning ahead: supervision should be used to anticipate the likely consequences of different courses of actions taken by the helper. This can be easily done by role-playing situations. This can enable the helper to see things from the perspective of the incest survivor and to consider different courses of action.

Discussion of personal issues: if issues raised by an incest survivor evoke painful memories for the helper, these should be addressed in supervision. If a helper remembers being abused as a child she/he should consider giving up the work with incest survivors until her/his own problems have been resolved. This should not, however, be undertaken is supervision but in another therapeutic environment. Supervision might cover how to hand over the work to another helper, without the incest survivor feeling this is like a personal rejection.

Sharing the secret: when an incest survivor discloses new information about her past, the burden of the secret passes to the helper. This is a stressful experience, especially if the disclosure is particularly horrifying. The helper can feel that she/he alone now holds the secrets of the abuse. Supervision then becomes an important place for sharing these secrets whilst maintaining their confidentiality and enabling the helper to maintain objectivity. Sometimes, a helper will find it difficult to wait until the next supervision session to share the disclosures made by an incest survivor. Good support is vital during this period. To share, in confidence, an incest survivor's disclosures is not a further betrayal of trust, it is one means of breaking the silence surrounding childhood sexual abuse.

Difficulties with believing: these should always be raised in supervision as an incest survivor will be hypersensitive to any suggestion that she might not be believed. Clarifying any reasons for doubt on the part of the helper is crucial. These reasons might include:

- disclosure of abuse which is more horrifying than any previous disclosure;
- any doubt that an incest survivor has about the occurrence of an incident. This in turn can influence a helper's ability to believe;
- knowledge that an incest survivor has lied in the past;
- lack of emotional reaction in a survivor, suggesting that nothing really happened.

We know that incest survivors often react unemotionally during disclosures of sexual abuse, and previous untruths do not mean that sexual abuse did not occur. It is essential that the helper believes a woman who says she has been sexually abused; any doubts should be reserved for discussion in supervision.

Preparing for disclosure: during supervision it is sometimes possible to anticipate the likely content of a woman's future disclosures; she may have had nightmares, or express unspecific fears about people, situations or events. The helper may be able to help her to connect these feelings with her early experiences and can be enabled to examine any anticipated disclosures in the safety of a supervision session. Any distressing or strong emotional reactions can then be dealt with before having to hear the disclosure from the survivor herself.

Effects of a survivor's disclosures on a helper: these should be examined in relation to the helper's own life. They may be difficult to discuss, particularly if they affect a sexual relationship. If work with a woman is intruding significantly, the helper must look for ways of letting go, and she/he should not continue to carry a survivor's pain and past into personal relationships. A variety of methods can be used to help. These include:

- a deliberate period of relaxation;
- writing notes or thoughts about the woman;
- discussion of her 'secrets' with a colleague, support person or partner as soon as possible;
- a hot bath/shower;
- taking some vigorous exercise e.g., swimming, jogging.

The 'style' of the helper. This may involve taking a close look at how the helper organizes the meetings with a survivor, and the style and method used in the work. We suggest that work with incest survivors has to be both active and creative. Sitting back with minimal intervention from the helper often allows the woman's passivity to dominate the session and so reduce the pace of the work. Being active means that the helper may sometimes exaggerate her/his facial expression and tone of voice so that an incest survivor begins to learn that talking in a flat monotone with little facial expression does little for communication with others. It may have been a useful way in the past to avoid communicating with others, but she will get more from them if she can learn to communicate differently.

Creativity in work with incest survivors is important. Methods and ideas for achieving a particular goal with an incest survivor should never be disregarded just because they are different from a helper's normal way of working; sometimes, the most unexpected idea causes a breakthrough.

Example: Norah was shown a picture from a newspaper depicting a small unhappy girl. It was contained in a charity advertisement for the N.S.P.C.C. This immediately helped her to recognise how she had felt as a child — unhappy, helpless and small. From that moment on, she stopped blaming herself and rarely expressed any guilty feelings again.

Sharing these ideas in supervision is useful as it can often lead to development of new techniques, or of different methods to use with a particular woman.

Sharing literature and new methods: Supervision provides a good forum for helpers to share and discuss new literature on sexual abuse; it is also useful for discovering new ways of dealing with the issues which women raise.

Questions for supervisors: Supervisors might find it helpful to ask these questions of the helper in supervision:

   – what were your reactions to the situation?
   – what made this situation easy/difficult for you?
   – what issues does it raise in relation to your own childhood?
   – how might your feelings affect the process of helping this incest survivor?

Models for Supervision

Helpers should consider the type of supervision which will be most useful to them and to try to arrange this if it is available. There are three possible alternatives outlined in Table 10.1, together with their advantages and limitations.

Table 10.1:   Models for Supervision: Advantages and Limitations

Model	Advantages	Limitations
One-to-one	Trust established with supervisor	Supervisor may feel wider pressure
	Personal material more easily disclosed	Can't check out how common feelings are
	Confidentiality more easily ensured	
Group (peer group)	Common issues identified	Not enough time for in-depth discussion
	More scope for new ideas and approaches	Less likelihood of helper disclosing personal issues
Group (with a leader)	Approaches from other settings shared	Common ground may be limited
	Supervision may be more structured	Supervision may feel more like training session
		Less time available for individual women's problems

The ideal situation may be a combination of one-to-one and group supervision, the latter occurring less frequently and taking place with a pre-planned agenda.

Support for Working with Incest Survivors

Support can be gained from a variety of people. It can include:

- letting off steam when you get home after a difficult session with incest survivor/s;
- letting friends/partner/colleagues know why you are feeling angry, upset or elated after a session;
- asking for a hug, cup of tea, some advice, or a ready ear after a session.

Making Links with Other Resources

It is easy for helpers who are working with incest survivors to feel isolated and un-supported, unless they are working in a setting where the main focus of work is sexual abuse. In order to give the best resources to incest survivors, it is essential to pool skills, knowledge and resources. Finding just one other person with an interest in this type of work can be the trigger for support, joint training sessions, seminars, or case discussions to share ideas on ways of working. Making links could start by finding out about all the resources available locally for incest survivors. A letter could be sent to clinical psychologists, psychiatrists, social workers, health visitors and others working in the field of mental health and support for women (e.g., Rape Crisis, Women's Aid, hostels for women). The letter might ask about any work undertaken with incest sur-vivors, the support and training available for this work and any interest in joint seminars or training.

This chapter has outlined the main issues concerning training, supervision and support for work with incest survivors. It is our view that no-one should undertake such work without adequate minimum training. A system of support and supervision should also be established otherwise helpers may find themselves feeling confused, doubtful and burnt-out.

11 Conclusions

Coming to terms with the experience of childhood sexual abuse is a long process. Many women are now embarking on that process, and they show great determination and courage in their ability to recover from their childhood experiences. We hope that this book will encourage more incest survivors to seek help and that it will enable helpers in a variety of settings and organizations to feel more confident about working with incest survivors.

It is inevitable that, with new knowledge and ideas, helpers will remember women with whom they have worked in the past. They may wonder if the women were incest survivors, or if they could have helped them in a more positive way. Whilst these thoughts and feelings can be acknowledged, it is also important to look towards the future, to try to ensure that any woman who discloses a history of sexual abuse receives help and support which they find useful.

The process of helping an incest survivor is likely to challenge helpers in a variety of ways. Methods of working may need to be re-assessed and assumptions about the nature of the family and the status of childhood may need to be questioned. As a result of this re-evaluation and a clearer understanding of the issues raised in this book, helpers will hopefully be able to listen to incest survivors in ways which are better able to meet their needs. Many incest survivors will seek help having had a history of contact with psychiatric services. For some, they have been given psychiatric diagnoses on the basis of symptoms which have not been linked to their experience of childhood sexual abuse; such diagnoses are often unhelpful, misleading and they have served to isolate women even further. More recently, however, two psychiatric diagnoses have been identified in relation to a history of sexual abuse: 'post-traumatic stress disorder' and 'multiple personality disorder'. The diagnoses themselves, together with issues they raise, are beyond the scope of this book, but interested readers should refer to Gil (1988) for further information and discussion.

With more incest survivors deciding to seek help and talking about their experiences, some women will consider taking legal action against their abusers, many years after the abuse has stopped. If this happens, helpers may find themselves supporting women through a difficult legal process, with all its attendant publicity and distress.

Knowledge about child sexual abuse and its effects is still hampered by a lack of research in a number of key areas. Firstly, our knowledge about the frequency of child sexual abuse is limited by the lack of large-scale surveys of both men and women. This is particularly so in Britain. Not only is there a need for sensitive research questions and methods, but researchers need to acknowledge that child sexual abuse often remains repressed until an event in the present brings it to the surface. Secondly, more information is needed on abusers — who they are and the reasons they give for sexually abusing children. Thirdly, the views of incest survivors themselves need to be sought and taken into account in a more positive way, in particular, information about women's previous experience of receiving help, how and by whom they would prefer to be helped in the future and which methods they have found most useful, need to be recorded and acted on.

Our final thoughts to anyone helping an incest survivor are:

- try to be creative, and do not disregard any therapeutic methods in the work just because they do not appear in textbooks;
- make sure that good support and supervision is arranged before starting the work, since the work can be both demanding and emotional;
- evaluate the work in the light of the woman's progress, new knowledge and experience;
- encourage women to write about their experiences as part of their recovery and as a means of helping other incest survivors;
- listen to and believe incest survivors. They have a great deal to teach their helpers and society at large about the experience of child sexual abuse;
- always bear in mind how difficult it is for a woman to disclose child sexual abuse. The helper should carefully consider their reactions and responses when a woman talks about her past.

Working alongside women who have experienced childhood sexual abuse is often a rewarding process, which offers hope for the future. Incest survivors are extremely courageous and resourceful women who have been weighed down by the burden of their past and as they start to recover, their burden gets lighter and they can begin to enjoy life — perhaps for the first time. The last words belong to a woman whose recovery is now well under way.

> At last I know I can be clean and whole again. There are times recently when I have been happy. Times when I have had the inner confidence to know I can be happy.

Appendix 1

Poems by Incest Survivors

The poems included in this appendix were all written by incest survivors. They cover a wide range of issues and feelings, and are a powerful testimony of the experience and effects of being sexually abused. They can be used in working with incest survivors or in training helpers for the work.

This poem describes some of the many perceptual disturbances experienced by incest survivors. It is taken from Ellenson (1986).

I still see the evil shadow in the darkness of the night from the bed where
    warmth and safety should have been my given right.
I hear the voice which calls my name or cries out in distress.
I'm terrified of being left alone in helplessness.
For in the blackness — in the night when I am all alone is when I hear the
    footsteps, bumps and breathing in my home.
Even when I sleep I cannot find escape or peace.
Nightmare earthquakes, floods and fires, vicious frightening beasts, threaten
    me or family and chase me out of breath.
And perhaps the worst of all of these are the dreams I dream of death.
Daylight drives the dreams away but not my haunting fear of furtive
    shadows in the halls, of unseen eyes that leer,
of sudden movements captured in the corners of my eyes,
of the evil presence, the unseen touch that chills my soul to ice.
I live in silence with all of these because I fear that maybe
if I told you of these awful things, you would think I'm crazy.

I   is for the isolation we feel
N   is for numbness and nothing feels real
C   is for the cuddles of which there were none
E   is for the emptiness and life's never begun
S   is for the sleepless nights seeming endless in a row
T   is for the tears that we were not allowed to show.

C   is for the comfort, a feeling we never felt
A   is for the anger at the hands we were dealt
U   is for the understanding which never came our way
S   is for the secret and the price we had to pay
E   is for the emotions we felt no right to claim
S   is for the scandal, the suffering and the shame.

P   is for the protection which we never received
A   is for the anguish that we may not be believed
I   is for the identity that we lost along the way
N   is for the nobody who is writing this today.

Put them together. The message is clear.
It's what we've all run from year after year.
But talking can help and I'm finding that out;
Yes even those times when I may have a doubt
It's hard to remember the message is right
During dark days and during dark nights.
It has to be faced and worked through somehow
At least that's how I feel right now.

By an incest survivor

For once I know just how I feel
I'm standing on the ledge
A feeling I know very well
I'm back on the knife edge.

What am I, am I a freak
To be stared at in a fair
Or am I just a piece of meat
With everyone wanting a share.

I want to retract every word I said
For I just cannot see
How telling Tom, Dick and Harry will be
Of benefit to me.

What do they expect of me
What am I supposed to do
Walking into groups and say to all
'Have I got news for you'

What am I supposed to say
When they're playing fast and loose
'Hey everybody, what do you think
I'm a victim of child abuse'.

Why did I open this powder keg
I'm regretting the day I did
I just want it over and done with
But I can't find the lid.

                              By an incest survivor

The following poems are from Sisk and Hoffman (1987)

Caution: There's a Child Inside[*]

There is a child inside me, and though she's very small,
There was a time not long ago she seemed not there at all.
Then one day I was asked to tell a little of my past.
As I spoke and walls came down, a little comfort the child had found.
Hiding no longer would keep her content,
        though protecting her had been my intent.
Frantically now she tried to reach out
        to see what this feeling had all been about.
For while I was thinking I just couldn't cope.
Someone had given the child some hope.
Here began the struggle, you see,
        between this little child and me.
For she had to be quiet and remain inside,
        so her guilt and shame I could hide.

Now someone has told her she wasn't to blame;
    and there wasn't a reason for her to feel shame.
Even though she still felt guilt and shame,
    she clung to that hope just the same.
I continue to fight her for I feel I must,
    for I see her slowly beginning to trust.
And I don't want her to hurt for I remember too well,
Her painful experience, of which I tell.
But this one who continues to listen to me,
    reaches into the child and tells her she's free.

*My adult vs. the child**

Each night as the adult lays her in bed
    her childhood fears play in her head.

She tries hard to block out fear
    as the child's blue eyes begin to tear.

The childs sits up as the adult ways to lay,
    the adult now explaining her fears away.

The child is still frightened yet tries to behave,
    in fear of the adult, as for now, she'll obey.

But as the adult begins to rest,
    the child's little mind flashes to the molest.

The child still trembling now silently screams,
    the adult still sleeping begins to dream.

The adult now sees, again the screams she can hear.
    Now she too trembles and awakens in fear.

And for awhile they both sit quivering in fright,
    as the child continues to experience each night.

But somehow between all the silent screams,
    the adult starts to realize it's only a dream.

Yet the child is still screaming for to her it is real,
    though the adult can numb-out, the child still can feel.

The adult now stifles the silent screams,
    in order to gain control of her dreams.

The child now looking for someone to hold her,
    finds only that the adult ever ready to scold her.

Not You But I*

You're the one who made me hurt,
    Yet I'm the one who feels like dirt.
You're the one who is to blame,
    Yet I'm the one who lives in shame.
You're the cause of my nightmares,
    Yet I lay awake trembling, but what do you care?
And when I'd told what you had done,
    I'm the one mom chose to shun.
You're the one who made me cry,
    Then dared a tear to leave my eye.
How tough, how strong you must have been,
    You had total control when I was ten.

The Child in Me*

I didn't stop it because I didn't talk
    or maybe it's the way I walk.
Whose fault was it? Yours or mine?
    I dredge through my past to find a sign.
Each time I say it was his fault,
    some inside voice speaks out.
One small forgotten issue
    that seems to raise some doubt.
Who is that voice inside of me
    that refuses to let my innocence be?
I thought it was those criticizing words,
    that as a child I always heard.
But surprised I was to come to see
    they're words of the little child in me.

This Kind of Touch *

Tonight as I lay awake in bed
    my hands propped beneath my head,
Afraid to close my eyes in sleep,
    for fear that into my room he'll creep.
I see him standing at my door,
    as he has so many nights before.
He doesn't think I know he's there;
    he doesn't know I see him stare.
And as he moves beside my bed,
    his ugly touch I start to dread.
For I feel frightened when I see his hand
    reaching out, touching me.
And I think that if I'd never been touched,
    it would have been better
Than this kind of touch.

---

*Excerpted from *Inside Scars: Incest Recovery as Told by a Survivor and her Therapist*, by Shiela L. Sisk and Charlotte Foster Hoffman. Copyright 1987. Pandora Press. Used with permission.

Appendix 2

Useful Books

There are many books which can be used to help incest survivors recover from the effects of childhood sexual abuse. Some of these, together with a short description of their contents, are outlined below.

Personal Accounts

ALLEN, C. V. (1980) *Daddy's Girl*, New York, Berkeley Book.
   A useful first-person account of the author's experience of being sexually abused by her father. The book gives a good insight into the child's way of coping with the abuse, and the effects of it on her subsequent development.

ANGELOU, M. (1983) *I Know Why the Caged Bird Sings*, New York, Virago.
   First in a series of autobiographical accounts about the effects of being sexually abused by her mother's boyfriend at an early age, and how she became mute for several years afterwards.

BRADY, K. (1979) *Father's Days: A true story of incest*, New York, Dell.
   A personal account of sexual abuse by her father.

EVERT, K. and BIJKERT, I. (1987) *When You're Ready*, Walnut Creek, Launch Press.
   An account of the way Kathy Evert came to terms with sexual abuse by her mother. This book is especially helpful for an incest survivor who uses regression as a means of re-awakening her memories.

MATTHEWS, C. A. (1986) *No Longer a Victim*, Canberra, Acorn Press.
   Account of recovery from sexual abuse by her father. The book is particularly helpful for a woman who has no memories of her childhood abuse. It describes what happens when these memories start to emerge.

SISK, S. L. and HOFFMAN, C. F. (1987) *Inside Scars*, Gainesville, Florida, Pandora Press.

The account of a woman's recovery from sexual abuse by her stepfather. Gives a good insight into the process of therapy, both from the incest survivor's point of view and that of her helper.

SPRING, J. (1987) *Cry Hard and Swim*, London, Virago.

A personal account of a Scottish woman's journey in coming to terms with sexual abuse by her father. It describes how she sought and found help, together with the difficulties she encountered in the process. A readable and moving account.

WYNNE, C. E. (1987) *That Looks Like a Nice House,* Walnut Creek, Launch Press.

A story, with pictures, of a woman's recovery from sexual abuse.

Collections of Short Accounts

ARMSTRONG, L. (1978) *Kiss Daddy Goodnight*, New York, Pocket Books.

A series of personal accounts of sexual abuse.

BASS, E. and THORNTON, L. (Eds.) (1983) *I Never Told Anyone: Writings by women survivors of child sexual abuse*, New York, Harper & Row.

Series of personal accounts of child sexual abuse.

McNARON, T. and MORGAN, Y. (Eds.) (1982) *Voices in the Night: Women speaking about incest*, Minneapolis, Cleis Press.

Women, including lesbian women, talk about their childhood experiences.

WARD, E. (1984) *Father-daughter Rape*. London, Women's Press.

A series of personal accounts is contained in the earlier sections of this book.

Novels

HART, T. (1979) *Don't Tell Your Mother*, London, Quartet Books.

This book examines the effects of a father's sexual abuse of his daughter on the father, the mother and their daughter, and the subsequent effects of legal action on the family.

MOGGACH, D. (1983) *Porky*, Harmondsworth, Penguin Books.

This story of a father's sexual abuse of his daughter, and effects on her development into adulthood. This can be quite an upsetting book.

MORRIS, M. (1982) *If I Should Die Before I Wake*, London, Black Swan Books.

A very powerful book describing the life of a girl who was sexually abused by her father.

WALKER, A. (1983) *The Color Purple*, London, The Women's Press.

A moving story of a woman's early and adult years of abuse and her pathway to recovery, told in the form of letters.

Self-Help Books Written for Incest Survivors

BASS, E. and DAVIS, L. (1988) *The Courage to Heal*, New York, Harper and Row.
An excellent book packed with information and ideas for use in the recovery process from the experience of sexual abuse. Written for incest survivors.

GIL, E. (1983) *Outgrowing the Pain*, Walnut Creek, Launch Press.
A good little book explaining aspects of the healing process. Cartoon illustrations and a simple clear text make for easy reading.

HANCOCK, M. and MAINS, K. B. (1987) *Child Sexual Abuse: A hope for healing*, Crowborough, Highland Books.
This book examines recovery from child sexual abuse from a Christian point of view, and examines the religious and spiritual difficulties experienced by incest survivors.

MALTZ, W. and HOLMAN, B. (1987) *Incest and Sexuality*, Lexington, Lexington Books.
An extremely useful book for incest survivors, their helpers and partners. It examines issues relating to sexuality and suggests ways of working through sexual problems.

General Self-Help Books

DELVIN, D. (1974) *The Book of Love*, London, New English Library.
Concise and readable book about sexual problems and ways of dealing with them.

DICKSON, A. (1982) *A Woman in Your Own Right*, London, Quartet Books.
An excellent book on the issue of assertiveness in women.

DICKSON, A. (1985) *The Mirror Within*, London, Quartet Books.
A very readable book of women's sexuality. Lots of useful ideas for changing attitudes and behaviour.

KITZINGER, S. (1985) *Woman's Experience of Sex*, Harmondsworth, Pelican.
An excellent, readable book which places sex in the context of life, and includes material on a wide range of issues. Clear illustrations and lovely photographs.

LEVER, J., BRUSH, M. and HAYNES, B. (1980) *P.M.T. The Unrecognised Illness*, London, New English Library.
Useful, clearly written book about pre-menstrual tension.

MUELENBELT, A. (1981) *For Ourselves: Our Bodies and Sexuality*, London, Sheba.
Examines aspects of women's sexuality, with chapters on sexual orientation, sexual violence and sources of help available for problems related to a woman's sexuality.

PHILLIPS, A. and RAKUSEN, J. (1978) *Our Bodies, Ourselves*, Harmondsworth, Penguin Books.

An invaluable sourcebook on women's health issues.

REITZ, R. (1985) *Menopause: a Positive Approach*, London, Unwin Paperbacks.
Examines issues relating to the menopause, and how to deal with difficulties.

Other Useful Books

BURNS, D. D. (1980) *Feeling Good*, New York, Signet Book.
A useful book for dealing with problems of self-esteem. Looks at how to change the negative thinking patterns that are experienced by individuals with low self-esteem.

Books for Parents to use in Talking to Their Children

CORCORAN, C. (1987) *Take Care! Preventing Child Sexual Abuse*, Dublin, Poolbeg Press.
Straightforward, direct book examining the myths of sexual abuse and strategies for teaching children to be safe. Written from the principle that 'an informed child is a safe child'.

ELLIOTT, M. (1988) *Keeping Safe*, London, New English Library.
A practical guide for parents and other adults talking with children about a whole range of problems from sexual abuse to teenage drug-taking and AIDS.

FAGERSTROM, G. and HANSSON, G. (1979) *Our New Baby*, London, MacDonald Educational.
Useful book describing puberty, conception, pregnancy and childbirth through the story of a new baby's arrival in a family.

RAYNER, C. (1979) *The Body Book*, London, Piccolo Books.
A useful book describing the working of the human body for primary school children.

Books for Groups

ERNST, S. and GOODISON, L. (1981) *In Our Own Hands: A woman's book of self-help therapy*, London, Women's Press.
Full of ideas that can be adapted for use in an incest survivor's group. Guidelines for starting a self-help group are also included.

KRZOWSKI, S. and LAND, P. (Eds.) (1988) *In our experience*, London, Women's Press.
A useful sourcebook for groups and workshops run by women for women.

NiCARTHY, G., MERRIAM, K. and COFFMAN, S. (1984) *Talking it Out: A guide to groups for abused women*, Seattle, Seal Press.
 Although written for battered women, it has lots of useful ideas and advice for running groups.

Appendix 3

Contacts for Women who have been Sexually Abused
(October 1988)

Scotland

Aberdeen Rape Crisis Centre, P.O. Box 123, Aberdeen, Mon. 6pm–8pm Thurs. 7pm–9pm (answerphone) Tel. 0224 575560

Aberdeen Incest Survivors Group, c/o Aberdeen Rape Crisis Centre

Central Scotland Rape Crisis Centre, P.O. Box 4, Falkirk. Tel. 0324 38433

Central Scotland Incest Survivors Group c/o Central Scotland Rape Crisis Centre

Central Scotland Action Against Incest c/o Central Scotland Rape Crisis Centre

Dundee Rape Crisis Line, P.O. Box 83, Dundee. Wed. 7–9pm Tel. 0382 646377

Dundee Incest Survivors Group c/o Dundee Women's Aid, 22 Thomson Street, Dundee

Dundee Action Against Incest c/o Dundee Women's Aid, 22 Thomson Street, Dundee

Dunfermline Rape Crisis Line, P.O. Box 47, Dunfermline. Fri. 7–9pm Tel. 0383 739084

Edinburgh Rape Crisis Centre, P.O. Box 120, Edinburgh. Mon. 1am–2pm, Tues. 6–8pm, Thurs. 6–9pm, Fri. 11am–2pm, Sat. 4–6pm, Tel 031 556 943

Edinburgh Incest Survivors Group c/o Edinburgh Rape Crisis Centre. Wed. 6–8pm Survivors Line 031 556 9437

Edinburgh Action Against Incest c/o 61a Broughton Street, Edinburgh

Highland Rape Crisis and Counselling Line c/o IVOG, 38 Ardconnel Street, Inverness Sat. and Sun. 7–10pm Tel. 0463 220719

Kirkcaldy Incest Survivors Group, c/o The Volunteer Centre, 18 Brycedale Avenue, Kirkcaldy. Tel. 0592 204756

Strathclyde Rape Crisis Centre, P.O. Box 53, Glasgow G21 YR Mon., Wed., Fri. 7–10pm Tel. 041 221 8448

Glasgow Incest Survivors Group, c/o Strathclyde Rape Crisis Centre

Glasgow Action Against Incest, c/o 48 Miller Street, Glasgow

England

Avon Sexual Abuse Centre c/o Bristol RCL, 39 Jamaica Street, Stokes Croft, Bristol, BS2 8JP. Mon.–Fri. 10.30am–2.30pm Tel. Bristol 428331

Bristol Incest Survivors have their own magazine, Taboo, a highly professional production which may interest many other groups

Birmingham Rape Crisis, P.O. Box 558, Birmingham B3 2HL. 24 hour service, Tel. 021 233 2122

Cambridge Incest Survivors c/o Cambridge RCC, Box R, 12 Mill Road, Cambridge. Wed. 6pm–12midnight, Sat. 11am–5pm, Tel. Cambridge 358314

Coventry: One in Four, Box 8 c/o Coventry Voluntary Services Council, 28 Corporation Street, Coventry CV1 1AB. Tues. 11am–3pm Tel. Coventry 76606.

Grays Thurrock RCC, Bridge House, 160 Bridge Road, Grays Thurrock, Essex RM17 6DB Mon. 6pm–9pm, Tues. 7pm–10pm, Wed. 1pm–5pm., Thurs. 12 midday–4pm. Women's group and individual counselling. Tel. Grays Thurrock 380609

Harlow Incest Survivors Group and Crisis Line, Women's Centre, 93–96 Altham Grove, Harlow, Essex. Group meets Tues. 8pm–10pm. Crisis line opens Tues. morning and Wed. evening. Tel Harlow 21612

London:

Child Sexual Abuse Preventive Education Project (CSAPEP), c/o A Woman's Place, Hungerford House, Victoria Embankment, London WC2N 6PA. Tel. 01 671 9033

Incest Crisis Line. The line is open to survivors of both sexes, and the counsellors are both male and female. Tel. Richard, 01 388 2388.

Incest Survivors Campaign c/o A Woman's Place, (as above).

Information Service on Incest and Child Sexual Abuse (ISICSA), 24 Blackheath Rose, London SE13 7PN Tel. 01 852 7432

Kingston Women's Centre, 66 London Road, Kingston-on-Thames, Surrey. Women's group and girls' group. Tel. 01 541 1964

Lambeth Incest Survivors, South London Women's Centre, 55 Acre Lane, Brixton, London SW2. Drop-in every Tues. 11am–12pm, Tel. 01 274 7215

London Rape Crisis Line, P.O. Box 69, London WC1X 9NJ, 24 hour service, Tel. 01 837 1600.

Waltham Forest Incest Survivors c/o Waltham Forest Women's Centre, 109 Hoe Street, London E17. Tel. 01 520 5318

Women's Advice and Counselling Service, The Albany, Douglas Way, Deptford, London SE8. Tel. 01 692 6268

Taboo, P.O. Box 38, Manchester M60 1HG. Tel. 061 236 1323, Crisis Line, Wed. 4pm–8.30pm, Tel. 061 236 1712

Sheffield Incest Survivors Group c/o Sheffield Rape Crisis Line, P.O. Box 34, Sheffield S1 1UD. Mon.–Fri. 11am–4pm, Tues. 7.30pm–9.30pm, Thurs. 7pm–9pm, Tel. 0742 755255

Sussex Incest Crisis Line c/o Brighton Rape Crisis Project, P.O. Box 332, Hove, East Sussex, Tel. 0273 24316

Ireland

Belfast Rape Crisis Centre, P.O. Box 46, Belfast BT2 7AR. Mon.–Fri. 10am–6pm, Sat. and Sun. 11am–5pm. Tel. Belfast 249696

Dublin Rape Crisis, 2 Lower Pembroke Street, Dublin 2. Mon.–Fri. 8pm–8am, Sat./Sun. 24 hours. Individual counselling and self-help groups. Tel. Dublin 601 470

Mothers

Chris Strickland Tel. 0965 31432

The Authors

Liz Hall is a Senior Clinical Psychologist working in the Community Psychology Department of Grampian Health Board. She has been working with incest survivors in individual therapy since 1984. She is involved with teaching, training and supervising other helpers who work with incest survivors in Grampian Region.

Siobhan Lloyd is a Lecturer in Social Policy and Community Work in the Department of Social Work, University of Aberdeen. She has a particular interest in social policy and social work practice issues which affect women. She has been co-facilitating an incest survivors' group in Aberdeen since 1985.

Bibliography

ALLEN, C. V. (1980) *Daddy's Girl*, New York, Berkeley Book

ANGELOU, M. (1984) *I Know Why the Caged Bird Sings*, London, Virago

ARMSTRONG, L. (1978) *Kiss Daddy Goodnight*, New York, Pocket Books

ASH, A. (1984) *Father-daughter Sexual Abuse: The abuse of paternal authority*, Bangor, Department of Social Theory and Institutions, University of North Wales

BAGLEY, C. and RAMSAY, R. (1986) 'Sexual abuse in childhood; psychosocial outcomes and implications for social work practice', *Journal of Social Work and Human Sexuality*, 4, pp. 33–47

BAKER, A. W. and DUNCAN, S. P. (1985) 'Child sexual abuse: a study of prevalence in Great Britain'. *Child Abuse and Neglect*, 9, pp 457–467

BASS, E. and DAVIS, L. (1988) *The Courage to Heal*, New York, Harper and Row

BASS, E. and THORNTON, L. (Eds.) (1983) *I Never Told Anyone: Writings by Women Survivors of Child Sexual Abuse*, New York, Harper and Row

BECK, A. T. (1976) *Cognitive Therapy and the Emotional Disorders*, New York, International Universities Press

BECKER, J. V., SKINNER, L. J., ABEL, G. G. and TREACEY, E. C. (1982) 'Incidence and types of sexual dysfunction in rape and incest victims', *Journal of Sex and Marital Therapy*, 8, pp 65–74

BLAKE-WHITE, J. and KLINE, C. M. (1985) 'Treating the dissociative process in adult victims of childhood incest', *Social Casework*, 66, pp 394–402

BRADY, K. (1979) *Father's Days: A True Story of Incest*, New York, Dell

BRANDES, D. and PHILLIPS, H. (1977) *Gamesters Handbook*, London, Hutchinson

BRIERE, J. and RUNTZ, M. (1986) 'Suicidal thoughts and behaviors in former sexual abuse victims', *Canadian Journal of Behavioral Science*, 18, pp 413–423

BROWNE, A. and FINKELHOR, D. (1986) 'Initial and long-term effects: a review of the research', in FINKELHOR, D. (Ed.), *A Sourcebook of Child Sexual Abuse*. pp 143–179, Beverly Hill, Sage

BURNS, D. D. (1980) *Feeling Good*, New York, Signet Book

CAVALLIN, H. (1966) 'Incestuous fathers: a clinical report', *American Journal of Psychiatry*, 122, pp 1132–1138

CORCORAN, C. (1987) *Take Care! Preventing Child Sexual Abuse*, Dublin, Poolbeg Press

COURTOIS, C. A. (1979) 'The incest experience and its aftermath', *Victimology*, 4, pp 337–347

COURTOIS, C. A. and WATTS, D. L. (1982) 'Counselling adult women who experienced incest in childhood or adolescence', *Personnel and Guidance Journal*, 6, pp 275–279

DAVENPORT, S. and SHELDON, H. (1987) 'From victim to survivor', *Changes*, 5, pp 379–382

DEIGHTON, J. and McPEEK, P. (1985) 'Group treatment: adult victims of childhood sexual abuse', *Social Casework*, 66, pp 403–410

DELVIN, D. (1974) *The Book of Love*, London, New English Library

DE YOUNG, M. (1982) Self-injurious behaviour in incest victims: a research note', *Child Welfare*, 61, pp 577–584

DICKSON, A. (1982) *A Woman in Your Own Right*, London, Quartet Books

DICKSON, A. (1985) *The Mirror Within*, London, Quartet Books

EGAN, G. (1982) *The Skilled Helper*, (2nd edition) Monterey, Brooks/Cole

ELLENSON, G. S. (1985) 'Detecting a history of incest: a predictive syndrome', *Social Casework*, 66, pp 525–532

ELLENSON, G. S. (1986) 'Disturbances of perception in adult female incest survivors', *Social Casework*, 67, pp 149–159

ELLIOTT, M. (1988) *Keeping Safe: A Practical Guide to Talking with Children*, London, New English Library

ERNST, S. and GOODISON, L. (1981) *In Our Own Hands: A Woman's Book of Self-Help Therapy*, London, Women's Press

EVERT, K. and BIJKERK, I. (1987) *When you're Ready*, Walnut Creek, Launch Press

FAGERSTROM, G. and HANSSON, G. (1979) *Our New Baby*, London, MacDonald Educational

FARIA, G. and BELOHLAVEK, N. (1984) 'Treating female adult survivors of childhood incest', *Social Casework*, 65, pp 465–471

FIELDS, M. D. (1988) *Legal and Social Work Responses to Sexual Abuse of Children*, Paper presented at the Conference on Social and Legal responses to Child Sexual Abuse, University of Stirling, Institute for the Study of Violence

FINKELHOR, D. (1979) *Sexually Victimized Children*, New York, Free Press

FINKELHOR, D. (1984) *Child Sexual Abuse: New Theory and Research*, New York, The Free Press

FINKELHOR, D. (1986) *A Source Book on Child Sexual Abuse*, London, Sage

FINKELHOR, D. and BROWNE, A. (1986) 'Initial and long-term effects: A conceptual framework', in FINKELHOR, D. (Ed.), *A Sourcebook on Child Sexual Abuse*, London, Sage.

FLUGEL, J. (1926) *The Psychoanalytic Study of the Family*, London, Woolf

FORWARD, S. and BUCK, C. (1981) *Betrayal of Innocence: Incest and its Devastation*, Harmondsworth, Penguin

FROMUTH, M. E. (1986) 'The relationship of child sexual abuse with later psychological and sexual adjustment in a sample of college women', *Child Abuse and Neglect*, 10, pp 5–15

GELINAS, D. (1983) 'The persisting negative effects of incest', *Psychiatry*, 46, pp 312–332

GIL, E. (1983) *Outgrowing the Pain*, Walnut Creek, Launch Press

GIL, E. (1988) *Treatment of Adult Survivors of Child Abuse*, Walnut Creek, Launch Press

GOODWIN, J., SIMMS, M. and BERGMAN, R. (1979) 'Hysterical seizures: a sequel to incest', *American Journal of Orthopsychiatry*, 49, pp 698–703

GORDY, P. L. (1983) 'Group work that supports adult victims of childhood incest', *Social Casework*, 64, pp 300–307

GROSS, M. (1980) 'Incest and hysterical seizures', *Medical Hypnoanalysis*, 3, pp 146–152

GROSS, R. J., DOERR, H., CALDIROLA, D., GUZINSKI, G. M. and RIPLEY, H. S. (1980) 'Borderline syndrome and incest in chronic pelvic pain patients', *International Journal of Psychiatry in Medicine*, 10, pp 79–96

GUTTMACHER, M. S. (1951) *Sex Offenses. The Problem, Causes and Prevention*, New York, W. W. Norton

HANCOCK, M. and MAINS, K. B. (1987) *Child Sexual Abuse: A Hope for Healing*, Crowborough, Highland Books

HART, T. (1979) *Don't Tell your Mother*, London, Quartet Books

HAYS, K. F. (1985) 'Electra in mourning: grief work and the adult incest survivor', *Psychotherapy Patient*, 2, pp 45–58

HERMAN, J. and HIRSCHMAN, L. (1977) 'Father-daughter incest,' *Signs: Journal of Women in Culture and Society*, 2, pp 735–756

HERMAN, J. and SCHATZOW, E. (1984) 'Time-limited group therapy for women with a history of incest', *International Journal of Group Psychotherapy*, 34, pp 605–616

HERMAN, J., RUSSELL, D. and TROCKI, K. (1986) 'Long-term effects of incestuous abuse in childhood', *American Journal of Psychiatry*, 143, pp 1293–1296

HERMAN, J. L. (1981) *Father-Daughter Incest*, Cambridge, Harvard University Press

JACKSON, S. (1978) *On the Social Construction of Female Sexuality*, London, Women's Research and Resources Centre

JAMES, J. and MEYERDING, J. (1977) 'Early sexual experience and prostitution', *American Journal of Psychiatry*, 134, pp 1381–1385

JEHU, D. and GAZAN, M. (1983) 'Psychosocial adjustment of women who were sexually victimized in childhood or adolescence', *Canadian Journal of Community Mental Health*, 2, pp 71–82

JEHU, D., GAZAN, M. and KLASSEN, C. (1985) 'Common therapeutic targets among women who were sexually abused in childhood', in VALENTICH, M. and GRIPTON, J. (Eds.), *Feminist Perspectives on Social Work and Human Sexuality*, pp 25–45, New York, Haworth.

JEHU, D., KLASSEN, C. and GAZAN, M. (1986) 'Cognitive restructuring of distorted beliefs associated with childhood sexual abuse', *Journal of Social Work and Human Sexuality*, 4, pp 49–69

JOSEPHSON, G. S. and FONG-BEYETTE, M. L. (1987) 'Factors assisting female clients' disclosure of incest during counseling', *Journal of Counseling and Development*, 65, pp 475–478

KEMPE, C. H. (1980) 'Sexual abuse: another hidden pediatric problem', in COOK, J. V. and BOWLES, R. T. (Eds.) *Child Abuse: Commission and Omission*, Toronto, Butterworth

KEMPE, R. S. and KEMPE, C. H. (1984) *The Common Secret: Sexual Abuse of Children and Adolescents*, New York, Freeman

KENWARD, H. (1987) Workshop on Child Sexual Abuse held in Aberdeen, October 1987, Personal Communication

KITZINGER, S. (1985) *Woman's Experience of Sex*, Harmondsworth, Pelican

KRZOWSKI, S, and LAND, P. (Eds.) (1988) *In Our Experience*, London, Women's Press

LEVER, J., BRUSH, M. and HAYNES, B. (1980) *P.M.T. The Unrecognised Illness*, London, New English Library

LISTER, E. D. (1982) 'Forced silence: A neglected dimension of trauma', *American Journal of Psychiatry*, 139, pp 872–876

LUKIANOWICZ, N. (1972) 'Incest. I Paternal incest. II Other types of incest', *British Journal of Psychiatry*, 120, pp 301–313

McCORMACK, A., JANUS, M-D. and BURGESS, A. W. (1986) 'Runaway youths and sexual victimization: gender differences in an adolescent runaway population', *Child Abuse and Neglect*, 10, pp 387–395

McFADYEN, M. (1989) 'The cognitive invalidation approach to panic', in BAKER, R. (Ed.) *Panic Disorder: Theory, Research and Therapy*, Chichester, John Wiley (forthcoming)

McGUIRE, L. S. and WAGNER, N. N. (1978) 'Sexual dysfunction in women who were molested as children: one response pattern and suggestions for treatment', *Journal of Sex of Marital Therapy*, 4, pp 11–15

MACLEOD, M. and SARAGA, E. (1987) 'Abuse of trust', *Journal of Social Work Practice*, November 1987, pp 71–79

MACLEOD, M. and SARAGA, E. (1988) 'Challenging the orthodoxy: Towards a feminist theory and practice', *Feminist Review*, 28, pp 16–56

McNARON, T. and MORGAN, Y. (1982) *Voices in the Night: Women Speaking about Incest*, Minneapolis, Cleis Press

MAISCH, H. (1973) *Incest*, London, Andre Deutsch

MALTZ, W. and HOLMAN, B. (1987) *Incest and Sexuality: A Guide to Understanding and Healing*, Lexington, Lexington Books

MASSON, J. M. (1985) *The Assault on Truth: Freud's Suppression of the Seduction Theory*, Harmondsworth, Penguin

MATTHEWS, C-A. (1986) *No Longer a Victim*, Canberra, Acorn Press

MEISELMAN, K. (1978) *Incest — A Psychological Study of Causes and Effects with Treatment Recommendations*, San Francisco, Jossey-Bass

MILLER, A. (1984) *Thou shalt not be aware. Society's Betrayal of the Child*, London, Pluto

MOGGACH, D. (1983) *Porky*, Harmondsworth, Penguin

MORRIS, M. (1984) *If I Should Die before I Wake*, London, Black Swan

MUELENBELT, A. (1981) *For Ourselves: Our Bodies and Sexuality*, London, Sheba

NAKASHIMA, I. and ZAKUS, G. (1977) 'Incest review and clinical experience,' *Pediatrics*, 60, pp 696–701

NELSON, S. (1982) *Incest — Fact and Myth*, (1st edition) Edinburgh, Stramullion

NELSON, S. (1987) *Incest — Fact and Myth*, (2nd edition) Edinburgh, Stramullion

NiCARTHY, G., MERRIAM, K. and COFFMAN, S. (1984) *Talking It Out: A Guide to Groups for Abused Women*, Seattle, Seal Press

O'HARE, J. and TAYLOR, K. (1983) 'The reality of incest', *Women and Therapy*, 2, pp 215–229

OPPENHEIMER, R., HOWELLS, K., PALMER, R. L. and CHALONER, D. A. (1985) 'Adverse sexual experience in childhood and clinical eating disorders: a preliminary description', *Journal of Psychosomatic Research*, 19, pp 357–361

PETERS, S. D. (1984) *The Relationship Between Childhood Sexual Victimization and Adult Depression among Afro-American and White Women*, Unpublished doctoral dissertation, University of California, Los Angeles

PHILLIPS, A. and RAKUSEN, J. (1978) *Our Bodies, Ourselves*, Harmondsworth, Penguin

RAYNER, C. (1979) *The Body Book*, London, Piccolo Books

REITZ, R. (1985) *Menopause: A positive approach*, London, Unwin Paperbacks

ROCKLIN, R. and LAVETT, D. K. (1987) 'Those who broke the cycle: Therapy with non-abusive adults who were physically abused as children', *Psychotherapy*, 24, pp 769–778

RUSH, F. (1980) *The Best Kept Secret: Sexual Abuse of Children*, Englewood Cliffs, Prentice-Hall

RUSSELL, D. E. H. (1986) *The Secret Trauma: Incest in the Lives of Girls and Women*, New York, Basic Books

SCOTT, A. (1988) 'Feminism and the seductiveness of the real event,' *Feminist Review*, 28, pp 88–102

SGROI, S. (1982) *Handbook of Clinical Intervention in Child Sexual Abuse*, Cambridge, Lexington Books

SGROI, S. M., BLICK, L. C. and PORTER, F. S. (1982) 'A conceptual framework for child sexual abuse', in SGROI, S. (Ed.), *Handbook of Clinical Intervention in Child Sexual Abuse*, pp 11–17

SHELDON, H. (1987) 'Living with a secret', *Changes*, 5, pp 340–343

SISK, S. L. and HOFFMAN, C. F. (1987) *Inside Scars: Incest Recovery as Told by a Survivor and Her Therapist*, Gainesville, Pandora Press

SLOAN, G and LEICHNER, P. (1986) 'Is there a relationship between sexual abuse or incest and eating disorders?', *Canadian Journal of Psychiatry*, 31, pp. 656–70

SPRING, J. (1987) *Cry Hard and Swim*, London, Virago.

TSAI, M. and WAGNER, N. N. (1978) 'Therapy groups for women sexually molested as children', *Archives of Sexual Behaviour*, 7, pp 417–427

TSAI, M. and WAGNER, N. N. (1979) 'Women who were sexually molested as children,' *Medical Aspects of Human Sexuality*, 13, pp 55–56

WALKER, A. (1982) *The Color Purple*, New York, Pocket Books

WARD, E. (1984) *Father-daughter Rape*, London, The Women's Press

WEST, D. J. (Ed.) (1985) *Sexual Victimization*, Aldershot, Gower

WINESTINE, M. C. (1985) 'Compulsive shop-lifting as a derivative of childhood seduction', *Psychoanalytic Quarterly*, 54, pp 70–72

WORDEN, J. W. (1983) *Grief Counselling and Grief Therapy*, London, Tavistock Publications

WYNESS, J. (1985) *Anxiety and Its Management*, printed for Area Clinical Psychology Services, Aberdeen,Grampian Health Board

WYNNE, C. E. (1987) *That Looks Like a Nice House*, Walnut Creek, Launch Press

Index